WILDLIFE PHOTOGRAPHY FIELDCRAFT

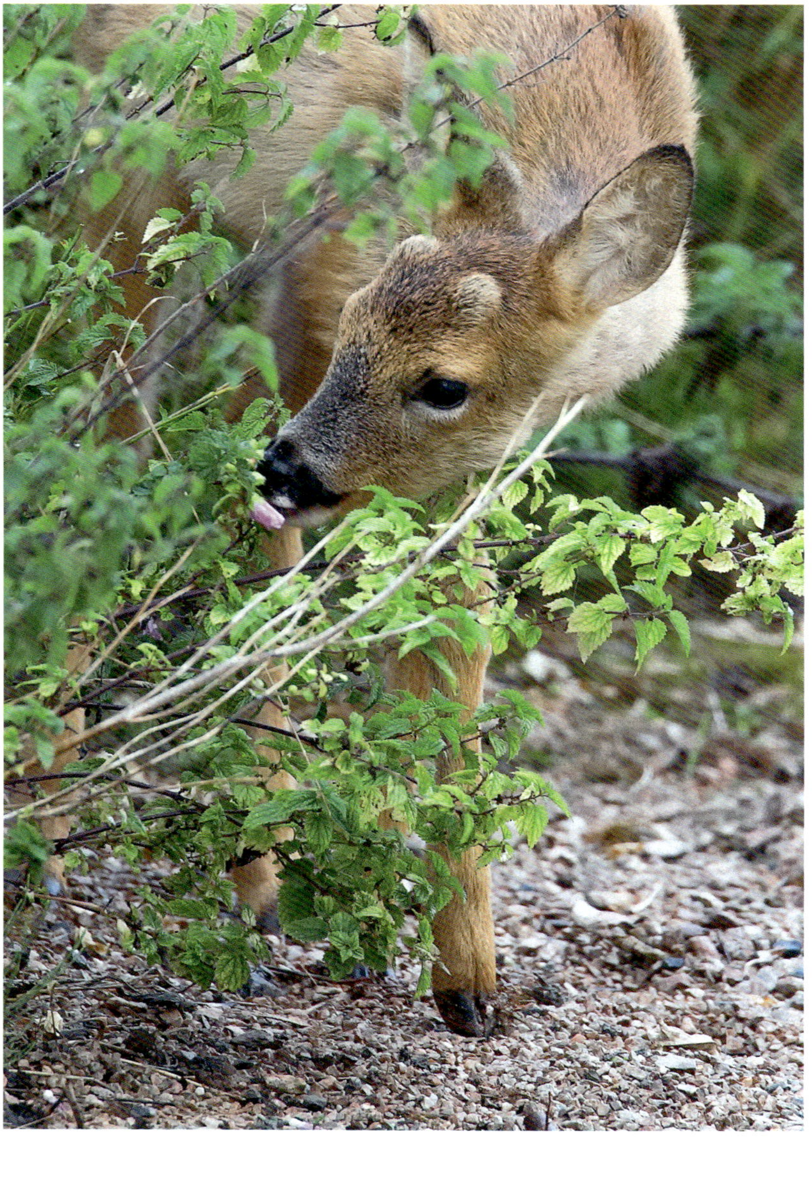

WILDLIFE PHOTOGRAPHY FIELDCRAFT

HOW TO FIND AND PHOTOGRAPH WILD ANIMALS

SUSAN YOUNG

Pelagic Publishing

First published in 2022 by
Pelagic Publishing
20–22 Wenlock Road
London N1 7GU, UK

www.pelagicpublishing.com

Wildlife Photography Fieldcraft: How to Find and Photograph Wild Animals

British Library Cataloguing in Publication Data
A catalogue record for this book is available from the British Library

ISBN 978-1-78427-393-4 Pbk
ISBN 978-1-78427-394-1 ePub
ISBN 978-1-78427-395-8 PDF

https://doi.org/10.53061/IKQP9992

Cover photo: Red Squirrel © Susan Young
Design and typesetting: Christopher Bromley

FSC www.fsc.org MIX Paper from responsible sources FSC® C113523

Frontispiece: A young Roebuck with the first sign of antlers

Contents

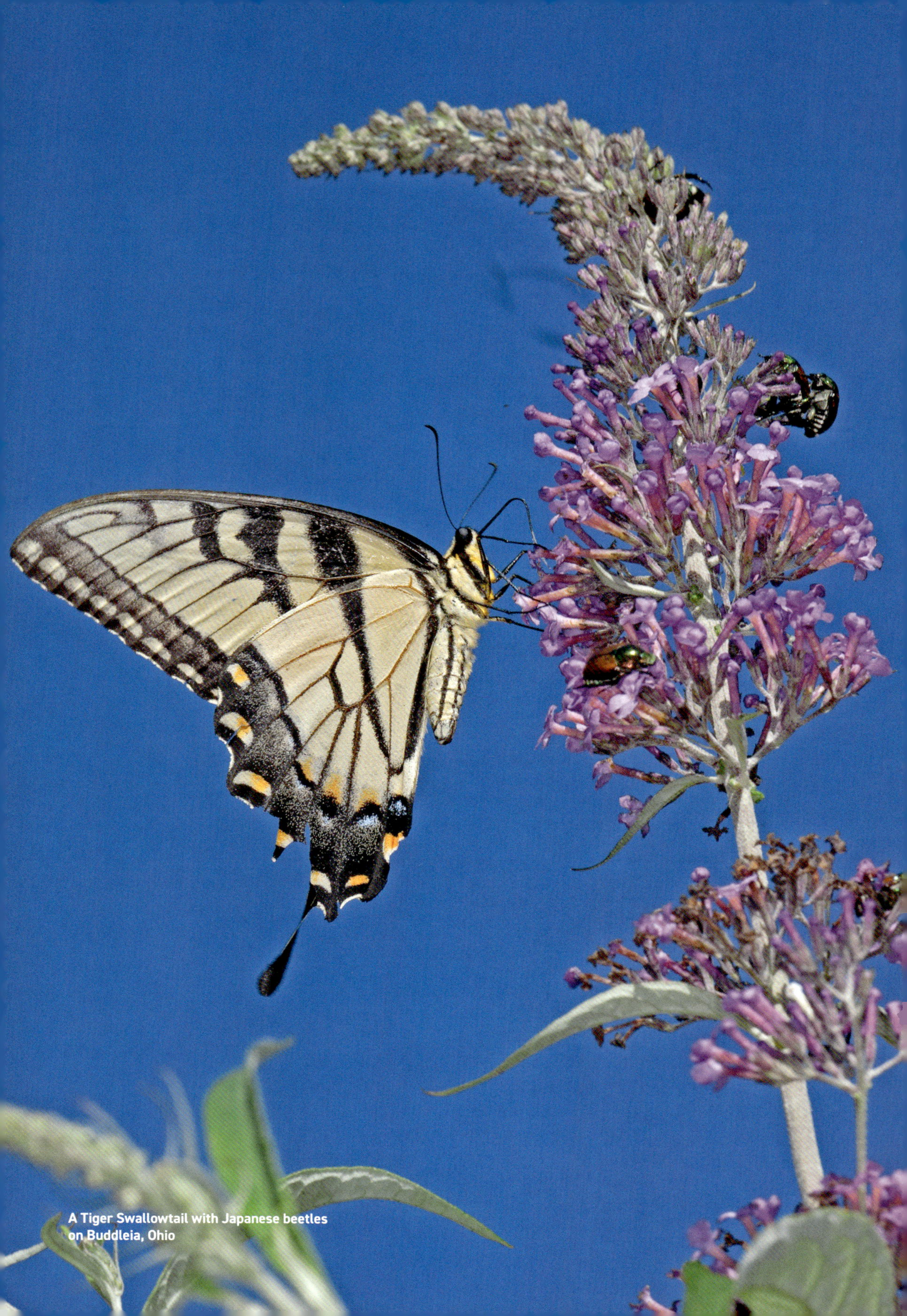

A Tiger Swallowtail with Japanese beetles on Buddleia, Ohio

Preface

When I first started wildlife photography some years ago, I soon realised what everyone eventually discovers: finding the wildlife is the most difficult part. Even if you do succeed in locating interesting subjects to photograph, getting it to keep still or to come within range of a camera lens can sometimes seem almost impossible.

At that time, I avidly read books written by wildlife photography experts, hoping for the answers – but I found very few. Apart from 'use a hide' or 'wear suitable clothing', there was very little information on how to actually locate animals. Even today, not much has changed. This may be because some photographers wish to keep their secret finds to themselves, whereas others may wish to protect the wildlife itself. There is always a dilemma around giving out too much information, because there is the risk that without using care and being aware of the sensitive nature of wildlife, it may be disturbed as a result.

Still, even with fieldcraft knowledge, wildlife photography requires a great deal of patience and persistence, particularly in the UK. This book does not claim that you will be able to take pictures of the most elusive animals, but it does aim to equip you with the knowledge required to increase your chances of getting great images. The patience and persistence has to come from you.

I have been lucky enough to be able to call on the expertise of wildlife fieldcraft experts and will share their secrets with you, as well as my own. Wildlife photography fieldcraft is not just about creeping around in bushes, although this is the common perception. It is mainly about research: finding out the facts and putting them to good use. This book describes the relevant research that is required, and gives details of how it should be put into practice. I have also sought with this guide to emphasise ethical photography, and I hope that those who read it will follow ethical guidelines and aim to capture images of wildlife without disturbing it.

So, finding the animal is only the first, if most difficult, step. In order to produce images worthy of the hours of hard work and the patience you have put in, it is important that your camera equipment is correctly used – therefore, I have included essential information on this. Preparation before taking the shot is often neglected, with some photographers relying on Photoshop or other post-processing software to correct substandard images (Adobe Lightroom is less complex and a very suitable choice, favoured by many photographers). This is not helped by the fact that many books on wildlife photography perpetuate the myth that expensive equipment and a deep knowledge of editing software is required to create good images. Nowadays, digital cameras produce images that require very little alteration, as long as time has been taken to prepare beforehand. Accordingly, I have included only the basic details of processing. That is all you really need. It is true that good-quality equipment helps, but the most important aspect is your persistence and willingness to research your subject.

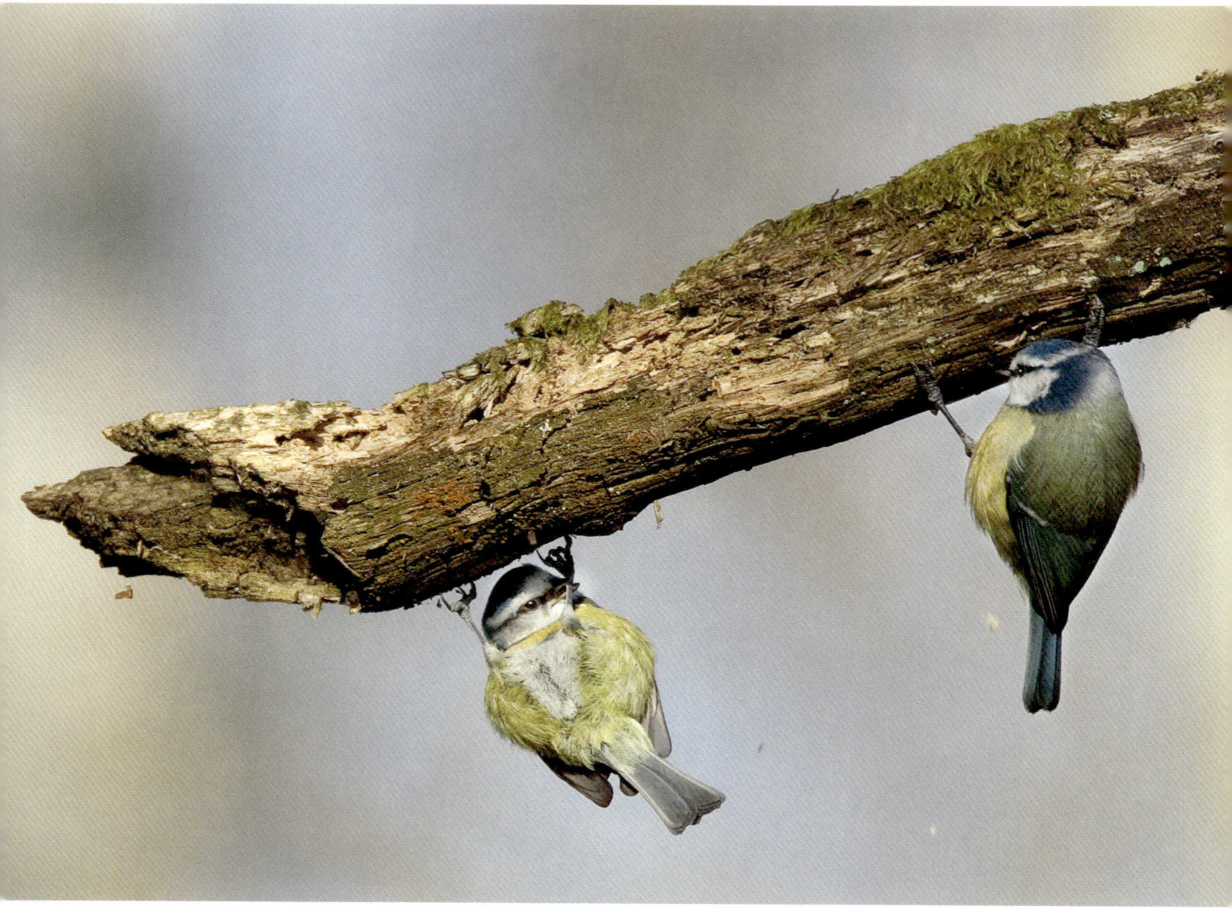

A Blue Tit shows off (the bird on the left then fell off the branch, but no harm done)

Introduction

This section defines the scope of the book with regard to the wildlife subjects described and the more technical photographic topics covered.

The method of finding wildlife subjects to photograph can seem like a 'dark art', but the truth is very different. Many professional photographers and wildlife film-makers rely on the local knowledge of others to source their subjects. For most of us, this is neither possible nor desirable for day-to-day wildlife photography, and the best route to success is to develop your own local knowledge.

This book is unique among wildlife photography books as it gives a clear strategy for developing this knowledge and how to use it. This introduction provides an overview of that strategy. It highlights the research required before going out to photograph, and once in the field.

It us impossible to produce an exact list of steps, as these will vary from species to species, but the chapters on each type of wildlife give more detail. To further clarify the strategy, there are several case studies which offer a detailed description of how I put the strategy into practice.

The aim of the book is thus to guide the reader towards developing their own strategy for successful and rewarding wildlife photography.

Scope

The book is divided into chapters covering different groups of animals. Birds and mammals are the most popular subjects with photographers and as a result take up the greatest part. The basic research required for each subject is described, together with details of sources for the necessary information. Examples show how to put the research into practice, and in some instances case studies are included, demonstrating the detailed steps taken by the author in pursuing a particular photographic subject.

Birds have been classified according to habitat, as there are often some similarities in behaviour between species. Although it is acknowledged that some birds occupy more than one habitat type, the huge number of species dictates that some simplifying method be used.

There are relatively few mammal species in the UK, and behaviour varies dramatically from one to the other. As a result, the book has a section for each of the commoner mammal species, together with some limited information on the very rare and elusive ones.

Butterflies and dragonflies are included, but the subject of smaller insects is not as popular with photographers as that of birds and mammals, and thus has not been covered. It is true that insect photographs often win wildlife photography competitions, and may be of interest to naturalists – but specialised macro-photography and lighting is required for high-quality images, and these do not fall within the scope of this book.

Nor is this intended as an in-depth guide to digital photography, as many other books are available on this subject. However, the basic considerations are outlined so that you will know on which aspects to concentrate, should you wish to pursue this in more detail. Camera equipment and basic techniques are covered, with some relevant websites listed. The all-important fieldcraft equipment is described, with details of how to set up hides, together with a section on making simple hides using PVC pipe. Finally, an Appendix gives a list of nature reserves, books and other useful information that may help to increase your chances of success, as well as discussing ethical, legal and safety issues that sometimes arise.

Some of the photographs included in this book are intended to illustrate techniques – but the majority aim to show what can be achieved, and to hopefully inspire you to overcome the difficulties inherent in the challenging yet rewarding pursuit of photographing wildlife.

How to use this book

The strategy for finding wildlife as described in this book hinges on researching the basic details, habits and behaviour of the target species and considering how this knowledge can help the photographer. Real-life situations and case studies are described in step-by-step detail, to expand on this strategy and give the photographer practical tools to increase the chances of success.

Basic facts

The detailed information in these sections is an amalgamation of facts from the Royal Society for the Protection of Birds (RSPB), the British Trust for Ornithology (BTO), the Mammal Society, the Wildlife Trusts and many other sources, together with my own experience. Only reliable sources based on science or personal observation have been used, as general information to be found on the Internet is not always reliable. It should be noted that some facts, such as bird population numbers, can even be very different on equally reliable websites, presumably due to differing methods of data collection.

Description

A photographer is normally expected to know what has been photographed, so description is one of the most useful facts to have at the fingertips. It is also necessary to know if appearance changes at different times of the year. For example, deer can be very dull in colour in winter, which can make it difficult to distinguish similar species. Conversely, birds are more colourful in the breeding season and images produced at this time can be much more attractive.

Weight

This is used mainly for mammals, as it gives an indication of how large the animal actually appears. For instance, Otters and Beavers are roughly the same length, but Beavers are much bulkier as shown by the much greater weight.

Weight can also affect the quality of tracks. Hence, mouse tracks are difficult to see, whereas deer generally leave clear tracks due to their much greater weight.

Nesting

Knowing when and where birds nest, and what the nest looks like, helps the photographer in identifying the bird species. Careful use of information about the time of year that egg-laying takes place and how long before the nestlings fledge, will ensure that the photographer can avoid disturbance.

Feeding

Information about diet gives an indication of where you might see the animal when it is hunting for food. For example, fish eaters such as Otters and waterbirds are likely to found feeding near water, whereas flying-insect eaters will feed on the wing.

Breeding

As nesting applies to birds, the term breeding used here refers to other animals. Knowing the breeding season alerts the photographer to potential courtship rituals, such as the deer rut, and the resulting photographic opportunities. Knowledge of the time of year that birth takes place is vital to capture images of the young at a time when disturbance is less likely.

Habitat

One of the first steps to finding a particular species is knowing the animal's favoured habitat. This can greatly reduce the number of sites to visit and can help pinpoint the most likely areas to look.

Distribution

Few species are found in all parts of the UK, so this information is vital to direct your initial search. This information also tells you where *not* to look for your target.

Population

Population figures given are for the UK. If you are just starting out on wildlife photography, it makes sense to begin with a target that is relatively numerous. Early success can be a great motivator, and is much more likely with a common species. Photographic technique can be honed until the photographer is ready to tackle more elusive subjects.

Questions

I have used the question sections to expand on the basic facts or to highlight issues of relevance to a particular species. These are all issues that I discovered over time and the answers to the questions can increase the photographer's chances of success.

Identifying such questions for yourself can be difficult to enact, and requires practice, but it can give you a competitive edge and may also reduce potential disturbance.

Equipment

Camera, lens and ancillary equipment must be chosen with a target in mind. Lenses, in particular, are often subject specific. A long telephoto lens will give better quality images of birds, whereas a shorter focus lens is adequate for large subjects that can be viewed at close quarters.

Flash can improve photographs of skittish butterflies, but may disturb more sensitive subjects.

As such, research on your target species will inform equipment choice, making satisfactory images more likely. However, the most important piece of equipment is the photographer and his or her attention to detail – and careful research of the subject.

Habits

Learning the habits of wildlife will give rise to greater photographic opportunities. Knowing whether your subject is diurnal or nocturnal is obviously vital so that you are present at the correct time. Is the species often solitary (such as Roe Deer) or gregarious (Fallow Deer)? It is easier to find groups of wildlife, and interactions make more interesting opportunities. With experience you will learn the habits of a greater range of subjects, which makes photography more successful and hence rewarding.

In the field

Research before going out to photograph is important for the reasons given, but it is also vital to be aware of opportunities and problems that present themselves once you are at your chosen site. These sections describe what to look for, how to behave and how the 'indoor' research can best be put to use for various species.

If possible, it is better to select several locations, so that if you are unsuccessful in one, you may have better luck in another. It is a good idea to try to find a source of local knowledge, as that is the quickest way to narrow down your search. Birdwatchers, photographers and wildlife websites can all be useful sources of information, but if you are visiting a nature reserve, the reserve rangers will know exactly where the animals are. Rangers are usually great lovers of nature, and as long as you show consideration for wildlife, and make it clear you will put the welfare of the animals first, they will be only too happy to help. The best way to meet knowledgeable naturalists, or reserve rangers with local knowledge, is to volunteer for conservation work at a reserve, go on a wildlife course at your nearest field centre, join your local Wildlife Trust group, or meet up with your local birdwatching club.

Case studies

In order to clarify how the outline above can be applied to different species, this book features case study examples throughout. These show in detail how I used researched facts and observation to find target species, and the steps taken to photograph them. This is vital information and gives an indication of what is actually carried out on site. Case studies are intended as a useful resource for the beginner, but I believe can also help hone the skills of the more experienced photographer.

For someone starting out in wildlife photography, finding out exactly what steps a successful photographer takes to get good images can be very helpful. That is the kind of information that I would have loved to have been given when I started out, but instead I had to go through the long, drawn-out process of discovering everything for myself. I have written detailed case studies to give just the kind of detail that is so often not available.

The steps taken in these case studies are ones that you can apply in your chosen area and, with experience, adapt to your chosen species.

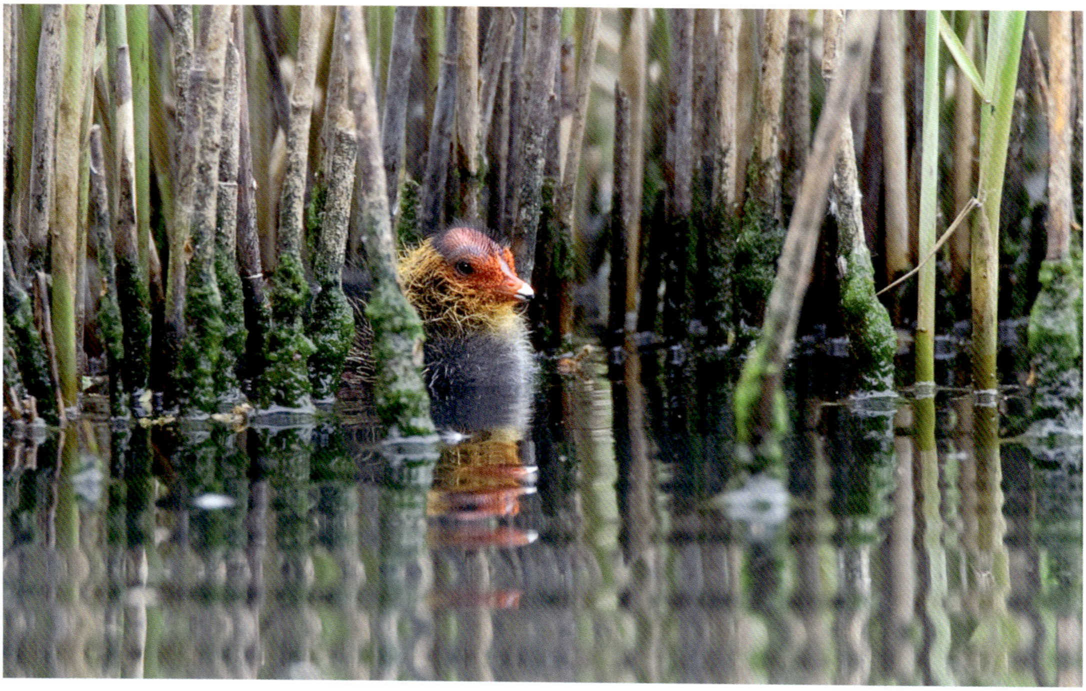

Coot chick hiding in reeds

Getting started (for the novice)

Becoming familiar with an area is important for finding wildlife, and it is better to get to know one site well than to visit many that are unfamiliar. It is tempting to think that the glowing descriptions of a nature reserve will make it easier to find wildlife there, but that is rarely the case. It is only with familiarity that those special photographic opportunities will arise.

Finding an animal can be difficult; getting a photograph is more difficult, and getting a good photograph harder still. My computer recycle bin is full of inferior images, and some days I have a 0–1% success rate – so experience is not a guarantee that winning images will always be taken. However, any success is very sweet indeed, and that is what makes wildlife photography worthwhile.

Initial research

1. **Decide whether you wish to photograph birds, mammals or other forms of wildlife**
   Camera equipment and techniques vary a great deal depending on what you want to photograph, so this is an essential step. It is true that you may encounter several types of wildlife – for example, you may see dragonflies whilst

looking for birds – but in my experience, you will obtain much better images by concentrating on one particular type of wildlife at a time. This will allow informed decisions as to which lenses to carry, probably the most important equipment choice for an outing. For the purposes of this introduction, I will use the example of heathland birds, but the principles apply to most wildlife.

2. **Decide where to look**
   For many bird species, this is simplified by selecting a habitat and considering the birds likely to be found there – bearing in mind that some birds can be found in more than one habitat, and the species encountered will vary depending on the season.
   You may wish, for instance, to visit a heathland area.

3. **Find information on your chosen habitat and/or species**
   The more information you have, the better your photographs will be.
   Use a bird guidebook or an Internet search to find out which birds are likely to be found on heathland, for the purposes of this example. This will help you to confirm your selection of habitat, as you may discover that the birds of greatest interest to you are to be found in a different area.

4. **Find locations with your chosen habitat**
   The Internet is a marvellous resource for finding good locations at which to try and capture images.
   Heathland, for example, is relatively rare, and unless you are lucky and live close to such an area, the best method is to research nature reserves. But the Royal Society for the Protection of Birds (RSPB) website, for instance, classifies birds by habitat, and gives a list of reserves of that type. Heathland habitats can be found at the RSPB reserves at Dingle Marshes in Suffolk, Farnham Heath in Surrey and also in the Pembrokeshire Coast National Park in Wales, among others. Upland heath or moorland can be found in National Parks such as those in Scotland.

5. **Select a convenient location and find out which species are to likely be present**
   Selecting a location can be difficult, as there are so many areas to choose from, but the nearest is a good place to start. This more detailed information on a specific site is necessary so that you can concentrate on a particular species. For example, the RSPB website shows that Aylesbeare Common in Devon lists Dartford Warblers, Nightjars, Stonechats, Yellowhammers and Tree Pipits, among others.

6. **Collect the basic facts about a species**
   This includes appearance, birdsong, size, feeding habits, season likely to be present and UK population. This is necessary in order to identify the birds you see, when you are likely to see them and in which parts of your chosen location they are likely to be found. Birdsong is a primary method for identifying birds. There are several CDs available for learning birdsong.

7. **Ask the right questions**
   This step involves a more detailed study of the facts, including habits, behaviour, tracks or signs of presence. For instance, some of the questions pertinent to nesting birds are:

   - **Is the bird Schedule 1 (protected by special laws)?**
     If the bird is protected, you must get a licence to photograph near the nest, unless you can demonstrate that you will not cause disturbance to the bird.
   - **Where are the birds located on the site?**
     Ask yourself whether there is any local knowledge you can use. Many professional photographers and film-makers (including those who work for the BBC) rely on local knowledge to help them find wildlife. If you have only a short time in an unfamiliar area and wish to photograph a difficult-to-find species, you may wish to hire a guide.
   - **At what time of year do they nest and where are the nests likely to be? Can I photograph in a position that will not disturb the birds?**
     Birds are most active during nesting time, especially when feeding young. This is the best time to look for birds. Avoiding disturbance to the birds also applied to those not protected by special laws.
   - **How long are the eggs incubated and do both birds sit on the eggs?**
     This knowledge is required so that you can calculate when the chicks will hatch and when the parents will start feeding. As there is less activity, there is less chance of seeing birds while they are sitting on eggs. Furthermore, as the birds are likely to be easily disturbed at this stage, it is better to wait until the eggs have hatched.
   - **Do both parents feed the chicks?**
     If they do, there will be more activity and a better chance at getting a photograph when the birds change over duties.
   - **How long after hatching will the birds fledge and leave the nest?**
     Getting pictures of newly fledged chicks is worth the wait. In the case of very sensitive or protected birds, photography should always wait until the nest is empty and birds are being fed away from the nest.
   - **Decide on the equipment you require**
     Choosing the best equipment is crucial. For example, a 500 mm lens is good for the photography of small heathland birds, together with some camouflage equipment. A Canon Prime 500 mm lens can cost up to £10,000, but there are other manufacturers that produce good telephoto lenses at a much lower cost, and the addition of extender lenses can increase the range of compatible devices.

Second-hand equipment can also be a good choice. There are specialist online retailers that will advise you. If they also have a shop, then you can visit them and reassure yourself that they are the experts they claim to be. One of the best, in my experience, is Mifsuds here in Devon.

There are photographers who always have the best equipment and make sure you know about it, but as I say several times in this book, good equipment does not make a bad photographer any better. And first-rate photographs can be taken with modest equipment.

In the field

Decide on the best season to visit your chosen site

With heathland birds, for example, the best time is spring when the nesting season starts. Male birds will usually perch on top of bushes or trees and sing, either to attract mates or to ward off rivals. They are most visible around dawn.

If at all possible, visit the site several times before taking photographs

It is best to visit early in the morning, for instance, when looking for heathland birds. Male birds sing in the open much more commonly at sunrise, and tend to have a favoured perch. Walking the site in advance enables you to select suitable positions for photography. You can decide whether a seat and net or a portable hide would be best for remaining hidden from the birds.

Decide on any special techniques before taking the photograph

Generally speaking, a large aperture with a telephoto lens correctly used gives sharp images with a diffuse background. You should also be mentally prepared for 'grab' shots, as birds may sing close to you as you walk to your chosen site, offering a perfect photographic opportunity.

Establish the bird's habits

Try to gather information from research or, better still, from observation, to establish the habits of the particular species of interest. This knowledge will lead to a greater number of photographic opportunities.

Case studies

Case studies are featured throughout with real-life step-by-step details of how I found individual species.

Chapter 1

BIRDS

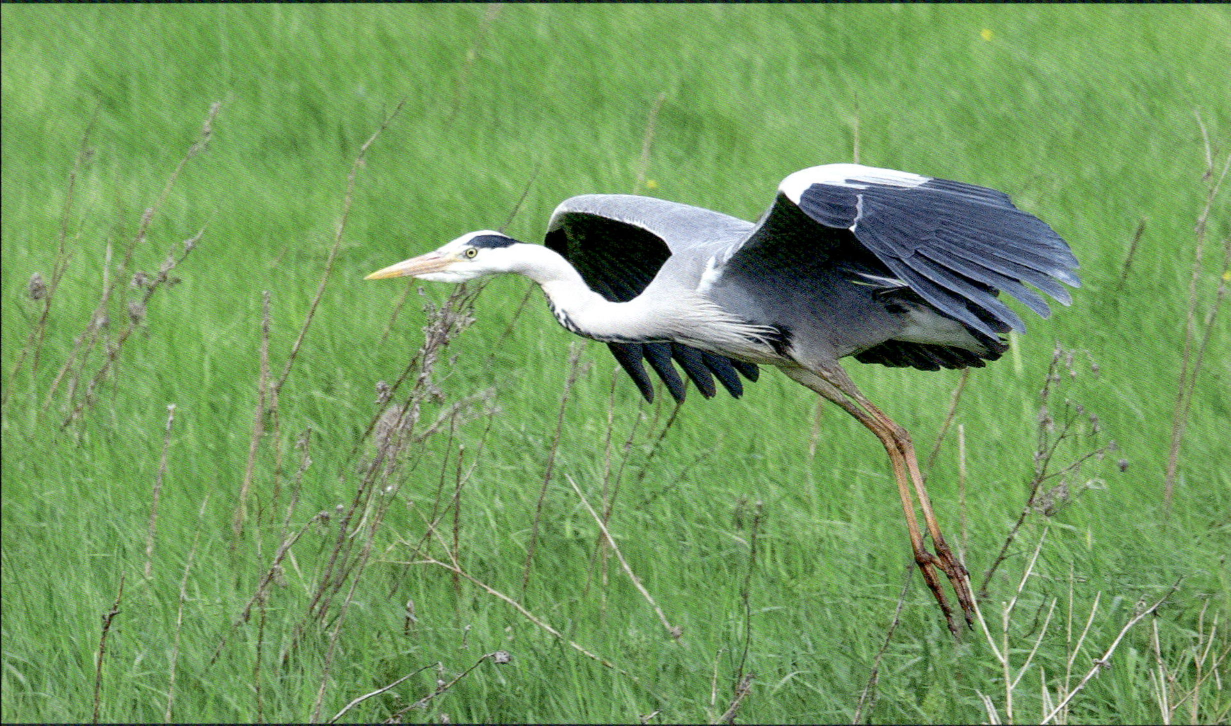

A Grey Heron takes off

Garden birds

Some photographers can be rather scathing about capturing images of garden birds, but a high-quality shot of a garden bird is better than a poor-quality image of something rarer. So, although this section is aimed at the newer photographer, the more experienced photographer and naturalist may also benefit.

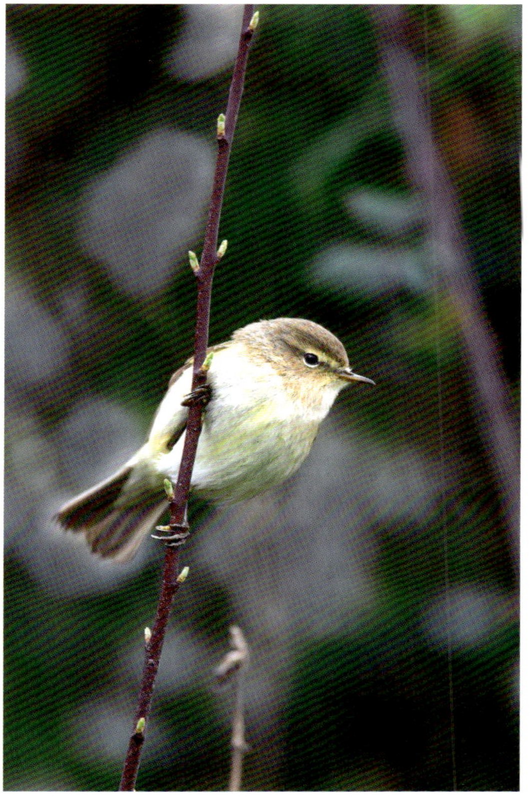

Chiffchaff

Initial research

Location

Any garden, whether urban or rural, can attract birds. Even a windowsill with some food on it will not go unnoticed.

Species

The variety of birds you might see in your garden depends on many factors:

- **Where you live:** Data from the British Trust for Ornithology (BTO) Garden Bird Watch 2020/21 showed that, as well as the common garden birds, some Scottish gardens had Yellowhammer, Siskin and Hawfinch; those in Greater London saw Jay, Great Spotted Woodpecker and Ring-necked Parakeet; whereas Welsh gardens had sightings of Goldcrest and Bullfinch. Here in Devon, coastal gardens in the south sometimes have Cirl Buntings, and snow on Dartmoor brings in flocks of Redwings.
- **Whether your garden is urban or rural:** Rural gardens with woods, water and rough meadowland attract an enormous range of birds as a result of the variety of habitats available. Even urban gardens, however, with good wildlife planting, can attract a range of species.
- **The size of your garden:** A bigger garden will attract many more birds, as long as the extra space is used to supply varied habitats. Two acres of mown grass will not attract very many species.
- **The plants growing in your garden:** The correct type of plant will appeal to certain species of birds. For example: nettles are caterpillar food and many birds rely on caterpillars to feed their young; seed plants such as Teasel, Knapweed and Sunflower will attract the seed feeders; shrubs with berries will attract other birds; shrubs and hedges provide nest sites. The BTO and the RSPB have advice for making gardens bird-friendly.
- **If you have a pond:** Ponds are attractive to birds as they need to bathe to keep their feathers in good condition, and also require a source of drinking water. Even a small pond in a shallow container

will supply the necessary water for drinking and bathing.

- **If there are trees and shrubs in your garden:** A wide range of trees is advised. Evergreens give cover and nesting sites, Rowan, Hawthorn and Cotoneaster provide berries, and Crab Apples are another source of food for birds. The best trees and shrubs are those which are native to the UK.
- **Whether you are near woodland, the coast or open fields:** If woodland is near, your garden will attract birds such as Jay, Great Spotted Woodpecker, Nuthatch and Long-tailed Tit. Rare species as well as common may be found in coastal areas, especially if on a migration route. Open fields with grazing animals will appeal to Barn Swallows and other flying insect catchers, but large monoculture fields will not attract many birds.
- **The type of feeder you have:** Nut feeders, seed feeders and a table for ground-feeding birds will satisfy a greater range. There are several good companies supplying bird food (including the RSPB), and they give good advice as to which bird species prefers which food. Even with feeders, a small tree or shrub nearby is valuable for cover.

If you live in the centre of a town, you will probably be able to attract Sparrow, Starling, Robin, tits, finches and more. If you live in a rural area and have a large garden with a pond and trees, you will attract a much wider range of species.

I am fortunate in having a large garden in South Devon, surrounded by fields and woodland. It includes several ponds, areas dedicated to wildflowers, a variety of habitats and a small wood, which is a continuation of a much larger wood. I have seed and nut feeders in several locations plus a log feeder, groups of evergreen trees (for cover), plantings of Sunflower and Knapweed, clumps of nettles, a large number of hedges both evergreen and native, cherry plum trees and other native fruit trees.

The following birds have been present at some time in my garden: Dunnock, Great Tit, Blue Tit, Coal Tit, Long-tailed Tit, Greenfinch, Chaffinch, Goldfinch, Chiffchaff, Treecreeper, Goldcrest, Wood Pigeon, Rook, Jackdaw, Carrion Crow, Robin, Mistle Thrush, Song Thrush, Redwing, Nuthatch, Great Spotted Woodpecker, Green Woodpecker, Bullfinch, Pied Wagtail, Grey Wagtail, Blackcap, Barn Swallow, Wren, Spotted Flycatcher, Blackbird, Grey Heron, Mallard Duck, Pheasant, Buzzard, Sparrowhawk and Tawny Owl.

However, although rural areas generally have a greater variety of wildlife, suburban and urban areas can be host to numerous species too. When I lived in a large suburban town in Hertfordshire, my small garden even hosted the rare Snipe and Lesser Spotted Woodpecker on several occasions.

Basic facts

As you will be waiting for the birds to come to you, rather than looking for a particular species, the basic facts in this garden birds section tend to be more general than later portions of the book. Garden bird facts are based on answers to the following questions:

- **Which birds are seed eaters and which are ground feeders?** A large range of bird species are attracted to feeders, so this is the obvious place to start. Seed feeders will attract mainly tits and finches, but I have some very athletic Robins that also use them. Nut feeders will attract the same birds, plus Nuthatch and woodpeckers, if you are lucky.

  Wagtails, Dunnock, Blackbird and other larger or less acrobatic birds are generally ground feeders. I do not usually put out food for ground feeders, as those birds can pick up enough seed discarded by fussy/messy seed eaters. Other species, such as the Chiffchaff, do not use feeders at all in my experience, so a good range of garden trees, shrubs and plants is required to attract the widest range.
- **Which birds are native breeding species and which are migratory?** The Fieldfare, Redwing, Waxwing, Chiffchaff, Barn Swallow, House Martin and Brambling are some of the migrant birds that visit gardens. Even some native breeding species have numbers swelled by migrants.

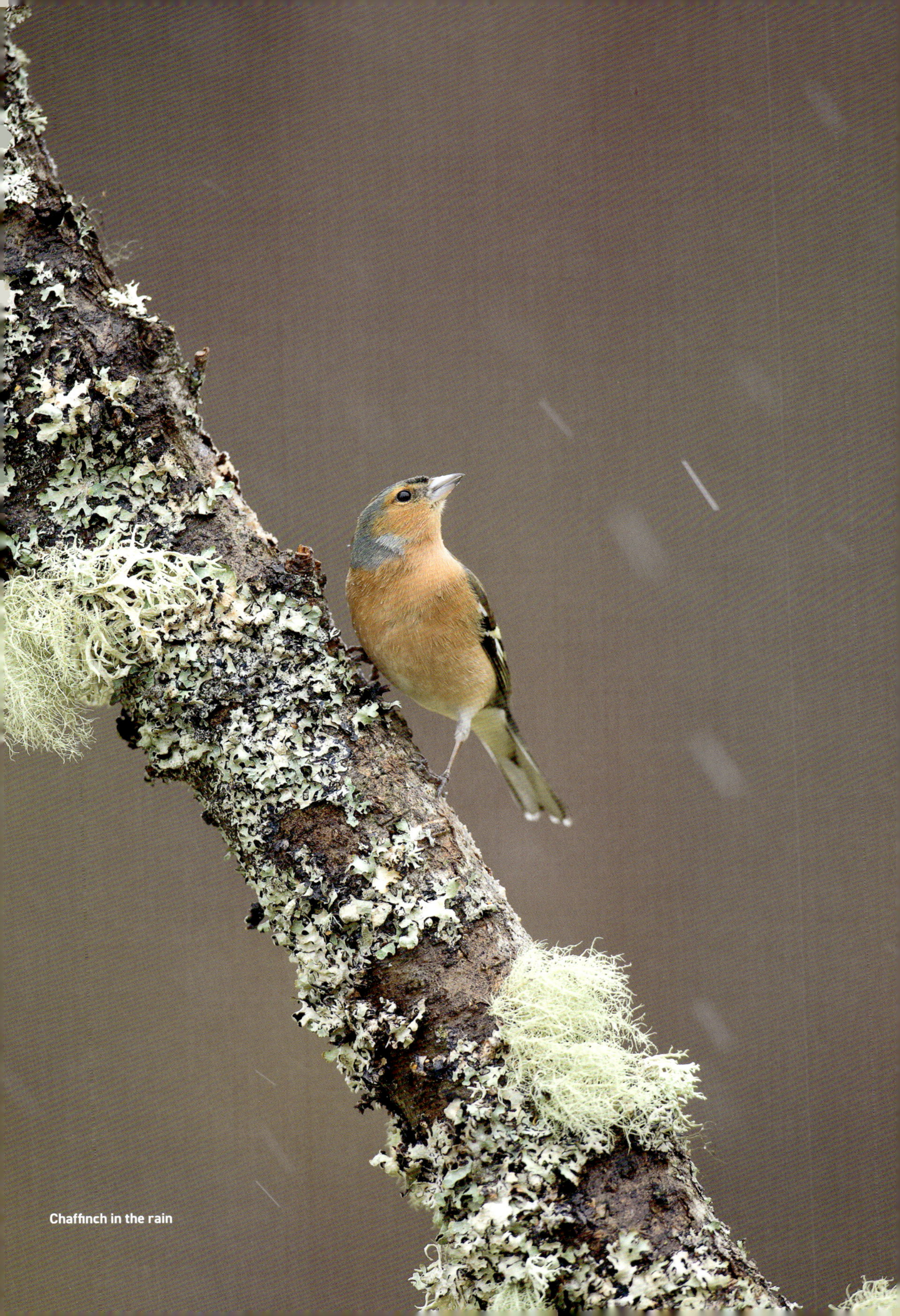

Chaffinch in the rain

- **What time of year is a migrant species likely to be seen?** The Fieldfare, Redwing, Waxwing and Brambling arrive in autumn and leave in spring. The House Martin, Chiffchaff and Barn Swallow arrive in spring and leave in autumn.
- **What type of habitat is a particular bird likely to need for nesting?** This is very varied and depends on the species. To give some examples: the Chiffchaff nests low down in bramble clumps, Barn Swallows nest in barns, Blackbirds nest in shrubs. The BTO and RSPB have more detailed information on this. Providing suitable nest sites is important in attracting photographic subjects.

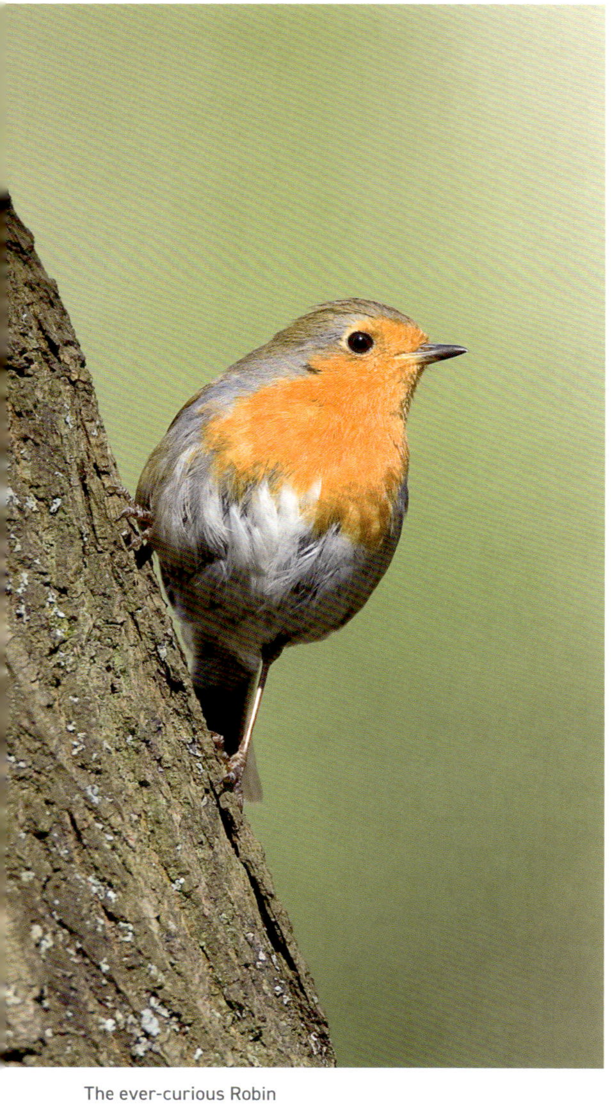

The ever-curious Robin

- **Which birds use nest boxes?** Regular nest box users are Robin, Pied Flycatcher, Tawny Owl, tits and others. The BTO has details of which species use nest boxes, and the type of box they prefer.
- **What type of natural food attracts which birds?** Thrushes like snails, so damp corners are needed. Blackbirds like berries and Redwings like fruit trees, whereas Bullfinches are attracted to fruit blossom, especially the cherry plum. Study the information given by the RSPB and BTO to ascertain what kind of natural food will attract the garden bird you would like to photograph.
- **Does my chosen species have any special habits?** This information can be obtained by research, but observation is also important. For example, Barn Swallows like to swoop down and drink on the wing, so a pond with a long, narrow section of clear water will attract them. They also like to sit on the roofs of glasshouses, as the heat from the glasshouse attracts flies and also warms the birds on a cool morning.

  The Chiffchaff may not use a feeder, but it does use ponds. It often hovers above the water surface first, giving interesting photographic opportunities. Look out for them on hot summer days.

This is the sort of knowledge that you can build up over time, and initially it is easier to concentrate on trying to produce conditions to attract the birds you are most interested in. If you are particularly interested in photographing a certain species that you know can be found in your locality, try to include items in your garden that will attract that species. For example, I was aware that Goldfinches were seed eaters and were fond of Teasel seed, thistle seed and the seed of Knapweed, so I sowed Teasels and Knapweed and left small clumps of large thistles unweeded. Each autumn I now regularly see flocks of Goldfinches feeding, particularly on the Knapweed seed.

In the garden

Perches

For the best, most natural images, set up an attractive perch close to a feeder, or place a feeder near a tree. Try to catch the birds as they approach the feeder for shots in flight. A lichen-covered branch makes an attractive perch and can be tied to a post near a feeder. If you have several feeders, you will attract more birds, and if you remove all but one when taking photographs, the birds will often alight on the perch to wait their turn. Alternatively, perches with blossom can be very successful, or a garden fence can be used instead. If you have Barn Swallows near you, you may see the young birds sitting on a fence, waiting for the parents to feed them.

Behaviour

Many people are unaware of the fact that parent birds continue to feed their young for some time after they have left the nest. Be especially vigilant in April and May and you are likely to see parent birds showing their young around the good feeding places, taking them to the feeders and, in other cases, bringing them food. There is a definite pecking order among birds – for example, a Great Tit will often intimidate a Blue Tit at the feeder to chase it off, a Nuthatch will drive off a Great Tit, and a Great Spotted Woodpecker will scare off everything smaller. Such behaviour can give rise to photographs with that little bit extra.

Hides

Some form of hide will greatly increase the number of birds you will see. It is surprising just how many different species are around but only seen when you sit quietly for some time. A hide near a pond will be more successful than a hide in the middle of the grass, as even nervous birds will come at some time or other for water, especially if it is hot. Chapter 5 has detail on hides.

Tripods

For small birds, a 500 mm lens is often required, but with a good hide, you may be able to get close enough to use shorter focal-length lenses. I would always advise the use of a tripod, as you may have to sit (or stand) for some time, and this method avoids sudden movements as you swing the camera up to your eye.

Background

One advantage of 'home grown' birds is that you have much greater control over the background to your photographs. When positioning a feeder and hide, try to ensure that the background is a good colour and is pleasantly out of focus. The easiest way to do this is to focus on the perch or feeder and take a picture without the birds being present. That way you can change your position until a soft-focus background of an even colour is obtained. Backgrounds of blurred blossom can look very attractive, provided that the colours do not clash with the plumage of the bird itself.

Angle of light

The angle of light also has a bearing on the quality of the image, so you have to consider the time of day you are most likely to take photographs, and where the sun will be at that point. Generally speaking, early morning is best as the birds are hungrier, and the light softer, but midday in summer will attract more birds to a pond. Experiment with taking photographs at different times of day throughout the year to get the best combination of sun position and height in the sky. This will help you decide where to put your feeders and hides.

Birds of rivers, lakes and wetlands

There is a wide variety of bird life in river, lake and wetland habitats, each having its own group of species, from the small to the large.

Initial research

This and the following sections on birds are more specific than the previous 'garden birds' section, as it is assumed you will go looking for particular birds in their preferred habitats.

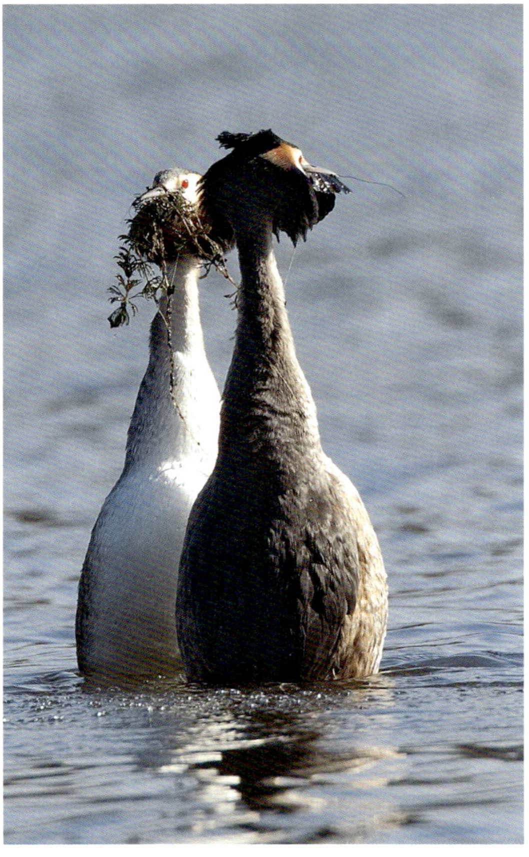

Great Crested Grebe courtship dance on a Devon lake

Habitat

A large number of bird species can be found in rivers, lakes and wetlands. Rivers are home to Dipper, Grey Wagtail and Kingfisher, as well as a host of smaller birds; lakes bring in a variety of ducks and geese, plus Grebes, Coots and Swans; wetlands can attract birds such as Redshank, Curlew and Little Egret. It is easier at this stage to select only two or three birds to research, in order to prevent information overload.

Many rivers and lakes have useful paths nearby, although these often attract dog walkers. I love dogs, but they are a menace to photographers, as they are very curious and always want to investigate what you are doing, resulting in them frightening off any birds. In dog walker areas, you have to arrive on the scene very early to avoid this conflict.

Wetlands tend to be much quieter, but they can be difficult to walk through. Wildlife reserves are a better bet, as they often have boardwalks and hides. Research a reserve thoroughly before visiting; maps and guides are usually available online.

Location

You may be lucky enough to have a river or lake near you, but if not, suitable locations can be found on the RSPB website, among Wildlife Trust reserves or at other nature reserves. For example, a quick Internet search will reveal nearly 70 suitable RSPB reserves from Marazion Marsh in Cornwall to Loch of Spiggie in Shetland. The Wildlife Trust website has a great deal of useful information on wet habitats and the species you might find there.

Species

It is easy to be overwhelmed by the vast amount of information, and finding a suitable location is only the first step. The task will be made easier by narrowing your focus to the particular species you would most like to photograph. To make the following steps more useful, I will take the Great Crested Grebe as an illustration. The principles applied will be very similar whichever species you prefer.

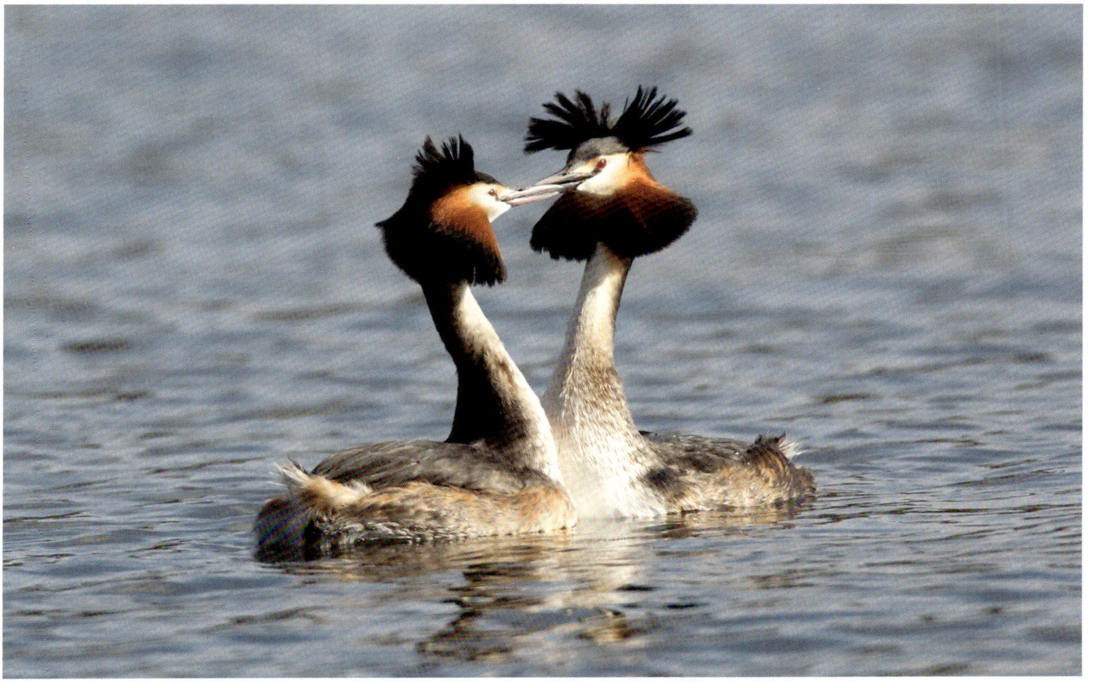

Great Crested Grebe pair in courtship mood

Great Crested Grebe

Basic facts

Description: Adults have a long white neck and red eyes. They have striking black and chestnut feathers in the breeding season, but are pale and nondescript at other times. Body length is 50 cm. Obviously, studying identification is important so that you recognise the birds, but in this case their appearance will also indicate the best season to look for them.

In the breeding season, the birds execute complex courtship routines on water, culminating in a 'dance', in which the birds stand upright while treading water. This is often carried out with beaks full of vegetative material, and is a wonderful routine to photograph.

Nesting: Nests are usually built from February to May, next to water. They are made from reeds and weeds. Up to four large white eggs are laid. If the nest is preyed upon, a later laying may take place. Avoid photography near where the birds are sitting on eggs, as disturbance may cause abandonment. This is one good reason for getting a good long-range telephoto lens.

Eggs take about four weeks to hatch, and the young fledge after another four weeks.

Feeding: Fish, insects, amphibians. This means the birds will hunt on water.

Habitat: Great Crested Grebes breed on fresh water, such as lakes, gravel pits or former quarries.

Distribution: They are found in most of the UK except for northern Scotland.

Population: About 4,900 pairs.

Questions

How does the description assist the photographer?
As well as the overall description helping to confirm you are looking at the correct bird, change of feather colour with season is also important. For the Great

Crested Grebe, winter plumage is very dull, so early spring, during the breeding season, is the best time to photograph. The young have different plumage from the parents, so extra observation is required.

What is the significance of the nesting details? Nests are often easily seen, but care should be taken not to disturb the adults sitting on the eggs. Photography is easiest, and safer for the bird, if attempted when the young have fledged. Knowledge of the nesting details allows you to calculate how long to wait before returning to photograph, once you notice that eggs have been laid. For the Great Crested Grebe, allowing six to eight weeks after the adults are first seen sitting on eggs should allow photographs of the fledged young, although the parents may move them to a safer position for a few weeks once the chicks have fledged.

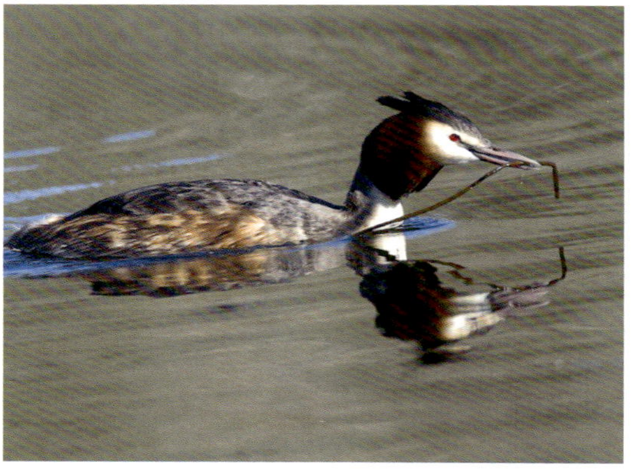

Great Crested Grebe with nesting material

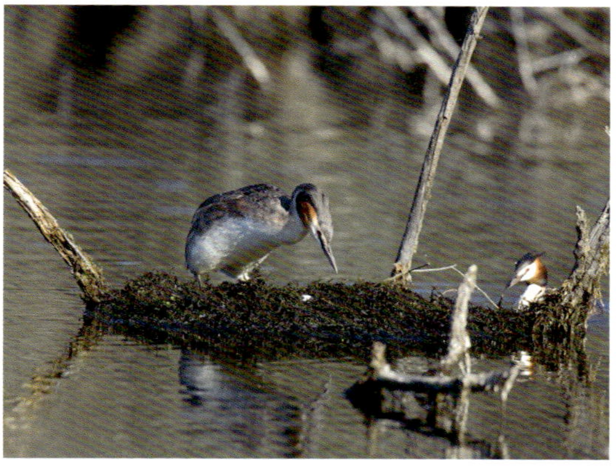

Grebe pair at their nest, with one of the two eggs on view

How do the feeding details assist the photographer? Most waterbirds fish in the water, during which they will almost always be in sight.

What is the best habitat for photography? Former quarries are popular with waterbirds, as they usually hold fresh water. Try to find waterbodies that are long and narrow, as the birds often swim in the middle when disturbed, and in rounder lakes may be too far away for high-quality images. Waterbodies that are very small will generally attract fewer birds, as they will feel threatened without a large expanse of water to escape to. Mallard ducks are the exception, and can choose quite small ponds.

What is the significance of the distribution? This information guides you as to where your chosen species is likely to be found, and more importantly where it will *not* be found. In the case of Great Crested Grebes, the photographer shouldn't have to travel too far – there should be a habitat near to most people.

Why is population important? Great Crested Grebes are reasonably common and should not be too hard to find. Rare species require much more work in both research and time in the field, and their pursuit is more suited to the experienced photographer with plenty of free time.

Equipment

A portable hide is not very practical for the photography of grebes and other waterbirds. They tend to choose large bodies of water and swim around them, so your hide could end up in the wrong position. Grebes are not particularly nervous birds, especially if they are present in parks, as they become used to people, but they will tend to stay in the middle of the waterbody if they are disturbed. I have found that sitting on a small stool with a camouflage net over me works very well, and the birds come quite close.

A 500 mm lens plus an extender will be required for large waterbodies, but in small lakes a 300 mm lens may be sufficient – although take care not to get too close to the birds. A tripod is a must, as you will have to sit for some time.

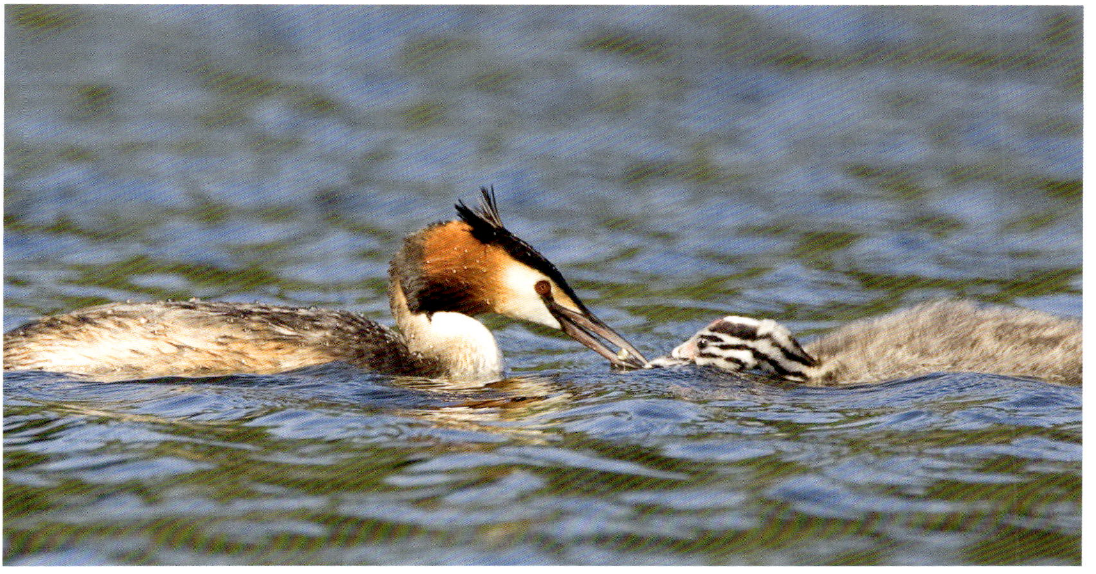

Great Crested Grebe feeding one of its young

Habits

The courtship display of the Great Crested Grebe is relatively easy to photograph, although some patience is required. The birds may swim around for some time catching fish; then a pair will suddenly start moving towards each other, heads lowered, making a distinctive staccato call. The mating dance may start, then stop almost immediately, or it can last for some time. For this species, the highlight is the 'penguin' dance, when the birds rise out of the water in an upright position holding weed in their beaks.

Once the young have fledged, they are often carried on the parent's back for a few weeks, although the birds may only do this if well hidden. However, this is such an attractive thing to photograph that it is worth returning regularly over a period of a few weeks to increase the chances of seeing it.

In the field

Having found a suitable location for your bird of choice, plan to have several visits, and walk round the site before even considering photography. That will show you where the birds are, and even if you disturb them initially, you will have a much better idea of where to position yourself when you have your camera and tripod to hand. Larger waterbodies with several pairs of birds will give more photographic opportunities. One of the big advantages of waterbirds over landbirds is that it is relatively easy to see their young, as they take to the water while still in their juvenile plumage. The colouring of young waterbirds is often very bizarre and photogenic. There are also many opportunities for seeing the young being fed by the parents, and watching them exploring. Parents are often very protective, which makes for many fascinating interactions. Sitting quietly beside a lake, with only a camouflage cloth over you, will allow you to take advantage of the many photographic opportunities on offer.

Another advantage of watery habitats is that there are also many landbirds around – look out for woodpeckers, Long-tailed Tits and Grey Wagtails, to name a few. The young of waterbirds can attract predators, so you may see birds of prey as well as Foxes. If you arrive early in the day and are very lucky, you may also see Otters or Mink.

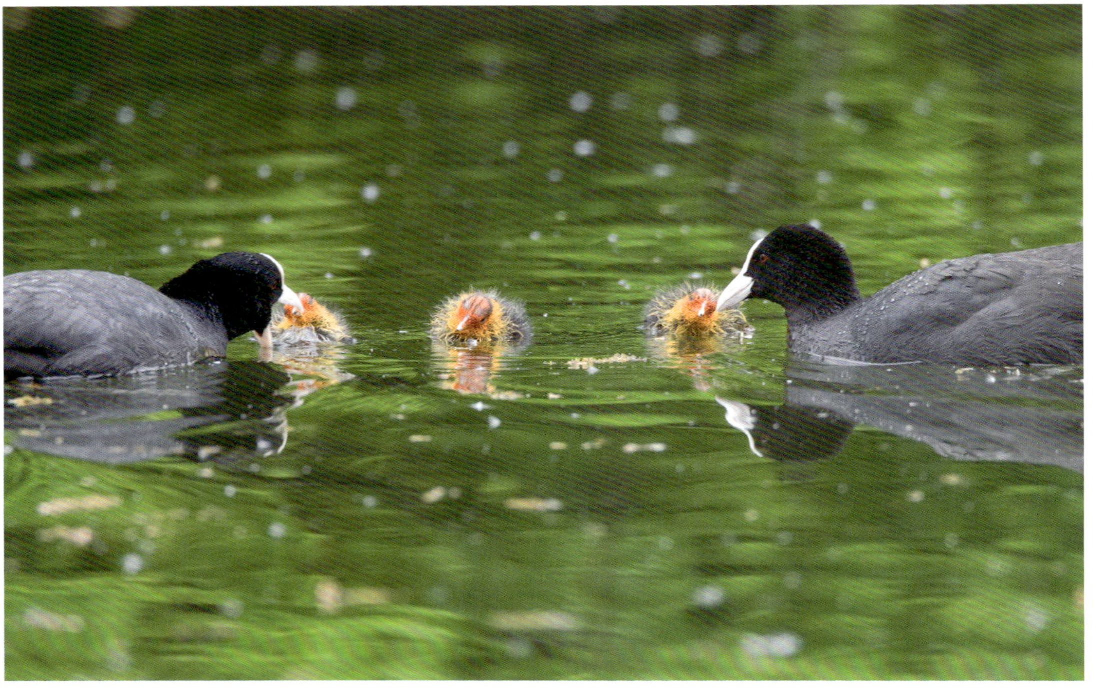

Coot pair feeding chicks

Once you have the relevant information at your fingertips, know where to go and are armed with the correct equipment, it is more than possible that your first few visits will not be successful. You may set out keen to photograph grebe courtship behaviour, only to find problems: there are no birds to be seen; it starts to rain, which dampens the birds' enthusiasm and leads to them floating about with heads under wings; some fishermen set up next to your chosen spot and frighten off the birds to the other side of the lake; a group of Canada Geese arrive, scattering all other birds; the birds put up a wonderful display, but behind a tree; the birds position themselves so that you are looking into the sun... and so on. I have experienced all of these and more. On the other hand, your first visit may present wonderful light, cooperative birds and a host of photographic opportunities.

Whichever species you choose to photograph, you should be prepared for difficulties – and that way, any success will be a bonus.

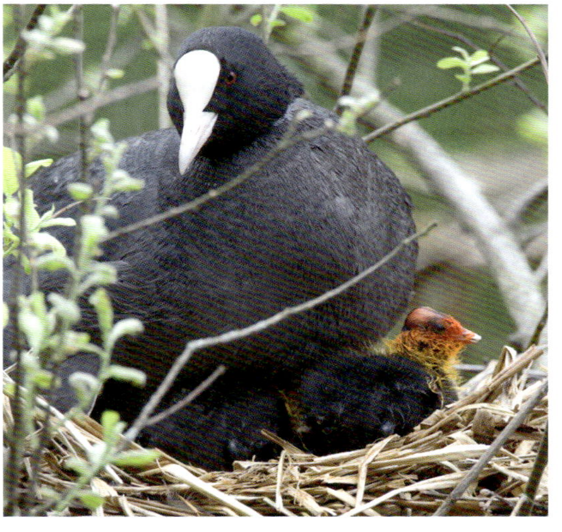

Coot with young on the nest

CASE STUDY: River birds – Dipper

Initial research

Location

I was very keen to photograph Dippers, and after talking to an ecologist who worked in the area, I was told that Dippers had been seen on the River Teign, which is very near to where I live. Although the Teign flows through a town (Newton Abbot), the upper reaches pass through private farmland with minimal disturbance. The river is fast-flowing and quite wide at all times of year. I consulted a map, looking for stretches of river that were not near habitation, yet had suitable public footpaths. In order to maximise my chances of finding Dippers, I studied the facts about the species and considered how this information could help me to locate and photograph the birds.

Dippers are not Schedule 1, thus a licence is not needed to photograph near the nest; however, it would be essential to ensure that my presence did not disturb them in any way.

Basic facts

Description: Dippers are dark brown birds with a white chest and a characteristic bobbing motion. They are 17–20 cm in length. They often fly close to the water surface. *This means the bird is a little smaller than a Blackbird. A white chest is uncommon, and with the dipping action is a good identifier. A Wren also performs a dipping action, but is much smaller.*

Nesting: Nests are built under bridges or on ledges in steep banks close to water. Nests are made of moss and lined with grass. *This indicates which sections of a riverbank are more likely to be chosen as a nest site. It might be possible to see the birds collecting moss.*

Up to five white eggs are laid from March to May. Incubation is by the female and lasts around 17 days. Nestlings fly after about 21 days. Both parents feed the chicks. *The fact that both parents feed the chicks means there will be more activity.*

Feeding: Aquatic insects and larvae. *It should be possible to photograph the birds in the water looking for food.*

Habitat: They prefer fast-running streams and rivers in predominantly rural areas. *This gives another indication of where to look for the birds. The map helped to pinpoint several stretches of the river worth investigating.*

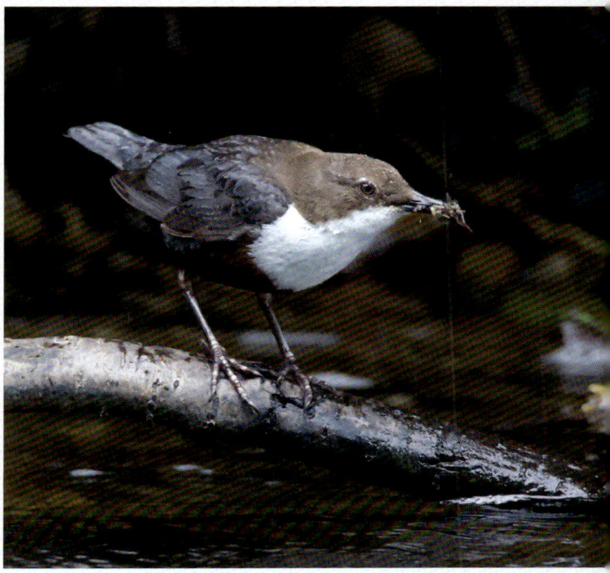

Dipper with food

Distribution: Upland areas of the UK and the south-west. *As I live in Devon, there is a good chance of seeing the birds.*

Population: Up to 18,000 breeding pairs in the UK, but very variable. *A reasonable number, so worth the effort.*

Equipment

Before making final decisions about equipment, I wanted to find out if the birds were present, and if so, where I should position myself to photograph them. *My initial thoughts were that a stool and camouflage cloth would be most suitable, if there was a good spot to sit.*

In the field

One morning at the beginning of May, I walked along the stretches of the River Teign bank that I had pinpointed on the map. I was looking for likely sites, based on the facts I knew about Dippers. One stretch, identified using the map, had a public footpath through private land, and passed close to the banks of the River Teign. I noticed that dog walkers used the path, so decided that a very early start would be required when embarking on a photographic trip, to avoid disturbance. One particular section was fast-flowing yet reasonably shallow, with rocky beaches, a stone bridge nearby, and large rocks in the river. There was also a steep bank on the opposite side, with no public access. This seemed to be a suitable spot to start looking for the birds. The river was reasonably wide, so I decided on a 500 mm lens and a tripod, based on the assumption that if the birds were nesting there, the nest would be on the other side of the river where the steep bank was situated. This first walk helped to narrow down suitable sites for photographic study.

A few days after my walk along the riverbank, I visited the site at 6.30 am, and selected a spot alongside the river on a part of the stony beach that featured vegetation to hide behind. It was located opposite the steep bank and close to the stone bridge, and thus fitted in with the type of area the birds prefer. I sat on a low seat and covered myself, my tripod and my camera with a camouflage net. I intended to sit for several hours, just to see what wildlife was around.

I had only been waiting for half an hour when two birds flew past, close to the water surface. Gradually they moved closer to the steep bank opposite me, and I realised they were Dippers. By studying their favoured habitat and choice of nesting site, I had chosen my spot well: they were building a nest directly opposite me on the steep bank. I was aware too that luck had also played a part, as even the best research can be fruitless.

Because I was low down, well hidden, quiet and hardly moving, the birds did not notice me, and even perched on a rock right in front of me, so close they were almost out of focus. I sat for some time photographing them as they gathered nesting material and flew up under the vegetation, presumably to a ledge on the bank. Initially they brought moss, which was washed in the river (I assume to bind the nest together), then dry grass.

I estimated that eggs might be laid within a few days of my visit, and adding the 17 days for the eggs to hatch, I returned four weeks later. I expected that by this time the eggs would have hatched and the parents would be feeding the young in the nest. The facts I had studied about the bird made it possible to work this out. My luck held, and I photographed both parents gathering food.

The habitat preferred by Dippers is also favoured by other bird species, and while watching the Dippers, I saw a Grey Wagtail and a Kingfisher. Because the river was bordered by woodland, I also found the nests of Great Spotted Woodpecker and Nuthatch, with very noisy inhabitants. They were obviously disturbed by the fact I was near their nests, so I did not stay to take photographs.

There is always a certain amount of luck involved in finding wildlife, but studying the details of the birds' habits can greatly increase the odds in your favour. With experience it becomes a little easier to find what you are looking for, but confidence is also very important. Once you have some success, you know it is worthwhile persevering, and you develop faith in your interpretation of the facts.

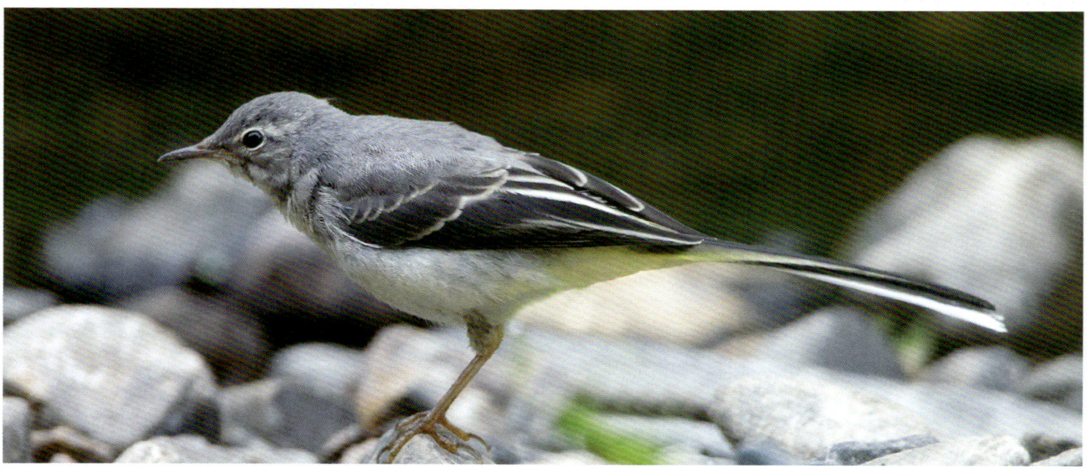

Grey Wagtails (this one is a juvenile) are often found with Dippers

Woodland birds

Woodland birds are a fascinating group: sometimes shy, sometimes noisy, and often colourful. The edge of woodland, where there is more light, is often the easiest part of the wood in which to photograph.

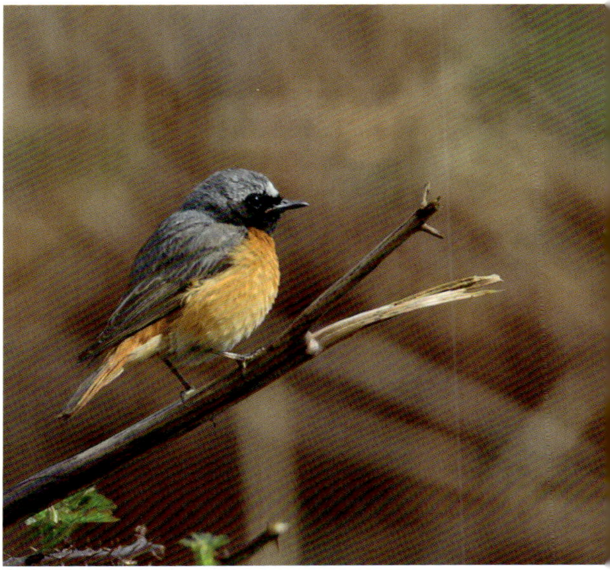

Redstart, Wales

Initial research

Location

There is no need to consult websites or books, as for most woodland birds all that is required is a broad-leaved wood of reasonable size (preferably more than one acre), with shrubs edging the wood, and water nearby. Parks and nature reserves almost always have suitable woods. The best type of woodland is ancient semi-natural woodland – in other words, woodland that has been present for hundreds of years. Such a wood is more likely to have a good range of the native plants that attract insects and provide food for birds. There is also a greater chance of there being rotting wood on site, which is a source of insects, and standing dead wood, which offers good nesting holes.

Species

The commoner broadleaved woodland species are Great Spotted Woodpecker (also found in coniferous woodland), Green Woodpecker, Blackcap, Chiffchaff, Long-tailed Tit, Nuthatch and Jay. Owls may also be present, and if the wood is on a rise, Buzzards also. These last two groups are included in the birds of prey section. Coniferous woodland, especially that of native conifers in Scotland, is host to rarer birds such as Crossbill, Goldcrest, Capercaillie and Crested Tit. If you are interested in the rarer species, it will be necessary to consult the RSPB and Nature Reserve websites for suitable locations, with the Cairngorms being a hotspot. There are several estates with hides set up for some of these birds, together with rangers who can be hired as guides. See the Appendix for details. For the purposes of this section, I will concentrate on broad-leaved woodland and use the Great Spotted Woodpecker as an example.

Great Spotted Woodpecker

Basic facts

Description: The Great Spotted Woodpecker is a large black-and-white bird with a red patch under the tail. The male also has a red patch on the back of the head. Body length is about 23 cm. The birds drum on wood in the breeding season to attract a mate and will tap when looking for food in trees. Their call is a short, sharp sound.

Nesting: The nest is a hole excavated in a tree, but nest boxes are also used. Four to six white eggs are laid from April to June and are hatched after 16 days. The nestlings are fed by both parents and are fledged after about 20 days.

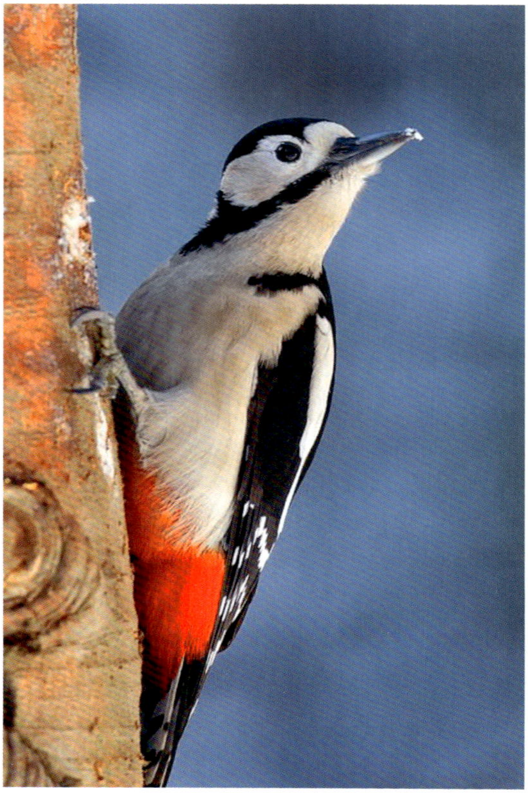

Great Spotted Woodpecker on a log feeder

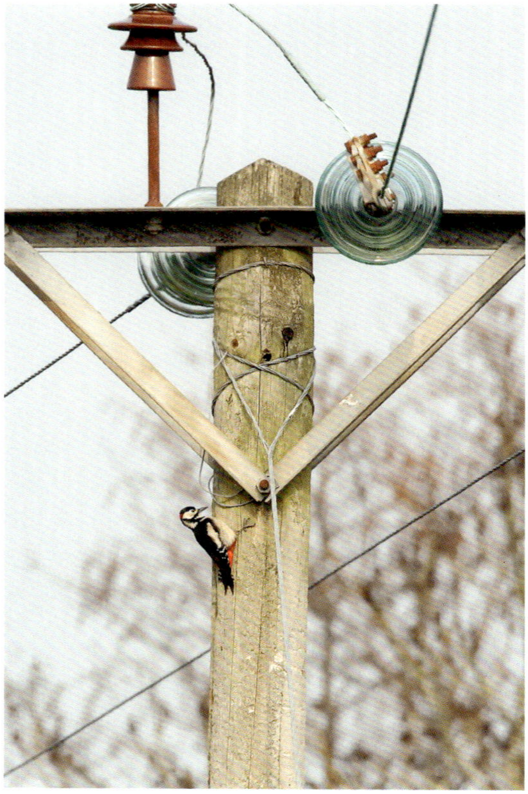

Great Spotted Woodpecker on a power pole

Feeding: Grubs, flies, small birds, nuts and conifer seeds. They will use bird feeders, but rarely feed on the ground.

Habitat: Broad-leaved or coniferous woodland, parks, wooded riverbanks.

Distribution: Common throughout the UK, except for some northern islands and Ireland.

Population: 30,000 breeding pairs (BTO), although opinions vary.

Questions

What is the best method of identifying the presence of the birds? The characteristic drumming in spring will make it clear in which area this species is located, and the call will indicate that the bird is close, but possibly alert to your presence. The sound of tapping on wood is another way to pinpoint the bird, although this can also signify the presence of the Nuthatch. If you walk slowly and quietly towards the sound, hiding between trees when possible, you can get quite close.

What is the best feeder to attract them? If you are reasonably close to even a small wood, peanut feeders are likely to attract Great Spotted Woodpeckers – but for the best pictures, use a log feeder.

Equipment

If you have woodpeckers in your area, or if you have permission to roam from a woodland owner, log feeders are the best way to attract these birds. Many of the best photographs of Great Spotted Woodpeckers are taken using log feeders. Log feeders are logs about two metres plus in height, with holes drilled in the side at an angle and filled with a nut mixture. If ivy or some other climber is planted at the base, the feeder will achieve a very natural look. Small birds of a more acrobatic nature will also use these feeders – an extra advantage.

Details of how to make a log feeder can be found at the end of this chapter.

Habits

The Great Spotted Woodpecker often drums on telegraph poles in spring to attract a mate, as they offer a more resonant sound than tree trunks. This is fortunate for the photographer – for unlike trees, poles are usually clear of vegetation, making it easier to get a clear shot. Even if you disturb the birds initially, they will usually return to their favoured pole. The birds are also fond of sitting on top of smaller trees in order to have a good look round. This will allow you to take some natural-looking pictures away from the usual log feeder setting.

In the field

The two main methods for photographing woodland birds such as the Great Spotted Woodpecker consist of using log feeders, or stalking the birds. 'Stalking' refers to the process by which you creep close to a subject without it being aware of your presence. As with many birds, it will be easier to find the woodpeckers in the breeding season. At this time of year their drumming advertises their presence, and they fly around much more frequently, initially when looking for suitable nesting sites and later when feeding young. This makes it easy to locate the birds.

If you decide to set up log feeders, first ensure that there is a good background that will give a pleasant colour and blurred appearance when you are focusing on the feeder. Woodpeckers are very sensitive to disturbance, and even a slight movement will send them flying off. A hide is advisable, if feasible, rather than just draping a

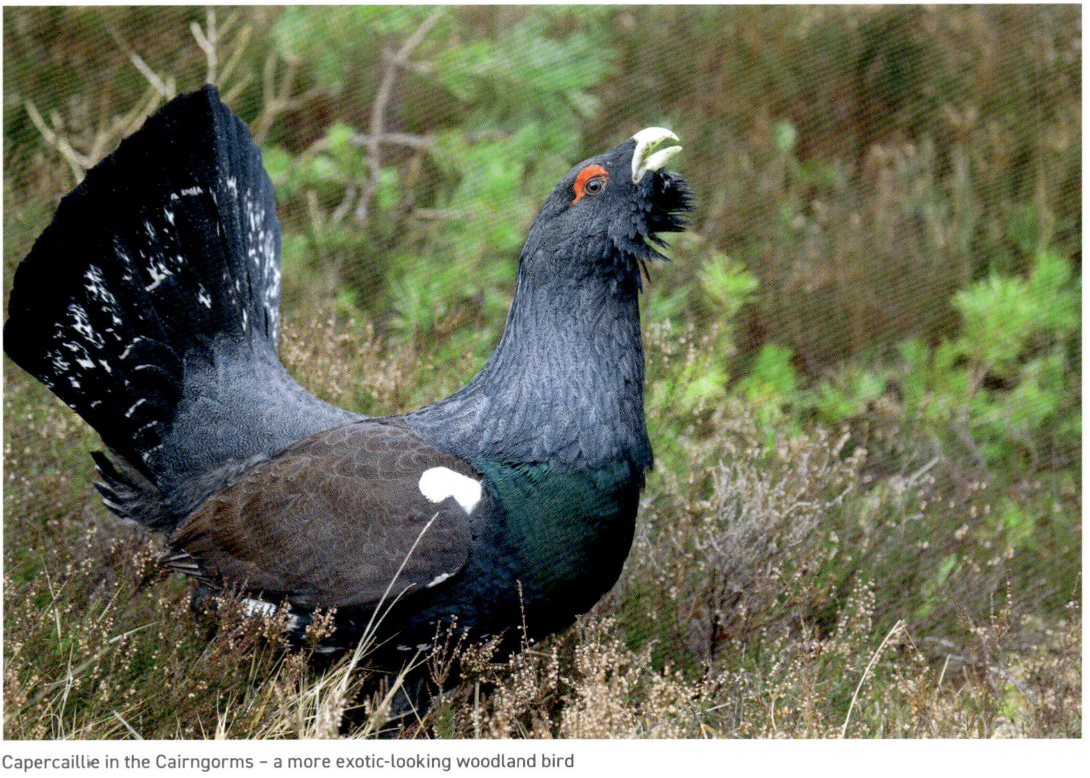

Capercaillie in the Cairngorms – a more exotic-looking woodland bird

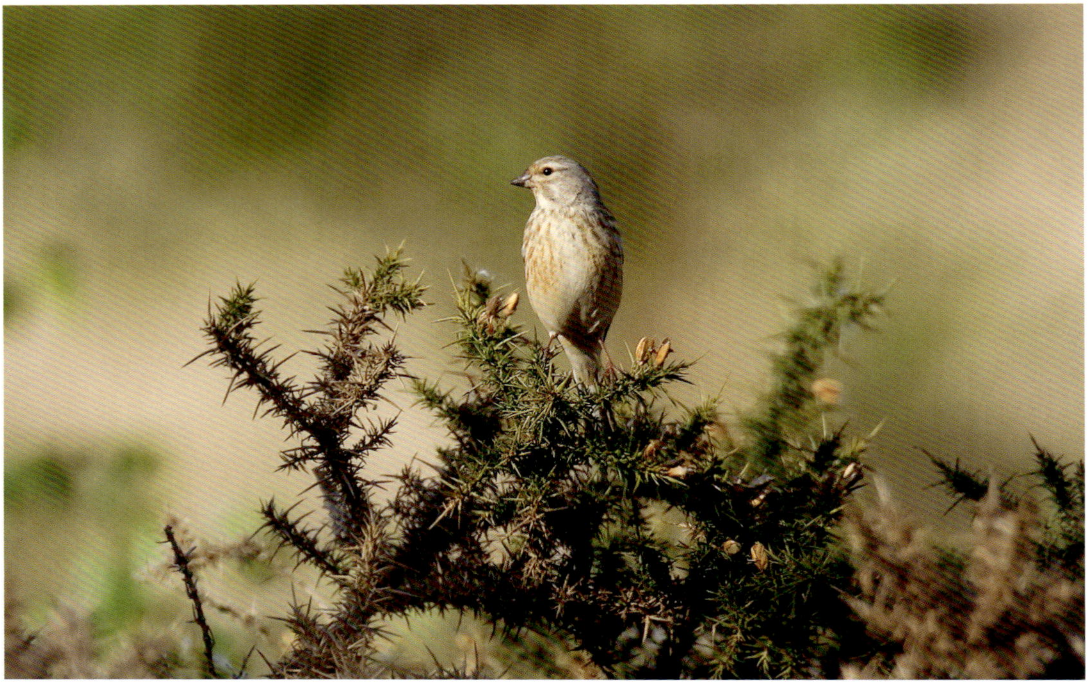

Linnet perched on gorse on Chudleigh Knighton Heath, Devon

camouflage net over yourself, as hides allow much better cover to prevent movement being seen. Use a camouflage net over the window opening so that only the camera lens pokes through, and try not to make sudden movements, as the birds may become startled and fly off. Position the feeder a minimum of five metres from the hide, and use a long lens. A 300 mm lens may be sufficient, but with a 500 mm lens you will be better prepared for shots of the smaller birds that are certain to visit the feeder and give additional photographic opportunities. A range of species will visit all year round, but there will be more activity in spring and early summer. The young birds are often shown the feeders by their parents.

It is possible to stalk the birds by creeping slowly, as described earlier, but even if you get close to the birds, the presence of tree branches and foliage can make it difficult to get a clear image. Handholding the camera is usually essential for this, which can be a problem as woods tend to be dark, making a fast shutter speed more difficult to arrange, even with a high ISO camera. If you persevere, however, you should eventually find the birds in a more exposed position with better light. Fortunately, much activity in spring can take place before the leaves are out.

Another solution I have found is to walk the site several times to establish where the birds are seen most often, then to sit and wait for them to come to you. A camouflage net and seat can work here, provided you are positioned close to a shrub or tree so that your outline is broken up and you are less obvious. My photograph of the Great Spotted Woodpecker on the electricity pole was taken in this way. I heard the drumming from a distance, and because it had a sharp resonant sound, I was sure the bird was using a pole. I looked for a line of poles, and eventually located the favoured pole of the bird. It flew off when I appeared, but I sat on my stool next to a hedge, with the camouflage net over me and the tripod ready. The bird came back after a wait of five minutes, and carried on drumming. It was possible to edge slowly closer to the bird, while still covered with camouflage, but I was limited by the fact that the poles were in a rather open environment.

It is also possible to locate woodpecker nests. These are round holes, of about 5 cm diameter, excavated by the birds in vertical tree trunks. However, be aware that the birds will be distressed if they know you are close to the nest. This will be signalled by incessant alarm calls from within the tree by the parent sitting on the eggs. Once the eggs have hatched, however, it is feasible to set up a hide nearby, as long as you are prepared to sit inside for some time. If the birds are obviously distressed, you should leave them in peace.

Other woodland birds such as Jay, Long-tailed Tit and Nuthatch can be photographed in similar ways, as they like peanuts and use log feeders – although I have to place whole nuts on top of the logs for the Jays. Jays can often be seen on the woodland floor eating nuts, so if you do not have a log feeder, sprinkling a few peanuts around on a regular basis will attract them. A pair of Jays in my wood soon became aware that I was putting peanuts out for the Badgers. As soon as they saw me approaching with the nuts, they rushed over to a nearby branch, and when they thought I had gone, they flew down to look for their treat. This became quite a problem as they ate most of them, so I now put the nuts under a stone, leaving just a few for the birds.

The Nuthatch has a very loud, distinctive call in spring, and will sit on a branch close to you, eyeing you up, when you first appear on the scene. If you are very quick, and lucky, you may be able to get clear shots of this species on a branch near you. Long-tailed Tits travel in small flocks, and will quite often come close by you, if you move very slowly or keep still. Again, a grab shot can be a lucky bonus.

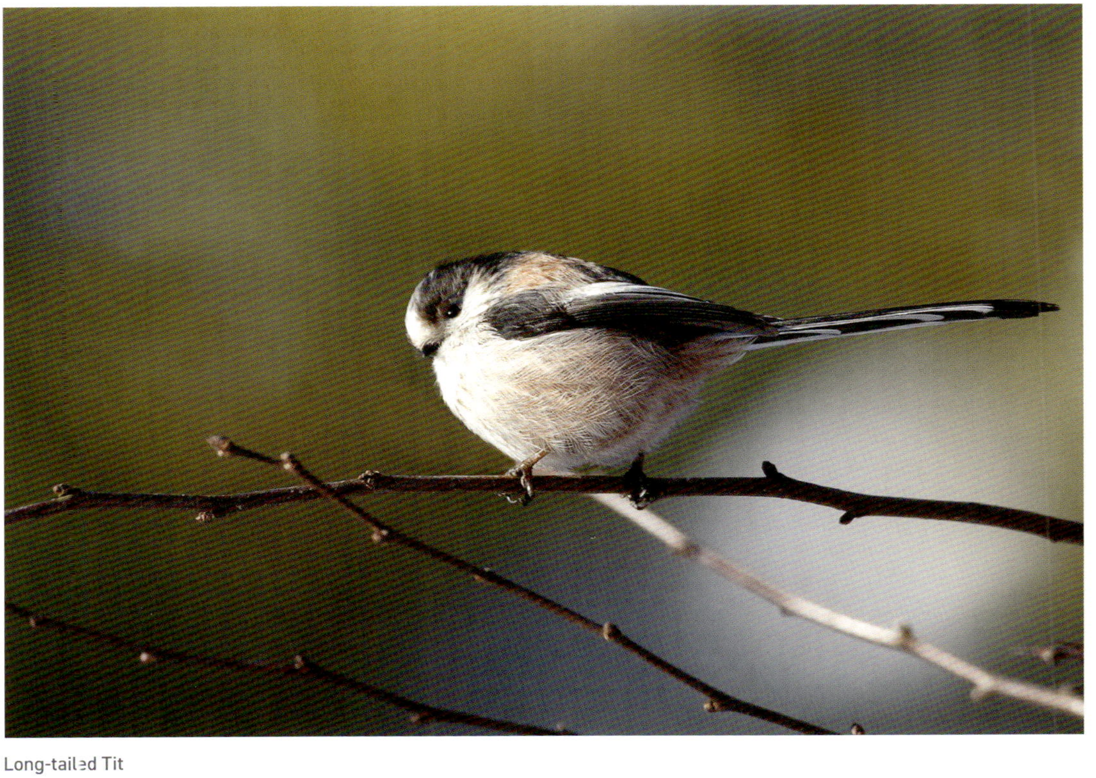

Long-tailed Tit

Heathland and moorland birds

Heathland, especially lowland heath, is a scarce habitat, and many heathland birds have declined in number as a result. This makes photographing them more of a challenge.

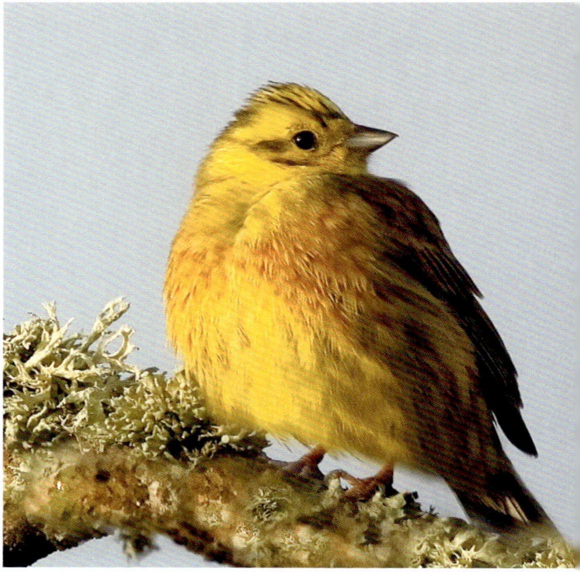

Yellowhammer

Initial research

Location

Heathland can be divided into lowland and upland heath. Lowland heath is a very scarce habitat; this can be an advantage as there are fewer sites to research, but also a disadvantage if the nearest is some distance away. Lowland heath is found in parts of Suffolk, Norfolk, south and west England, south and west Wales and parts of Scotland. Use the RSPB and Wildlife Trust websites to identify possible locations.

Upland heath is more commonly known as moorland, and is found in many National Parks such as Dartmoor, the Peak District, and those in Wales and much of northern Scotland. The scarcity of lowland heath and the generally isolated nature of upland heath can make bird photography in these habitats very challenging. Local knowledge is essential if you want to photograph anything other than the commonest species.

One thing to be wary of at all times, but particularly on heathland, is the presence of ticks. Above all else, do not sit on clumps of heather for any length of time, as you will take home more than you bargained for.

Species

Lowland heath attracts a wide range of species, but the star attractions are those which are becoming increasingly rare, as a result of the scarcity of suitable habitat. These rarities include Dartford Warbler, Nightjar, Stonechat and Tree Pipit. Upland heath tends to be more exposed and even desolate, especially when found at height. Depending on the location, moorland birds can include Ring Ouzel, Pied Flycatcher (in more wooded sections), Redstart, Wheatear, plus birds of prey such as Peregrine, Buzzard and Red Kite.

Although lowland heath is uncommon, some of its birds, such as the Yellowhammer, are quite accessible.

Photography of Nightjar can be extremely challenging. Although they are ground-nesting birds, they are so well camouflaged that it is almost impossible to see them during the day without regular daily forays to a suitable site. I did speak to one ranger who said that because he was colour-blind, he found it easy to spot Nightjars as he is more sensitive to changes in patterns of foliage. There are differing opinions on whether this is generally applicable, but is something worth pursuing for some photographers.

Nightjar are active at night – especially at dusk, when they carry out courtship display routines during the mating season – but night photography has its own challenges, even with the use of flash. I did venture out one evening to try and photograph them on nearby heathland. The birds frequently rose and flew nearby, but moved too fast for night photography. I did eventually capture one on an electricity cable using flash, but because the bird was some distance away, the image quality was not to my satisfaction. Under normal circumstances, I would have returned and persevered until I obtained good photos, but prowling round heathland in the dark is not my favourite occupation. You may be more successful.

Yellowhammer

Basic facts

Description: The male has a golden-yellow breast and brown back, with the female being duller. The outer tail feathers are white. Body length is 15–17 cm.

Nesting: The nest is made from dried grass and lined with hair, and can be on the ground or low down in a hedge. Three to five white eggs marked with purple are laid from April to June. The eggs are incubated by the female for about 14 days, and the young fledge after another 11–13 days. Both parents feed the young.

Feeding: Seed is the main food, with grain and small insects also taken.

Habitat: Heathland is preferred, especially if hedges, hawthorn and gorse bushes and scrub are present.

Distribution: Throughout the UK, especially in the east.

Population: Around 700,000 territories in summer (RSPB).

Questions

How is the bird detected? The song of the Yellowhammer is very distinctive, often described as 'a little-bit-of-bread-and-no-cheese'. A flash of bright yellow and the rusty-brown back show up well on heathland, downland or open country.

Equipment

The birds are quite curious and not particularly nervous, but as they are small, a 500 mm lens may be required. A camouflage net is advised, but a low seat is not suitable, as sitting down would make it difficult to see over the gorse bushes.

Habits

Yellowhammers can be seen most easily at dawn in the breeding season, when they will sing for some time from a favoured song post. During courtship the male may chase the female in a twisting flight.

In the field

As there are relatively few areas of lowland heath, it is easier to narrow down possible sites for this bird. If the approach to your heathland site is along lanes edged with hedges, you may see the birds flying in and out of them as you travel along. As with all sites, it is important to walk around several times in order to see which birds are present. The Yellowhammer may well gaze at you curiously as you do.

Make sure to arrive around sunrise in early May, and you may hear the bird singing from its favoured post. Once you have selected a suitable position, and are ready to take photographs, return another day before dawn and set up your tripod. If possible stand with your back to a tree and cover yourself and your equipment with a camouflage net. With luck, you will be near the bird when it starts its morning song.

Try to move very slowly if turning the camera towards the bird, as sudden movements will be noticed. On a good day, you should see other heathland birds such as Linnet and Stonechat. I have often seen Linnets and Yellowhammers on the same small tree ignoring each other, whereas the Stonechat seems to prefer the top of a bush for a solitary song post. The Yellowhammer can also be found on farmland, especially if grain is grown, but modern farming practices involve ploughing in stubble before winter, and this is quoted as one cause of the decline in numbers of this bird.

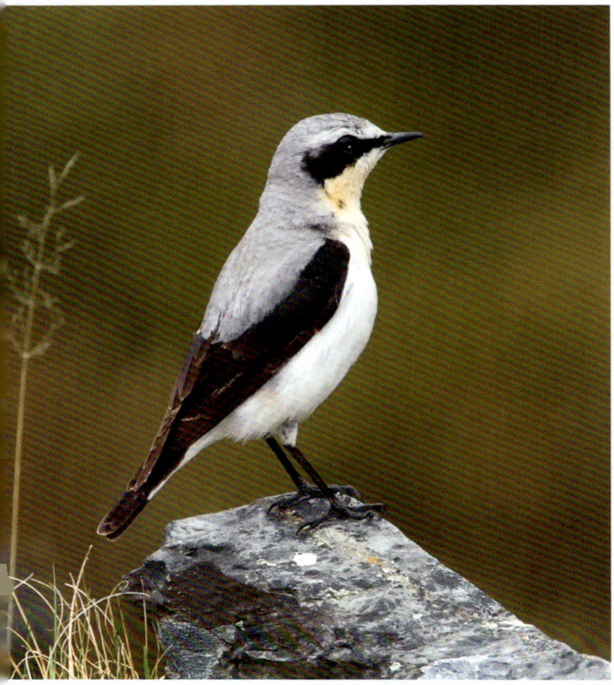

Male Wheatear

CASE STUDY: Moorland birds – Wheatear

This case study concentrates on Wheatear. Although Dartmoor, like other upland moorland areas, can be bleak, windswept and isolated, it offers many areas close to roads and paths yet still relatively quiet, especially if you are out early in the day. This case study describes how I found and photographed Wheatears with their young in April and May.

Initial research

Location

As Dartmoor is a National Park, there is a great deal of information on the official website about the species to be found and where to see them. With some basic Internet research, I was able to find several references to the birds found on Dartmoor, including Wheatear. *I had explored part of the area in South Dartmoor thoroughly on previous occasions and was aware of several small car parks up tracks, and away from the main road. The car parks were very quiet, and surrounded by rocks.*

Basic facts

Description: The male has a blue-grey back, buff chest and a black eye patch in the breeding season. The female is brown, as is the male in winter. Both have a white rump. Body length is 15 cm. *The male and female would be very different in appearance as I would be on site in the breeding season, April and May.*

Nesting: In the region of six pale blue eggs are laid April to June, and they are incubated by the female for 14 days.The birds fledge after another 14 days. Nests, which are to be found in rock crevices or rabbit burrows, are made from grass and moss, and may be lined with hair or feathers. Nestlings are fed by both parents. *I would be unlikely to see any nests as they would be underground or in rock crevices so would have to watch any adult birds carefully.*

Feeding: Insects and larvae. *The birds might be seen feeding on the ground.*

Habitat: Rough open ground such as downs and moors. *Dartmoor was an obvious place to look.*

Distribution: The Wheatear is a summer visitor, and is chiefly found in upland areas of northern and western Britain, including Ireland. *The BTO Bird Atlas also showed that Dartmoor is host to the birds.*

Population: 56,000 breeding pairs in the UK (BTO). *This is a reasonably common bird, and so a good subject.*

Questions

Is the nest site preference significant? Dartmoor is littered with rocks, giving many suitable nest sites. The car park I first considered was very quiet, and surrounded by rocks on three sides. *Their presence suggested that the area might be attractive to Wheatears in the nesting season.*

What would be the best time of year to look for the birds? The breeding season is the obvious choice as the male bird would be in his best plumage. *The birds start to arrive in April, so late April and early May seemed a good time to look for them.*

Is the fact that the nest may be lined with hair significant? Horsehair is a popular nest-liner, *so the presence of Dartmoor ponies may make nests more likely.*

Equipment

I was planning to use my car as a hide, so only required a beanbag to rest the camera on the car door windowsill. *I took a 500 mm lens.*

Habits

Wheatear like open habitats, although they nest in rocks or crevices, and can be seen chasing insects on the ground. This makes them easier to spot than some other moorland birds, or birds which hunt for insects in trees. That should also mean it's easier to get clear shots without vegetation in the way.

In the field

The car park I had chosen was very quiet, with vegetation and a stream nearby, plus plenty of grass and moss for nesting material. I had often seen Dartmoor ponies near the site, and thus knew there was a source of horsehair for lining nests – which, I was assured by a friend with horses, is a popular 'home improvement' technique for birds. As the car park was bordered with large rocks hosting many crevices, it seemed like a good choice for a possible Wheatear sighting. Car parks on Dartmoor, away from the main road, are generally quiet, provided that one arrives before the dog walkers. By sitting with one side of the car opposite the rocks, I was able to use my car as a hide. I perched my 500 mm lens on a beanbag on the car door, pointed the lens towards the top of the nearest rock and waited.

I had only been there for five or ten minutes when a male Wheatear appeared on top of the rock. He was quickly followed by a Meadow Pipit, a Pied Wagtail and, to my delight, a pair of Linnets. It is not often that one has such good luck, but my careful planning paid off. The male Wheatear appeared on the rock several times, but there was only a brief visit by a female. Because the eggs are laid from April to June, and as both birds were around, I concluded that either the female was sitting on eggs, the pair was seeking out a likely nesting place, or they were in the process of building a nest. The male flew down frequently to one spot to the left of the large rock on which it had perched, so I reckoned the nest site was in that area. The eggs take 14 days to hatch and the young take another two weeks to fledge, so I decided that if I returned in four to five weeks, I might see young.

Five weeks later

Five weeks later I returned, this time to another small car park closer to the area where I suspected the nest site might be, and just fifty metres from the first car park. I did not want to get too close in case I disturbed the birds, and once again used my car as a hide. My luck from the previous visit held, and I could see the male Wheatear feeding a youngster. As I watched, another appeared, begging for food.

Had I read about this several years ago, I would have thought that the success was dependent on years of experience and that it would take a long time to acquire that knowledge – but it was simply a matter of applying the basic facts about the birds to the environment, as I have outlined. This example is from Dartmoor, but the principle could apply equally to any nature reserve or wildlife area near you.

During a visit to Wales a year or two later, I was lucky enough to see the nest site of a Wheatear. The nest site was a hole in the ground on a south-facing bank. At first I saw a bird carrying dry grass and small feathers, and watched its progress. It landed on the same spot several times, and eventually I was able to locate the nest hole, as shown in the image below.

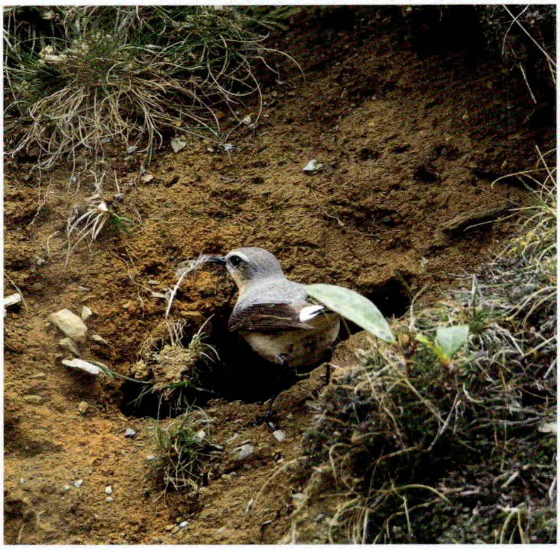

Wheatear at nest hole

Birds of coast and estuary

Our coasts are host to a rich variety of birds, and are one of the more rewarding areas for photographers to explore.

Initial research

Location

Coastal areas offer some of the best photographic opportunities available, as there is usually a large number of birds around, with the chance of some rarer species as well as a great variety of commoner ones. The Wildfowl and Wetlands Trust has several excellent sites around the UK, with Slimbridge on the Severn being the first and arguably the best for wading birds. The RSPB has many fine sites, with Minsmere in Suffolk one of the better known. The disadvantage of such sites, however, is that they can be very busy, so you have to arrive early to avoid the crowds during the peak bird season. If you prefer quieter surroundings, almost any river estuary will be worth visiting.

Many reserves contain hides in coastal locations, so it is worth looking to see if your chosen site has them. Birdwatchers can be very enthusiastic and regularly carry out 'official' bird counts from hides, or nearby. They are often very knowledgeable, and willing to help with identification. They can advise you of sites nearby that are worth visiting, which will save a lot of time in research. You are also likely to meet other photographers in hides, and they can be a source of useful information – although in my experience, they are not as knowledgeable as birdwatchers.

Cliffed coasts can offer enormous quantities of birds, with the Bempton Cliffs in Yorkshire being one of the more spectacular and accessible mainland sites. However, it is on islands remote from habitation, where pollution is lower and fish stocks higher, that the largest colonies of cliff-dwelling birds can be found. St Kilda in the Outer Hebrides, for instance, has 60,000 pairs of Gannets plus hundreds of thousands of other birds. The disadvantage of many island sites is that the birds can only be seen after a long trip by boat, sometimes in rough seas. Shetland, however, has many seabird colonies, most of which can be seen from the land: Sumburgh Head and Hermaness are among the better known. Several islands off the coasts of Wales and Ireland also have important seabird colonies.

If you are some distance from the main sites described, or do not fancy long boat trips in rough seas, you will be able to find seabirds in any of the coasts and estuaries in the UK, but in much smaller numbers.

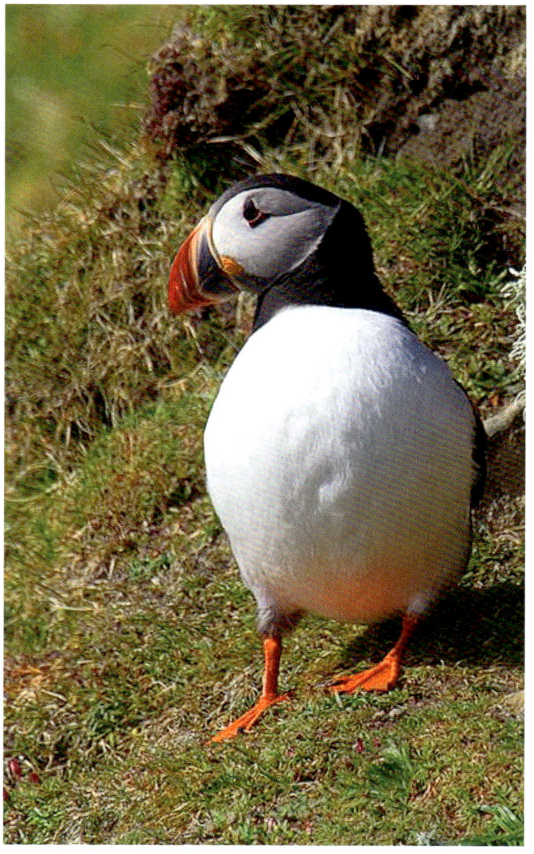

Puffin on Skomer Island, Wales

Species

The species seen will vary according to the site, depending on whether it is an estuary with wading birds or a cliffed location, and these are separated below. Generally the birds can be divided into those which fish by diving into the sea, either from a height or from the sea surface, and those which wade in shallow water, or at the edge of the tide. Plunge divers such as Gannets can give spectacular photographs, but you have to be very quick, as they dive at high speed. Guillemots dive from the sea surface, so are less spectacular to photograph. Wading birds are much easier subjects.

Estuary or beach: Slimbridge in South Gloucestershire, Minsmere in Suffolk, Dawlish Warren in Devon, for example.

In winter, Slimbridge is famous for the large number of migrant birds, especially Bewick's Swan. There are also large flocks of birds such as geese and ducks of various kinds, Golden Plover, Curlew, Dunlin, Lapwing and Greenshank in winter and spring.

Cliffs: Bempton Cliffs in Yorkshire, St Kilda in the Outer Hebrides, Skomer and Ramsey Islands in west Wales are good examples.

Cliffed coasts attract Gannet, Guillemot and Razorbill, often in great numbers, together with Cormorant, Puffin and a host of other birds, although many of these species are only present in spring and summer.

Puffins are popular spring and summer subjects and are present where there are suitable sites for digging burrows for nests. Skomer Island in west Wales and Sumburgh Head in Shetland have accessible Puffin sites, for example. Puffins are not nervous birds and it is possible to get very close to them.

Basic facts

There are so many interesting birds to be found on coast and estuary, and so many locations that it is easier to focus on one or two species at first. Reserves with a large number of birds often steer visitors away from the land-based breeding areas, as the birds here are easily disturbed. In addition some birds, such as the Arctic Tern and the Great Skua, are very protective of nests and will attack unwelcome humans. Although they will mostly avoid contact, this can be very disturbing for the photographer! Cliff dwellers are easier to view, and chicks can be seen, although it can be more difficult to get close. These are all important points to consider when homing in on a particular species.

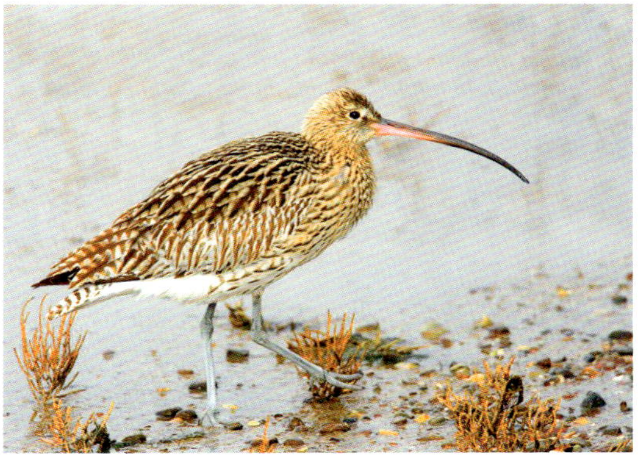

Curlew

Questions

When do the young leave the nest? Once you have selected a site and researched the species likely to be found there, it is advisable to find out when the young fledge, as you will be able to photograph parents bringing in food or see the young starting to forage for themselves. Cliff dwellers in particular can be interesting, especially at the time when the young plunge into the sea for the first time.

Which birds are present and when? Some species are winter visitors or summer visitors only, so this information is vital to gauge what you are likely to see and when. The Internet is a valuable resource, as most reserves give lists of birds seen per season.

Be aware that smaller birds such as Wheatear, Pied Wagtail and Linnet are also likely to be present around the fringes, so keep an eye open for them.

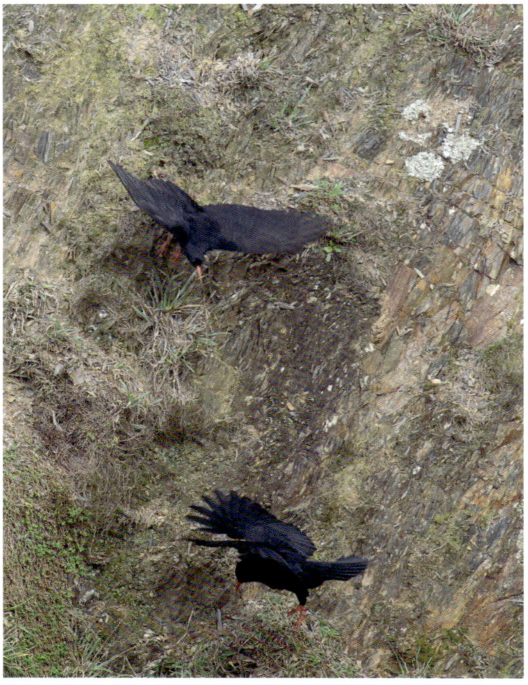

Choughs on a cliff in Wales. This is a rare and charismatic corvid species, with characteristic red feet and downcurved red bill.

Equipment

A long lens, 500 mm or so, will usually be required, especially as you may be further from the birds than you might like. Shorter focal lengths, however, are also useful for those birds which are closer, such as Puffins.

In the field

Waders

There are many species of wader, each with their own habits and presenting their own challenges to the photographer. If using a hide, the only problem is whether or not the birds will get close enough to you. The best time is generally from the hour before to the hour after high tide, as then the birds are usually closer inland, and are actively feeding at the water's edge. Cormorants, although not waders, often collect on small sandbars as the tide rises, and the smaller birds fly around in flocks before landing in a group. Sanderlings rush around in clusters at the edge of the water, and Redshank and other waders test small pools left behind by the receding tide. The larger birds, such as Little Egret, Grey Heron and Curlew, are active as the tide recedes, and these are among the most beautiful of the waders, in my opinion.

If you do not have access to a hide, beaches can be problematic as there may be little cover. However, some of the smaller birds are less nervous, and if you sit or stand still they may come to you. For extreme close-ups, the fanatical photographer will crawl on his or her stomach towards the birds. That is not something I am keen on, but it can be very successful.

Cliff dwellers

These birds are easy to photograph as they gather in large numbers (in the main sites), so there is always something interesting to observe. The main disadvantage is that it is not always easy to get close enough for clear shots, even with a 500 mm lens, but that does depend very much on the site. A tripod is generally required, but it may be more convenient to go without one, and balance your camera instead on a beanbag or on your camera bag, on a convenient rock. Be aware that cliff sites can be very windy, so do not put yourself or your equipment too close to the edge.

The large number of birds generally present on coastal sites can make it difficult to select one or two for a detailed study, but if you can get close enough this will not be a problem and you can take advantage of the many opportunities that will present themselves. Many island sites, even those close to the mainland, offer boat trips round the island, but photography on a boat brings its own challenges unless the sea is very calm. It does however allow one to get closer to birds such as Guillemots, which dive from the surface of the sea, and terns, which hover just above the water before diving. Ferry boats are a good compromise, as they tend to be larger and stable enough for photography, yet will still get you close to seabirds.

CASE STUDY: Estuary birds – Little Egret and Heron

Herons can be found on any waterway, but are often seen with egrets on the coast. The Little Egret is possibly the most beautiful of our native birds, although it is only in recent years that it has come to the UK in large numbers. Egrets are found mainly in the south, but the fieldcraft for the photography of egrets is similar to that for the Grey Heron, which is present in most parts of the UK. My ambition several years ago was to photograph these birds at close quarters in the wild at my local estuary, the River Teign. The steps I took to get good shots are described below.

Initial research

Location

Little Egrets are present on most of the estuaries in the south, but the main problem with photographing them at close quarters is that they are very nervous. As a result, it was obvious that finding a site with good cover would be essential. *The relatively narrow Teign estuary, which is lined with trees, fitted the bill exactly.*

Basic facts

Identification: The Little Egret is a large white bird with black legs and beak, and large yellow feet. Body length is 60 cm. The Little Egret is in the heron family, and is often seen in groups with Grey Herons. *Being fairly large birds, they are easy to see.*

Nesting: In April and May, large nests are made from twigs and branches, and established in tall trees near water. The birds often nest in heronries. Eggs are laid from April to May and take about three weeks to hatch. The young fledge about six weeks after that. *I was visiting in summer, so expected to see some juvenile birds.*

Feeding: Fish, insects, molluscs. *The birds would most likely be fishing in the water.*

Habitat: Little Egret are commonest on river estuaries, but are also found on lakes and reservoirs. Southern estuaries see the biggest concentration. *The Teign Estuary would be a suitable site to see groups of birds.*

Distribution: They are found mainly in England, especially along the southern coasts. *The Teign estuary is on the south coast of Devon.*

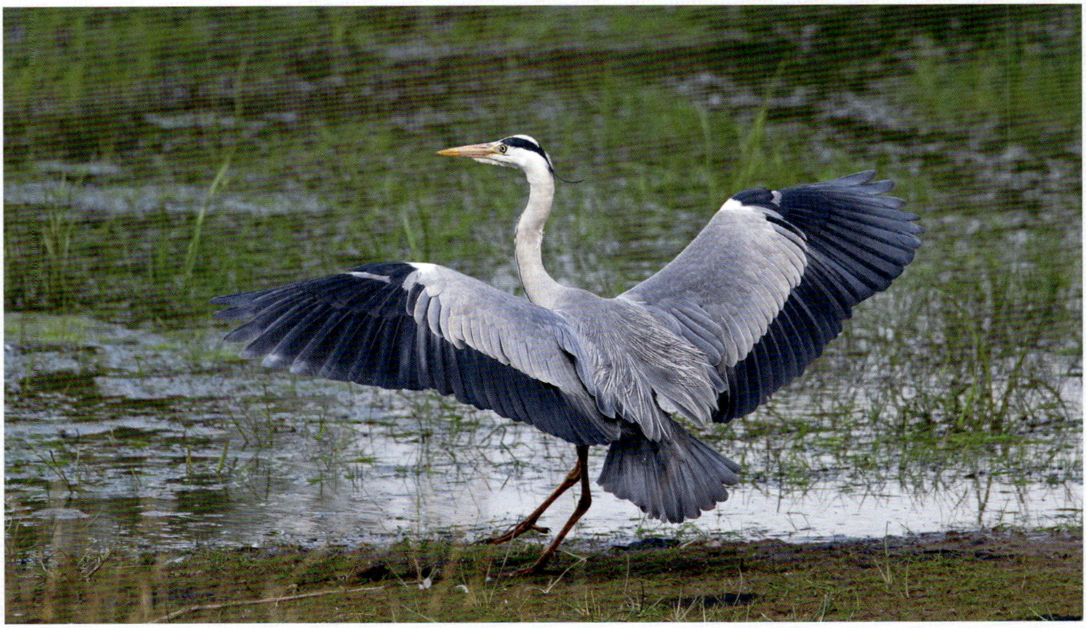

Heron with outstretched wings

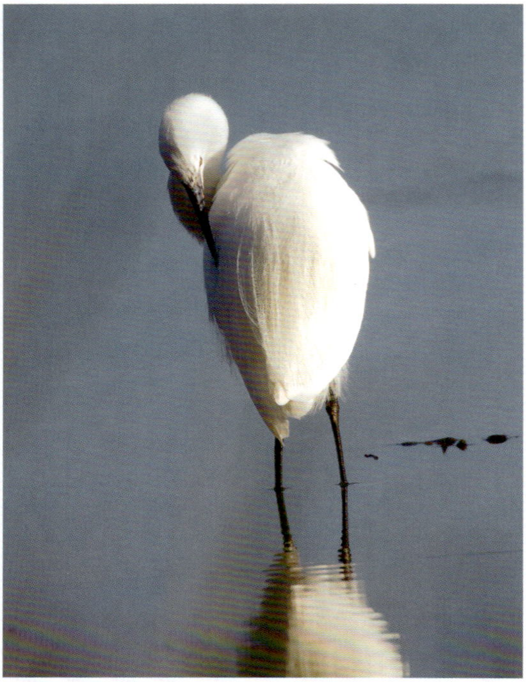

Little Egret preening

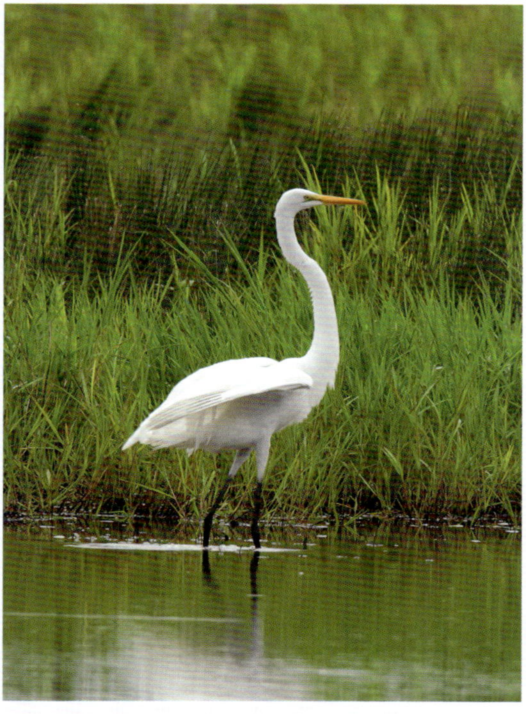

Great Egret

Questions

How are the birds affected by the tide? Because the birds fish in shallow water, they often roost in trees at high tide. They are at their most active on the receding tide. *This gives two different photographic opportunities to plan for.*

What time of year is the best to photograph them? Although some birds remain throughout the year in the south, summer is the best time to see them, when the numbers have been swelled by migrants. *In early summer, young may be present.*

Equipment

The Little Egret is quite a large bird, which would normally mean that a 300 mm lens would be adequate, especially if some form of camouflage is used, and the birds come close. However, because it is a nervous bird, I selected a 500 mm lens, since that would allow me to photograph more distant birds without the shutter noise disturbing them. As I expected to be standing for some time, the shore being very wet and unsuitable for sitting, *I decided that a tripod would be essential and that a camouflage cloth such as pigeon net should be used.*

Habits

Watching the birds fishing is fascinating. They stir up the water with one foot to disturb their prey, then stab down with their powerful beaks. They often collect in small groups, allowing the opportunity for interaction between birds. They also roost in trees when not fishing.

In the field

Before setting out to photograph the birds, I visited the estuary several times to familiarise myself with the problems that could arise. I also wanted to find out if there were any spots favoured by the birds, so that I could locate a suitable 'wait and see' position. The first problem to overcome was the tide. The Teign is a relatively narrow estuary and is affected a great deal by tides. High tides vary in height as well as time of day, and it was obvious that I would not be able to walk along the shore at the highest tides. It would be necessary to consult tide tables before I set off, to determine when there was a medium

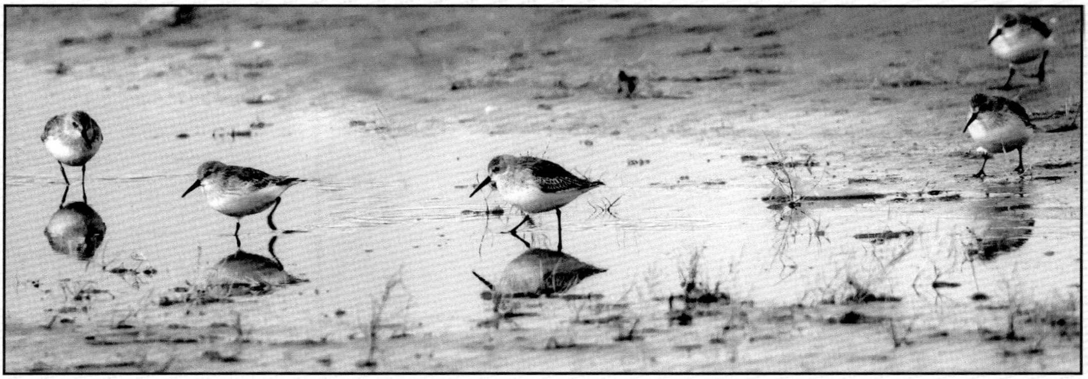

Sanderlings

high tide at a suitable time of day. The shore was very slippery with seaweed and wet rocks, so considerable care would be required when carrying camera equipment. Wellies would also be essential, as I soon discovered that the shore was very muddy and wet in places.

During my early visits to the site, I noticed that there were several dog walkers around, and that the dogs frequently ran into the water, frightening the birds. As a result, I decided that it would be essential to choose a day when a medium high tide took place around 6 am, as the dog walkers generally did not arrive until after 7 am.

I walked along the shore, looking for favoured fishing sites, and although the birds flew off when I came closer than 100 metres, I was able to pinpoint several favoured areas. One of these had a convenient tree overhanging the shore. As there was room to stand under the tree, it seemed like a good base for photography.

The birds usually roost in trees overnight as well as at intervals during the day, and by studying the shoreline on the access road to the shore, I saw several colonies in the trees lining the river. On my first photographic visit, the birds were obligingly arranged on a nearby tree, preening themselves in the rising sun before setting off for a day of fishing.

Once I had completed the initial field research, I returned at 6 am when it was a medium high tide. I positioned myself under the selected tree, set up camera, 500 mm lens and tripod, covered myself and my equipment with pigeon net and waited. After thirty minutes or so, the birds started flying past and several landed close to where I was standing. The tree together with camouflage net worked well, and the birds came very close without seeing me. In fact they came so close that they filled the frame of my full-frame camera. Although I had decided on a 500 mm lens, a 300 mm lens would have been satisfactory after all.

To test the importance of using a camouflage net, I returned on another day to the same spot, but without it. The birds started to approach me, then at the last minute turned and flew away. This was obviously because I was more visible without the net, despite being under a tree – a valuable lesson in the importance of camouflage.

Once the tide had receded, the birds collected in large clusters in the middle of the river, and it was possible to take some pictures of group interactions. Although it would have been possible to get images of egrets from day one, when they were in the middle of the river my aim was to produce images of individual birds that could be printed at A3 size. It should not be enough for you just to get any image. Aiming for the highest-quality possible makes wildlife photography really worthwhile.

Although the Little Egret is the commonest egret to be found in the UK, you may be lucky enough to see the Great Egret. This bird is larger, as the name suggests, and it has a very long neck, with a yellow bill and black lower legs and feet. Their numbers are on the increase, so they are worth looking for. Another species, the Cattle Egret, has also been appearing in parts of southern Britain in recent years, and has even bred in the south-west.

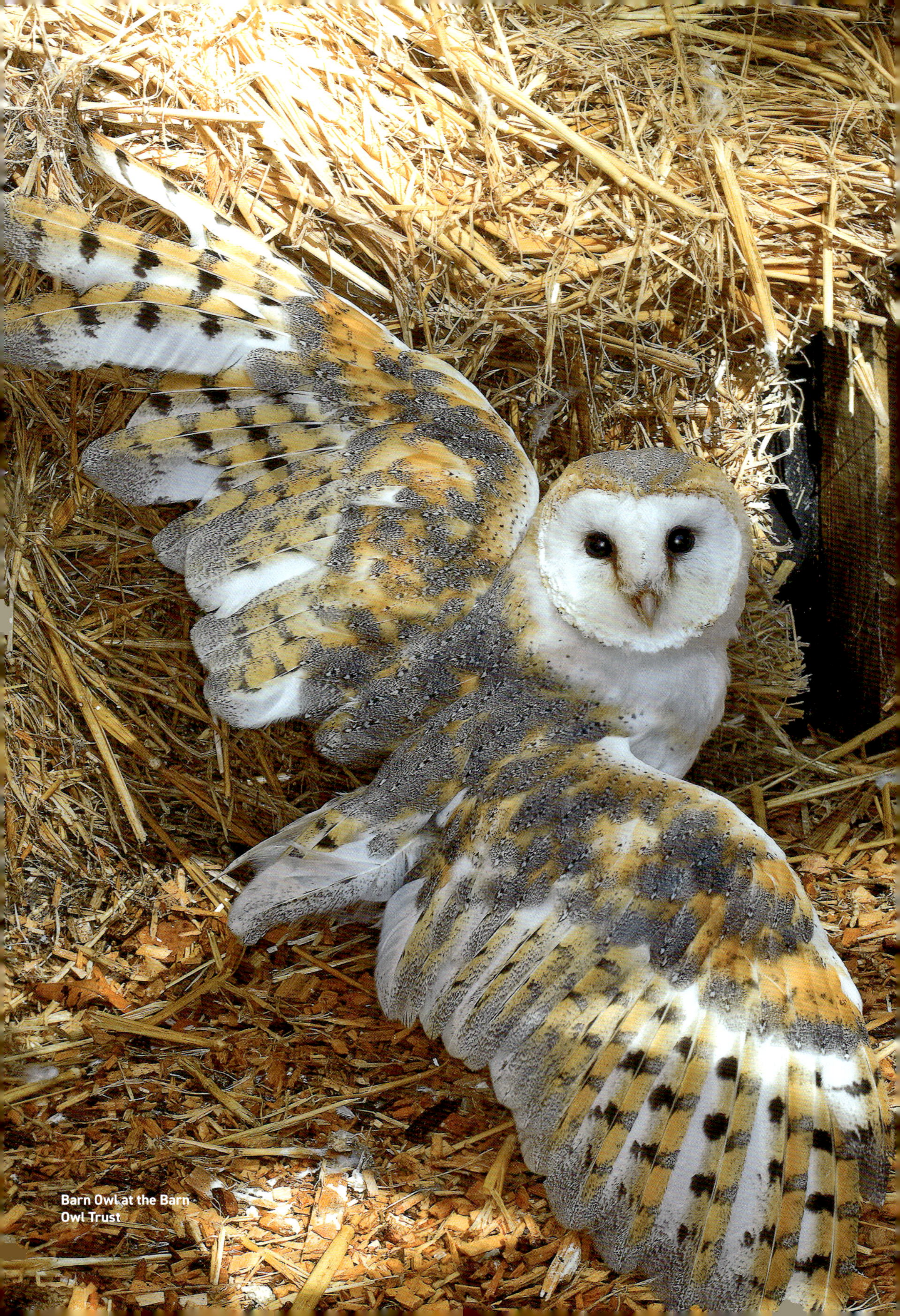

Barn Owl at the Barn Owl Trust

Birds of prey

For birds of prey (also known as raptors), the initial research comprises two components: general details applicable to most species, together with the facts relating specifically to each species.

Initial research

Birds of prey are by far the most difficult birds to photograph. The likes of Tawny Owl, Buzzard, Sparrowhawk and Kestrel are very challenging to capture on camera, even if their presence is known. Owls are mainly nocturnal so can only occasionally be photographed at dusk or dawn, and other birds of prey have such good eyesight it is impossible to stalk them. A bird that can spot the ultraviolet light from a urine trail left by a vole will certainly have no trouble in seeing a photographer coming from a long way off. As a result, research for bird of prey photography has to be much more comprehensive than for most other birds. Simply choosing a promising location is not sufficient. This section is therefore structured differently from the earlier sections on birds. Here I describe the field knowledge required in general, then describe several of the commoner species in detail. The Wildlife Trusts website has details of good places to see birds of prey under the section 'Where to See Wildlife'.

Most existing photographs of UK birds of prey are of captive birds, mainly because many professional photographers cannot afford the time required to obtain the same images in the wild. Towards the end of this section there are some 'Tips for finding birds' along these less onerous lines, but the challenge of photography in the wild is hard to resist for the amateur photographer who has time and patience. The key elements to successful bird of prey photography can be summarised as follows:

- You must first look for the habitat, and then the conditions, preferred by the bird of prey you wish to photograph.
- In those areas, you must look carefully for the signs that birds of prey are present.
- Having narrowed down the search area, you must move forward with a combination of keen observation and a great deal of patience in order to achieve any measure of success.

Habitats and preferred conditions

The habitats favoured by each species can be discovered through reading and Internet research, but in terms of narrowing down the search areas, word of mouth is the best method. The Internet has many sources of recent sightings, and nature reserve websites give some information on the birds of prey likely to be seen. To focus search areas further, one should study the topographic conditions preferred by various species. For example, large birds such as Buzzards and eagles need to conserve energy whenever possible, so that the balance of food in and energy out is maintained. Hilly country is often preferred as this can be a good source of *orographic lift* and *thermals*, for which the windward sides of hills are ideal. Wind is also a source of *dynamic soaring*. These three methods used by birds to gain lift are described next, together with details which will probably be of more interest to the experienced photographer or naturalist.

Orographic lift

Much is said about birds of prey rising on thermals, those warm 'bubbles' of air which rise above land heated by the sun. However, many birds of prey take off and soar on orographic lift, before circling on thermals. As a result, they are often only found on sites where this lift can occur, when the wind meets a cliff or hill and is forced up by the contours.

Birds of prey fight a constant battle between the energy they expend flying, and the energy they take in with food. If they get the balance wrong, they will starve, so they continually look for ways to reduce the amount of energy used. Rising on

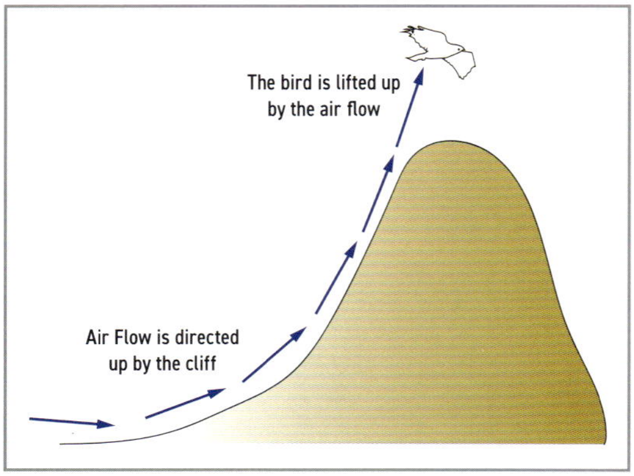

Orographic lift

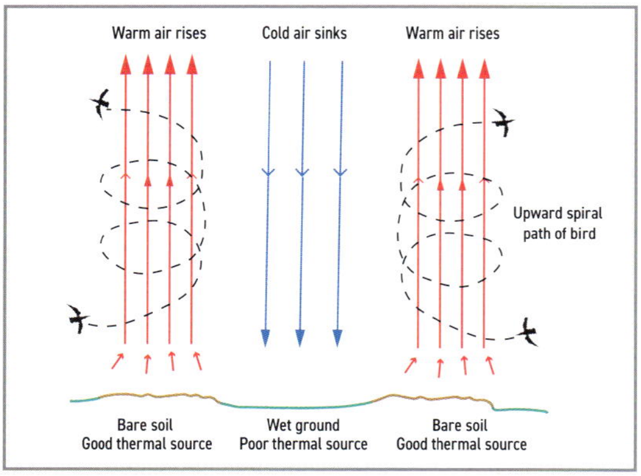

Thermal air current formation

orographic lift is a good method, as it means less wing flapping is required. Understanding the process of orographic lift makes it easier to find those birds of prey dependent on it. Buzzard, Peregrine and Red Kite, for example, are more likely to be seen where there are cliffs or high land masses including sea cliffs, and will rise on the side facing the wind. Wales is particularly rich with birds of prey. The Brecon Beacons area, for example, is ideal as it has many rounded hills with a steep windward face, as well as unspoiled countryside, rich in food sources. Once sites with suitable hills or cliffs have been located within your search area, you will be able pinpoint where the birds are more likely to be found. Knowledge of the other 'lift' methods employed by birds of prey will make it easier to know when to look for the birds.

Thermals

Once birds of prey have taken off, usually using orographic lift, they gain height using thermals, caused when different land surfaces heat up at different rates. Land surfaces, such as bare earth and buildings, heat up more quickly than water surfaces, for example, and the side of a hill facing the sun will be raised to a higher temperature than the side in shade. The warmed ground heats up the air above it, and as this hot air is less dense than the surrounding cooler air, it rises up in columns known as thermals. Birds can be lifted up in these currents of warm air without having to flap their wings. The width of each thermal depends on the surface of the ground underneath, and in order to retain the lift, birds have to fly in a spiral fashion so that they stay within the column of rising air.

By using thermals, birds can rise up without expending much energy. They can also travel for some distance horizontally, falling as they encounter cool air, then rising again when they find another thermal. This makes the search for prey a relatively low-energy process. Moreover, from their high vantage point, they are better able to spot prey and photographers.

Thermals will not be formed during wet weather, making it less likely that birds of prey will be seen then. However, on sunny days in summer, once thermals have formed, the birds may be seen, often mid morning and again in the afternoon. Thus in order to see Buzzards, for example, one should wait near a place that gives orographic lift, and at a time when thermals are likely to have formed. Thermals are much weaker in winter than summer as there is less heat available, so summer is the optimal time to see birds making use of them.

Dynamic soaring

The third method by which birds can rise with minimum energy loss is by making use of wind. By angling their wings and body correctly they can use the wind to give them lift. At first they fly into the wind, gaining lift from the increase in wind speed with height, but losing forward speed at the same time. When their forward speed is zero, they suddenly turn so that the wind blows them forward.

Here they lose height as there is no lift, but they gain in forward speed. They turn again and repeat the process, thus staying airborne without expending energy. This method requires some skill or they will simply be buffeted by the wind and blown off course. It is a tactic especially used by seabirds, but also by birds of prey, especially when conditions are not suitable for the formation of thermals.

Dynamic soaring is not dependent on sun, so this method is used throughout the year.

How does this knowledge help your photography?

In winter, when thermals are weaker due to less heat from the sun reaching the ground, the combination of orographic lift and dynamic soaring will allow the birds to rise, but the faster motion will make photography more difficult. However, if you understand how the birds fly, it may be possible to predict their position. If birds are using dynamic soaring, for example, their forward speed will be lowest just at the highest point before they change direction, and if you can predict where that will be by studying their flight, it will simplify photography.

Spring and summer offer the best photographic opportunities for making use of these flying methods. Not only is there more activity, but thermals are present more often, and the slow upward flight of the birds makes it easier to take photographs – although you have to do this before they get too high, or even a 500 mm lens will not be adequate.

Orographic lift can be quite strong at the top of sea cliffs or other steep scarps, with the result that birds can hover without having to flap their wings. This is a great advantage to birds such as Kestrel, which, without orographic lift, have to expend a great deal of energy flapping their wings in order to hover above prey. On sea cliffs where orographic lift is strong, they can be seen apparently suspended in mid-air, with wings outstretched, before suddenly diving down to attack. This stationary flight can make photography easier, as a lower shutter speed is required and thus a smaller aperture can be used, giving sharper images. Although the depth of field

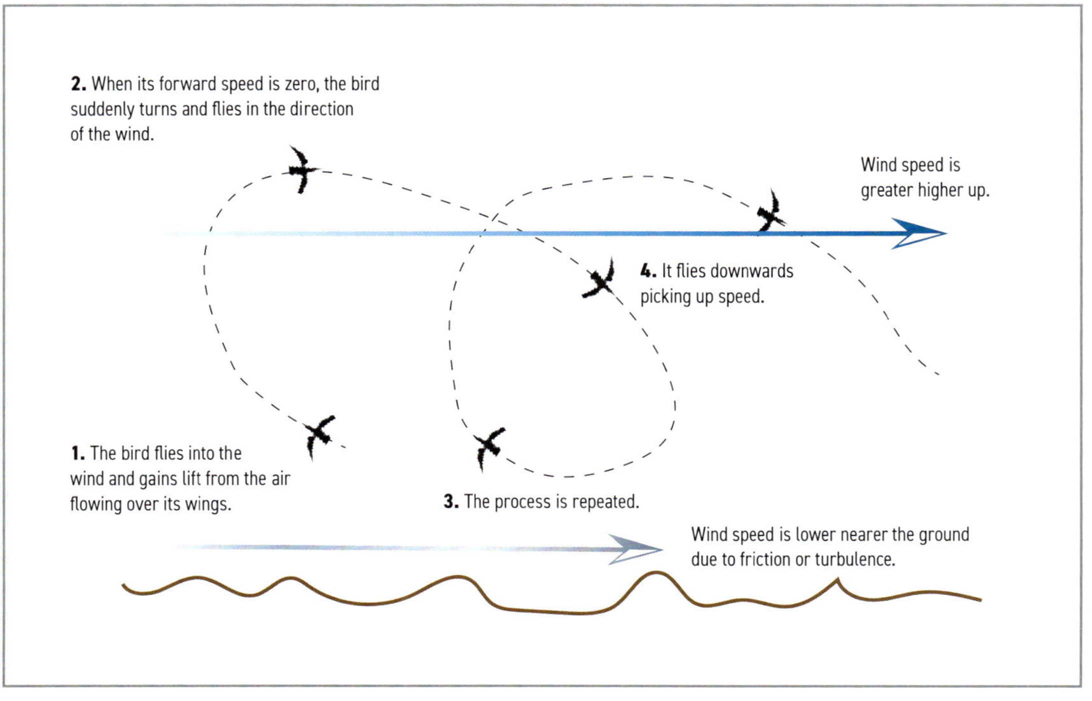

Dynamic soaring

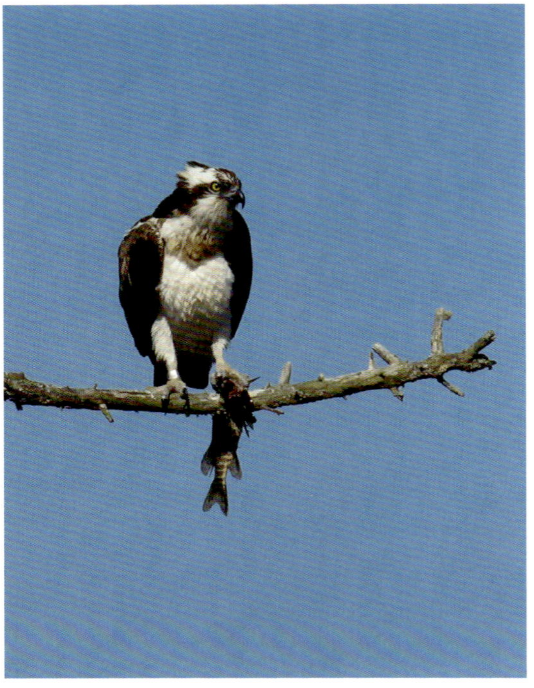

Osprey with fish in the Cairngorms

will increase with a smaller aperture, this is not usually a problem if the bird is photographed against the sky, as the background will almost always be pleasantly diffuse. The only disadvantage of photography on clifftops (apart from having to avoid falling off the edge) is that there may be less cover for you, with the result that the bird is more likely to move away to a 'safe from photographer' distance.

Reading the signs

Being able to read the signs that birds of prey are present is of great importance, as this allows you to reduce the number of areas to investigate. This is particularly crucial for the less common birds of prey. Typical signs are plucking posts, pellets and feathers, but the easiest sign to find, and the one which most quickly identifies birds of prey, is the bird's urine or faeces, consisting of white-wash-like splashes without solid matter. Look for leaves which appear to have been painted white and this will indicate the presence of a bird of prey, although that alone will not tell you which species.

Plucking posts

Birds of prey tend to use regular plucking posts, particularly during the breeding season. A plucking post is a favoured spot where the bird will take its freshly caught prey and pluck out the feathers or fur before either eating the prey itself, or taking it to feed its mate or young.

Fish eaters such as Osprey may eat the head from fish first before feeding their mate or young, thus prioritising the act of keeping themselves fed.

A variety of places can act as plucking posts: a dead tree, a large lateral branch, an earth bank, a gate post, a tree stump, or the root plate of a tree that has been blown down. One factor that these various places have in common is that they will generally be raised above ground level. They are recognisable by the fact that they are littered with fur and feathers, or in the case of Osprey, bits of dead fish.

By examining the feathers found at a suspected plucking post site, it is possible to determine whether the kill was by a bird of prey or by a mammalian predator such as a Fox. When a Fox has made a kill, it will remove the feathers, either where it killed the prey, or else under a bush where there is cover. Unlike a bird of prey's plucking post, these sites will be at ground level. Also, mammals tend to chew off the feathers of a bird, with the result that the feather shaft tips are broken and uneven. When a bird of prey plucks a bird, it pulls the feathers out of the skin, so that the feather shaft tips retain their point, and the feathers are scattered over some distance where the wind takes them.

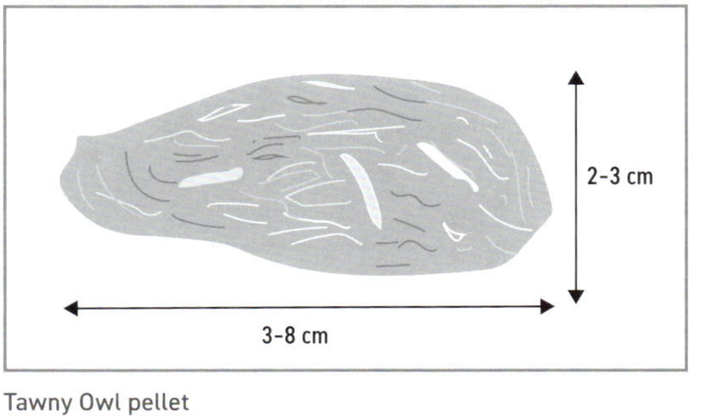

Tawny Owl pellet

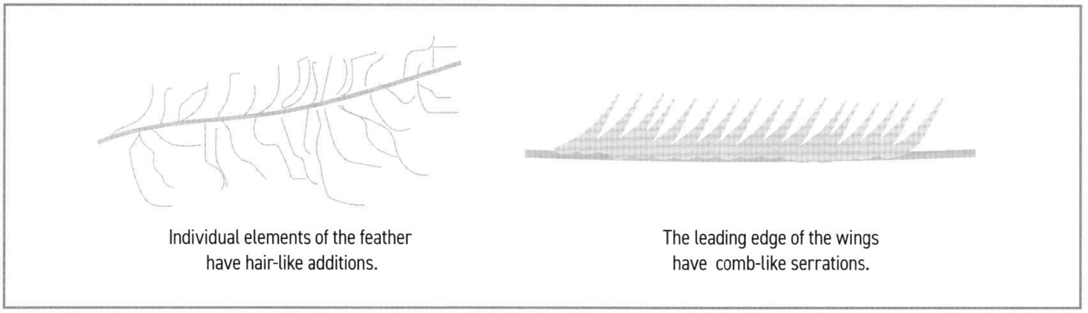

Tawny Owl feather detail

The photograph opposite shows an Osprey sitting on a lateral branch, having eaten the head of a fish. Ospreys are reputed to carry the fish head-first, possibly because it offers less wind resistance in that position. In the case of this photograph, the bird then presented the headless fish to its mate who was sitting on the nearby nest.

Pellets

Birds of prey regurgitate the indigestible parts of their food as pellets. The size, shape and content of the pellets can give a good indication of which bird of prey is present, although it can be difficult to separate closely related species. The sections on individual birds of prey that follow give some details of the main bird of prey pellets, but for more comprehensive information and photographs, consult the Helm Identification Guides *Tracks and Signs of the Birds of Britain & Europe*.

Owls tend to swallow their prey whole, as they mainly hunt small mammals or birds. As a result, owl pellets contain fur, feathers, bones and skulls. Other birds of prey, such as Buzzards, hawks and falcons, do not swallow their prey whole, with the exception of very small mammals. They usually pull off the head, pluck most of the feathers or pull off the fur, and then tear the flesh off the bone. As a result, very few bones are found in their pellets.

Pellets tend to be found under favoured perches or roosts, so discovering a collection of pellets can serve as a good indication of where to place a hide. Identifying the bird that produced the pellets is also important for the photographer, as this will indicate the best time to wait in said hide. For example, there would be little point in waiting during the day if the pellets belonged to a nocturnal bird of prey such as a Tawny Owl.

Feathers

Feathers can give a clearer indication of which birds are present in the area, so becoming familiar with the plumage of the main birds of prey can be very valuable to the photographer and naturalist. Most bird guides include some feather details, but for clearer identification, more comprehensive books such as the Helm Identification Guide are necessary.

Owl feathers, such as those of the Tawny Owl, have three features designed for silent flight. These tend to be more prominent in nocturnal owls, and can be distinguished through close examination. Owl feathers are furry due to fine 'hairs' that lend a fluffy appearance. This adaptation slows the air moving through the feather, thus reducing noise. Another feature is a velvety surface, which may be to reduce the noise of feathers moving over each other. In addition, the leading edges of the wings have comblike serrations, which are believed to reduce air turbulence. These adaptions for silent flight allow the owl to catch its prey unawares.

Activity cycles

Most birds have activity cycles, and becoming familiar with these can help in planning the best time for photography. For example, when a female

Sparrowhawk is on eggs, the male will hunt at first light, pluck the prey and then call the female to the plucking post to eat. He may then spend the rest of the day doing very little. If you have found a plucking post in spring, and suspect it to be that of a Sparrowhawk, it would be essential to set up your hide overnight and arrive before dawn, otherwise you would miss the activity.

When walking around a site, look for suggestions of activity and try to analyse the signs you see. Accumulations of pellets under a tree, for example, will probably indicate that birds are roosting there, making this a good position for a hide.

A favoured perch for owls is a lateral branch overlooking an area with bare earth and log piles. If there is an accumulation of white splashes on the leaves under the perch, this indicates that a bird of prey has used it. This was the case for the site in the photograph below. The presence of log piles means hiding places for mice and voles, which are the prey of the Tawny Owl. Bare earth paths close to the perch make it easier for owls to spot voles as they move around. A Tawny Owl is a likely bird of prey to use the perches shown, and a hide placed nearby would thus be a good site for an 'owl watch'. A trail camera could be used near the perch to give an indication of the frequency and timing of owl visits.

The following sections give more specific detail about the commoner birds of prey and how this can be of use to the photographer. For each species described, the facts are in addition to the general bird of prey details above.

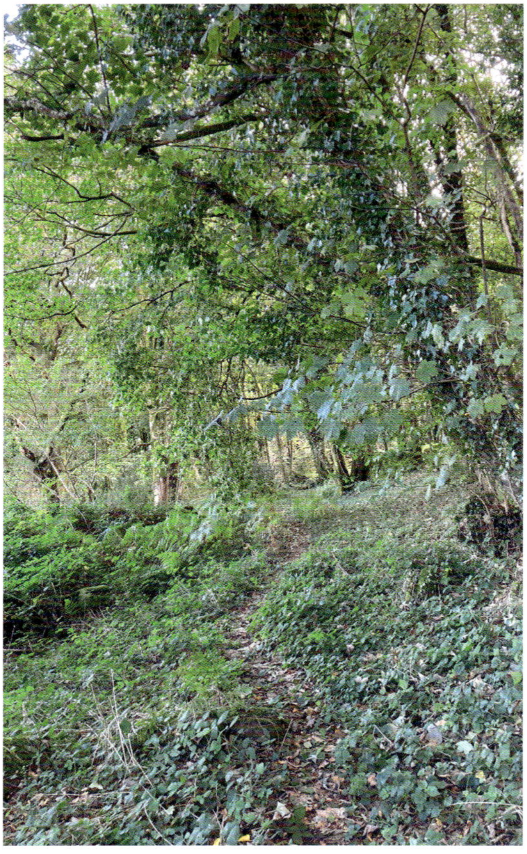

Suitable Tawny Owl perches

Tawny Owl

Basic facts

Description: The Tawny Owl has brown and white-marked feathers and a body length of 38 cm. It has distinctive 'kee-wick' (female) or 'hoo-hoo' (male) calls.

Nesting: The Tawny Owl does not build a nest but lays two to four white eggs in a tree hole from March to May. They will also use nest boxes. The eggs, incubated by the female, take 30 days to hatch. The young leave the nest after another 30–40 days.

Feeding: Food is mainly small mammals, especially mice and voles.

Pellets: They produce pellets that are 3–8 cm long and 2–3 cm wide. The pellets are light grey, compressed in shape, and contain bones mainly of mice and voles. Owl urine leaves white splats and there is no solid matter in the faeces, which also consist of white splats.

Habitat: Woodland, wooded parks and gardens.

Distribution: Most of England, Scotland and Wales.

Population: 50,000 breeding pairs in the UK (BTO).

Questions

Are there any special precautions to take with Tawny Owls? Never approach a Tawny Owl's nest with young in it, as the adults are very protective and can attack the over-curious photographer. The times for incubation and fledging are important as they give an indication as to when it might be safer to approach.

Is there any significance in food choice? The fact that voles are the favoured food means that the birds will perch in areas where small rodents are easier to spot, such as woodland edges.

Equipment

The equipment needed will depend on the method you choose to look for owls. If you choose the more ethical method of searching for a day roost, a camera with high ISO/low noise capabilities would be advised, together with the longest lens you can handhold easily. If you are lucky enough to find a suitable location where the owl roosts regularly, erect a portable cloth hide.

Habits

The Tawny Owl hunts at night, but young Tawny Owls can be seen in the early evening when they start to explore. The adult often sits on a branch overlooking grassland or bare ground, waiting for prey. These favoured branches will be signalled by white urine/faeces 'paint' on leaves below. Owls detect prey by hearing and sight, and often roost by day in trees. Pellets are often found in groups under a daytime tree roost.

The eyes are conical in shape and cannot move as ours do, so the owl has to turn its head to look in a different direction. The flexible neck allows the head to turn through 270 degrees to aid vision, but also to help channel sound to the very sensitive ears. The acute hearing of the owl makes life difficult for the photographer, with the result that stalking is unlikely to be successful, even in the dark.

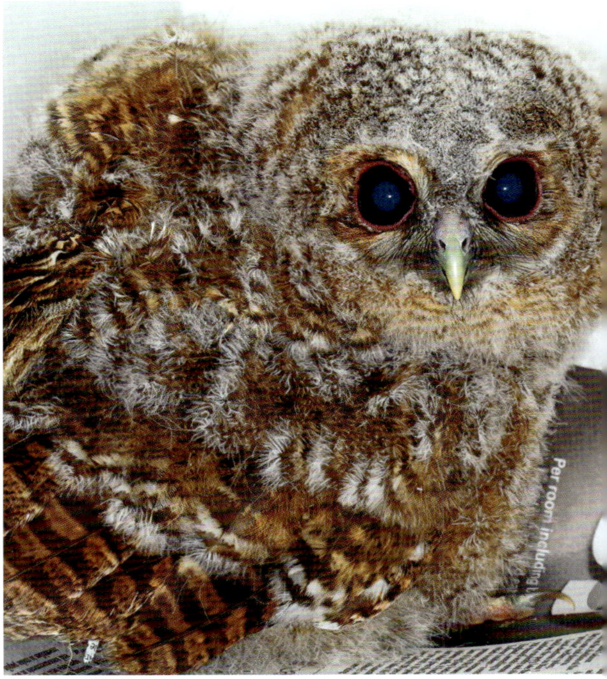

Young Tawny Owl at a wildlife hospital

In the field

As Tawny Owls are nocturnal, photography is difficult without resorting to less than ethical means, such as baiting or attracting the owl by imitating its call. You may have no objection to these methods, but they interfere with the natural behaviour of the owl. Some well-known photographers think nothing of baiting, and in fact I have seen photographs that to me look as if grain has been put out deliberately to attract rodents, so that the owl could be photographed just before it pounced on the unsuspecting prey. If you choose such methods, be aware that major wildlife competitions and wildlife magazines will ask if the animal was baited, which may put you at a disadvantage. In using live bait you would be causing unnecessary suffering, which contravenes the Animal Welfare Act 2006. On the other hand, putting out food such as dead mice on a regular basis could arguably be framed as no different to putting out bird feeders. One advantage of this approach is that once an owl comes to feed regularly, you will

NAME	SIZE	FEEDING	HABITAT	NESTING	POPULATION
LITTLE OWL Can often be seen sitting several hours before dusk. Local knowledge is the best method of finding them.	Length: 22 cm Wingspan: 56 cm	Insects, worms, small mammals	Open country, orchards, hedgerows	Small holes, nest boxes	6,000 pairs
BARN OWL They can be seen hunting early in the morning and in the evening, especially in winter. Good sites include Hickling Broad and Holme Dunes in Norfolk and Westhay Moor on the Somerset Levels.	Length: 35 cm Wingspan: 80–95cm	Small mammals such as voles	Rough, unimproved grassland	Barns and nestboxes	5,000 pairs, but uncertain
SHORT-EARED OWL These owls do hunt during the day, especially in winter. They are resident in northern England and Scotland, moving south in winter. They can be seen at Minsmere in Suffolk and Skomer Island in west Wales.	Length: 38 cm Wingspan: 100 cm	Mainly voles	Open moorland	Nests on theground	600–2,000 pairs
LONG-EARED OWL These owls are very difficult to find, as they are secretive and nocturnal. Local knowledge or some very good luck will be required to find them.	Length: 36 cm Wingspan: 90 cm	Voles, mice and some birds	Woodland near open ground	Old crow nests often used	2,500 pairs

Table 1.1 Rare Owls

know where to set up your hide or automatically triggered cameras.

The more ethical methods require much more effort and some care. They entail looking for the favourite evening or daytime roosts of the owl. First you have to find a wood with Tawny Owls. That is easy to do, as they hoot most evenings, especially in winter. The calls travel some distance, so pinpointing the source is not difficult. Once you have found their location, you will find that they often start to hoot from the same spot. If you are lucky, and the favoured perch is not in the middle of a leafy tree, you can get into position early and wait.

Daytime perches are harder to find as the owls generally rest there, and do not hoot from them as often. However, if you are lucky, they may be quite close to the evening hooting perch. The first time you spot them, the owl will most likely be disturbed and fly off, but if you are patient, sitting in wait may prove fruitful.

The surest strategy is to find a nest, and wait for the bird to fly in and out, but that is also potentially dangerous – although easier if a nest box you have placed is used. Owls can defend nests vigorously, and being silent fliers, can attack you before you are aware of their presence. Once again, however, patience and good preparation can win out. If you locate the nest, you can set up a hide during the day and be in position several hours before dusk. It is good practice to have someone come with you to the hide, and leave once you are inside. That way, if the bird is watching, it will see the disturbance arrive and then leave, so it will not realise you are still there – provided that you are quiet, of course. The same person should come and collect you when you have finished, otherwise the bird will become suspicious of the hide, having seen someone emerging from it without having apparently arrived.

A similar but possibly less dangerous method is to wait until the baby owls fledge. They sit around on branches calling for food, often in early evening when it is still light, and not only can they be heard, they can also be seen. The only problem with this, apart from protective parents, is that it takes place when there are still leaves on the trees, and it may therefore be difficult to get a clear view.

Although the scope of this book does not include triggering devices (other than trail cameras), it is possible to use these to photograph owls, if you are familiar with their regular flight paths. Set up an infrared triggering device attached to your camera, with flash, across a flight path. If you are lucky, the owl will fly past, break the infrared beam, and produce a photograph. Your computer's recycle bin will be full afterwards, as it will be difficult to ensure focusing is correct and that the owl is in the frame. This is a subject for another book, but I wanted to mention it here, so that you know there are various methods out there for the photography of owls.

Taking photographs in low light is a subject in itself, but using some lighting to help with focusing and then using flash to take the picture is the only sure method of getting sharp images when it is almost dark. Even the use of flash could be questioned as it might dazzle the owl, although a single flash is probably not a problem. Locating a daytime roost will mean that more light is present – but even in summer, woods can be quite dark places, so a camera with a low noise at high ISO is required if flash is to be avoided. As with all difficult subjects, dedicating time to your subject is the best, if not the easiest, way to find success. The amateur photographer can score here, as professional photographers who have to make a living from photography can rarely justify long periods of searching. To summarise, there is no sure-fire, easy way to photograph owls, but if it were easy, there would be no challenge.

Other owls

The Tawny Owl is by far the commonest owl, and the other species of owl are much more difficult to find. Some details are given below. Bear in mind that the field signs are similar for all owls.

Buzzard

Basic facts

Description: Buzzards have dark brown feathers above, and paler feathers with dark bars below. There is a great deal of variation in colouring, with the young often being white underneath. Body length is 50 to 60 cm, with the female being larger than the male.

Nesting: They build a large nest from sticks, usually in a tree, and lay two or three eggs from April to May. The eggs hatch after about 36 days. The young leave the nest after another 6–8 weeks, then stay with their parents for an additional 6–8 weeks.

Feeding: Buzzards eat small mammals including rabbits, as well as pigeons and earthworms. The birds can be seen looking for earthworms in large fields that have been newly ploughed. Despite their bird of prey status, Buzzards eat earthworms more often than one might expect.

Pellets: They produce pellets 4.5 to 6 cm long and 2.5 to 3 cm in diameter, which mainly consist of fur with very few bones. Buzzard urine and faeces consist of white liquid without solid matter.

Habitat: Woodland, moorland, mountains, farmland, some coastal areas. (See the notes on orographic lift above for further details of habitat.)

Distribution: Wales, mainly western England, and Scotland.

Population: Possibly more than 50,000 pairs. Probably the most frequently seen bird of prey.

Questions

How safe is it to approach Buzzard nests? Do not stray too close to nests. Buzzards have been known to attack those who come too near.

How do I know when the young have fledged? The young birds are likely to be heard calling for food, and they may be seen learning to fly from about July to September. It is usually easier to photograph younger birds, as they tend to stay in the region of the nest for some weeks.

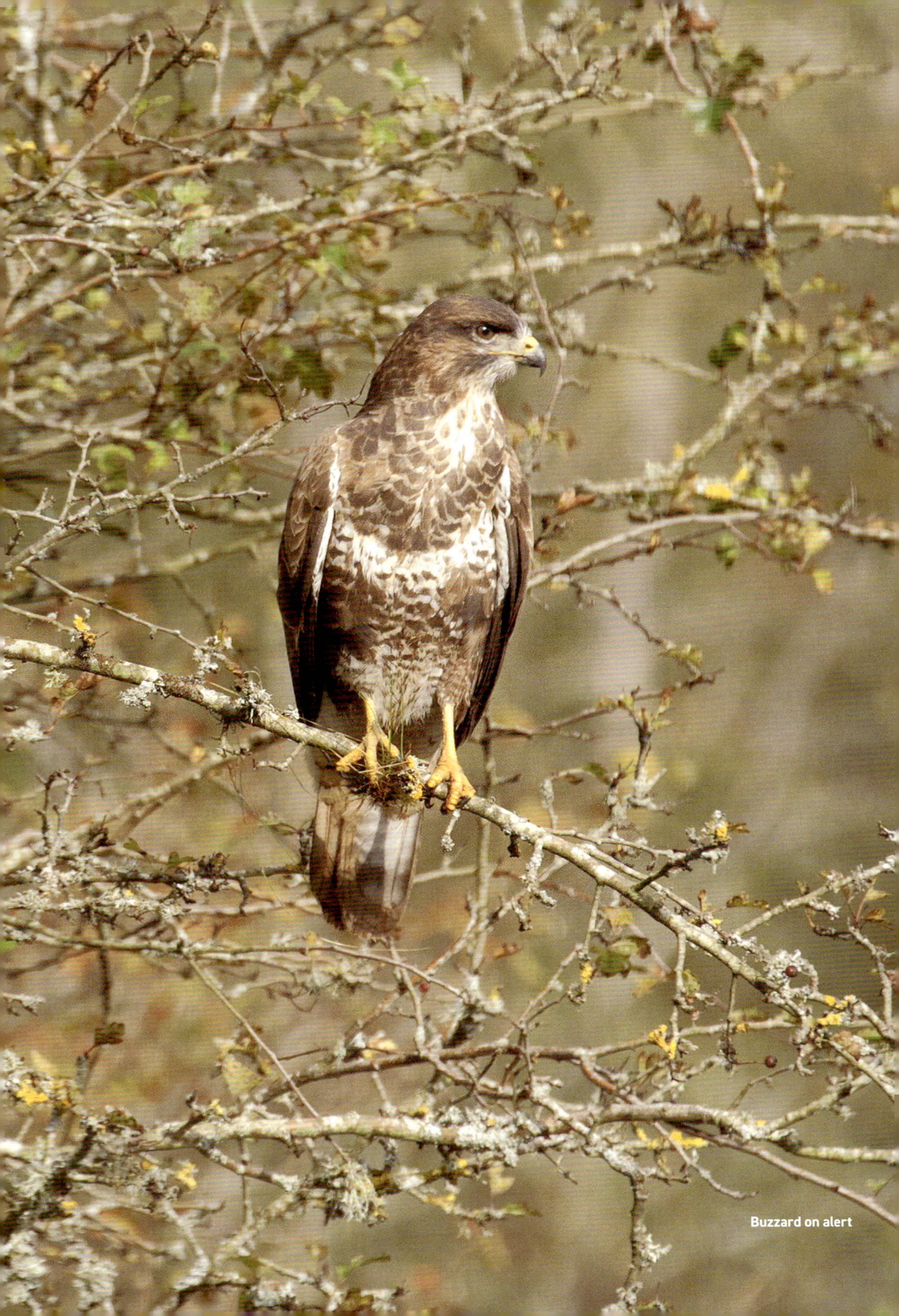

Buzzard on alert

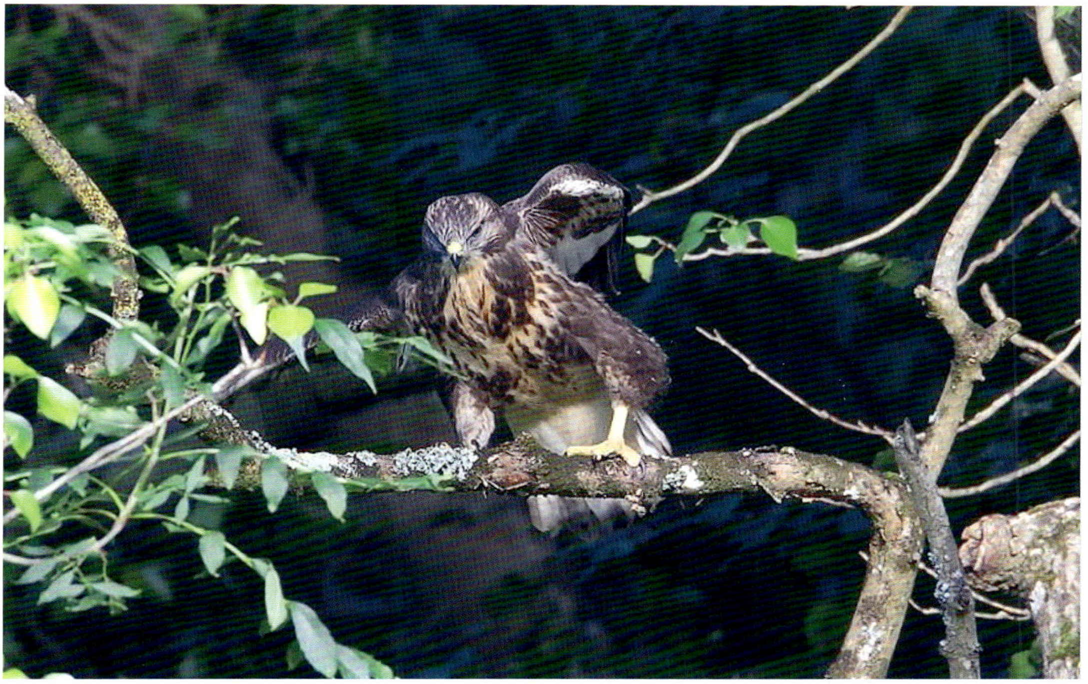

Unsteady Buzzard fledgling

Habits

Buzzards hunt by day, soaring and moving in large spirals as they rise on thermals. With the right strength of wind, a Buzzard can sometimes appear to be hovering above the ground: it can angle its wings such that lift from the wind exactly cancels out gravity, without the wind giving the bird any forward speed. Buzzards have very keen eyesight, and can detect prey from great distances. Once one has spotted a source of food, either by hovering, circling or viewing from a post or branch, the bird will stoop down at speed to pounce on its prey. It has a distinctive, plaintive call, heard most when it first starts to fly. This is a useful signal to the photographer to get ready.

In the field

Although flying comes naturally to birds, the more advanced soaring and riding of thermals is a learned skill. For several weeks in August and September a few years ago, a young Buzzard from a nest close to my garden was seen learning the more advanced flying techniques. The youngster found the process very difficult, and on several occasions I saw it being shown how to fly by a parent. At times the young bird flew just behind the adult, copying its wing and body angles. Practice on its own was less successful, and it evidently found it very difficult to rise much above the treeline. Dynamic soaring was even less successful at first, and early attempts blew the bird off course, causing it to land on the nearest tree, where it sat for some time looking very disgruntled.

Buzzards are relatively easy to find, as their call is very distinctive and carries some distance. The young bird shown above cried on and off for hours, when still in the nest and wanting food. If you locate a nest by following the calls, and wait around on days when orographic lift and thermals are likely, it will be relatively easy to get shots of a young fledgling bird at flying practice, or of the adult bringing food. Take care not to get too close, especially before the birds first start to fly. The adults can be aggressive if protecting young.

The young Buzzard pictured had only recently left the nest and was waiting, unsteadily, to be fed by its parents, calling frequently. The photograph was taken just before it fell off the branch. No harm done – it just fluttered down to the branch below. It could be heard crying loudly each day for food, especially in the evening.

Buzzards often sit on telegraph poles or lateral branches overlooking paths and roads, waiting for prey, and look like an easy photographic target. Often I have driven past such birds, then stopped and reversed to get a picture. However, although the birds quickly become used to traffic going past and learn to ignore it, the sight of a car stopping and reversing is not what they are used to seeing, and they always fly off. This is not because they have recognised a human, but because they have seen behaviour (from the car) that they regard as unusual. However, if you regularly see a Buzzard on the same lookout post, lying in wait may work. And if you have a large rural garden, erecting a tall post may well attract them. As I was writing the other day, a Buzzard landed on a tree above my garage and I was able to get a photograph through the window. Such events are rare, but it pays to be prepared at all times.

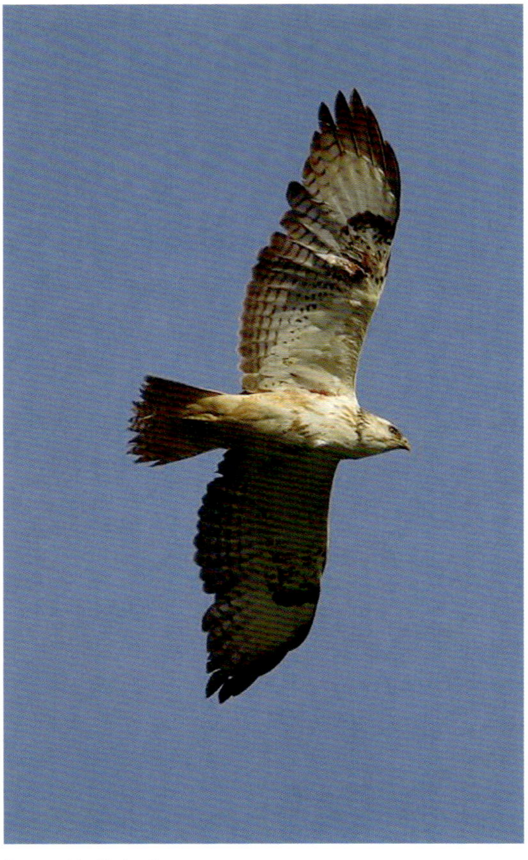

Buzzard in flight, Devon

The birds will tend to take off from the same position each time using orographic lift, especially when thermals are present, so lying in wait mid morning, mid afternoon or early evening will eventually prove fruitful. However, even if you have located a good Buzzard-sighting position, the problem of exposure adds difficulties. Photographing a dark bird against white cloud will usually overexpose the sky and underexpose the bird. Since often the photographic opportunities last no more than a minute, if that, you have very little time to sort out exposure. Because the birds usually move quickly, the technique of taking and blending several exposures is not an option.

My image of a Buzzard in flight (opposite) has the right features for a properly exposed shot:

- The bird was banking and was tilted towards the sun.
- The sun was behind the camera and lit up the underside of the bird. This allowed a high shutter speed to prevent motion blur.
- Because it was the young Buzzard (described previously) it had the pale underside often seen in young birds.
- I was already in place with the correct equipment on a tripod.
- The bird was also reasonably close.

Finding this combination of factors in the photographer's favour with a wild, un-baited bird is rare, and in this case I was watching for Foxes. I knew, however, that Buzzards frequently rose from the trees opposite where I was standing, so I was on the lookout for them, and was able to react quickly.

Sparrowhawk

Basic facts

Description: The male has grey upper feathers, and the female has brown upper feathers. Both have distinctive brown bars on pale underparts and a white eye stripe. Body length is about 35 cm, with females being larger.

Nesting: The female, usually on her own, builds a large nest from twigs in a tree, and lays four to six eggs in May.

Feeding: The favoured diet is small birds such as finches and sparrows, although the larger female may take thrushes and starlings. Not everyone will want to photograph a Sparrowhawk with its prey.

Pellets: The pellets produced are 2.5 to 3.5 cm long and 1 to 1.8 cm in diameter, are usually without bones and consist mainly of small, downy feathers. Both urine and faeces are white splats.

Habitat: Woodland, especially coniferous, farmland and gardens. You are most likely to see them in gardens, with bird tables being the great attraction because of the possible prey that feeds there.

Distribution: Most of the UK.

Population: 31,000 breeding pairs (BTO).

Habits

The Sparrowhawk hunts by flying alongside linear features such as hedges, and suddenly flipping over to the other side in order to surprise its prey. The Sparrowhawk will have several ambush points, and will visit these in turn. The commonest ambush point is a bird table, especially in an area where there are houses with further bird tables close by. Sparrowhawks use plucking posts, particularly during the breeding season.

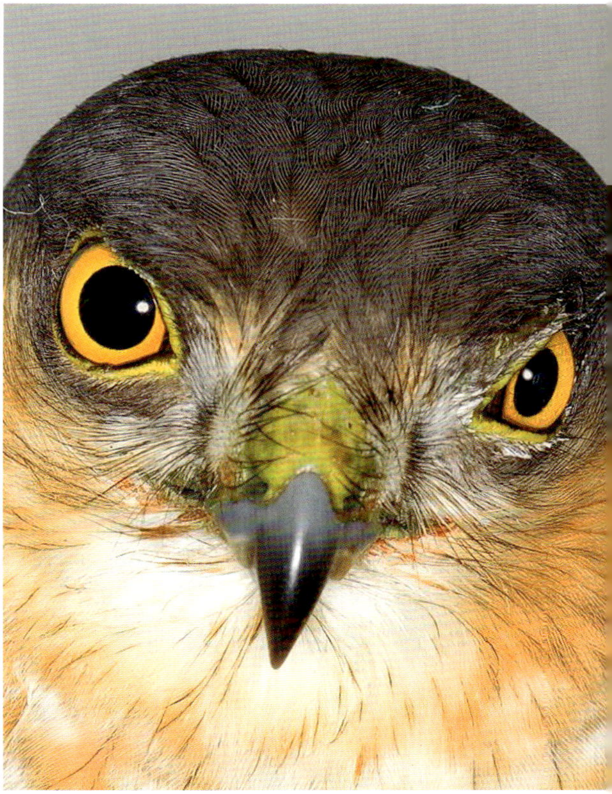

Prey's eye view of a Sparrowhawk

In the field

It is difficult to write hard and fast rules for finding Sparrowhawks, as they move very quickly and conceal themselves as much as possible – flying behind hedges, for example, before appearing to pounce on their victim.

However, Sparrowhawks are also seen sitting near their ambush points, and I have often heard people say that they have a Sparrowhawk which regularly sits on a gate or tree near them, no doubt waiting for prey. Such knowledge can be very valuable. Because they ambush their prey and move very rapidly, this is probably the only way to get good images of Sparrowhawks in the wild. Social media is a good method of finding those who are granted regular Sparrowhawk visits.

My closest recent encounter with a Sparrowhawk was at a time when the first brood of young Barn Swallows was starting to fly. Young swallows spend several days sitting around waiting to be fed, and the Sparrowhawk was obviously aware of this.

The first sign of its presence came when the adults started to make alarm calls and then flew towards the hedge near where several young birds were sitting. True to form, the Sparrowhawk suddenly flipped over the hedge, but any ambush attempts were thwarted by the alertness of the parents. About four or five adults flew just in front or just behind the Sparrowhawk to harass it, flipping over and back across the hedge with an agility that the raptor could not match. Eventually it flew off. When there are a number of baby birds around, keep a look out for Sparrowhawks, to make the most of photographic opportunities like this one.

Kestrel

Basic facts

Description: The Kestrel has a reddish-brown back, marked with dark flecks. The male has a grey head, with bars on pale underparts. Body length is about 35 cm, with the female being larger than the male.

Nesting: No nest is built, as the birds use a cliff or high building and lay three to five eggs from April to May.

Feeding: The Kestrel diet consists of small rodents and birds.

Pellets: Kestrels produce very light grey pellets, 2 to 4 cm long and 1 to 2.5 cm in diameter, which are mainly comprised of fur with very few bones. The urine and faeces ('mutes') consist of white splats.

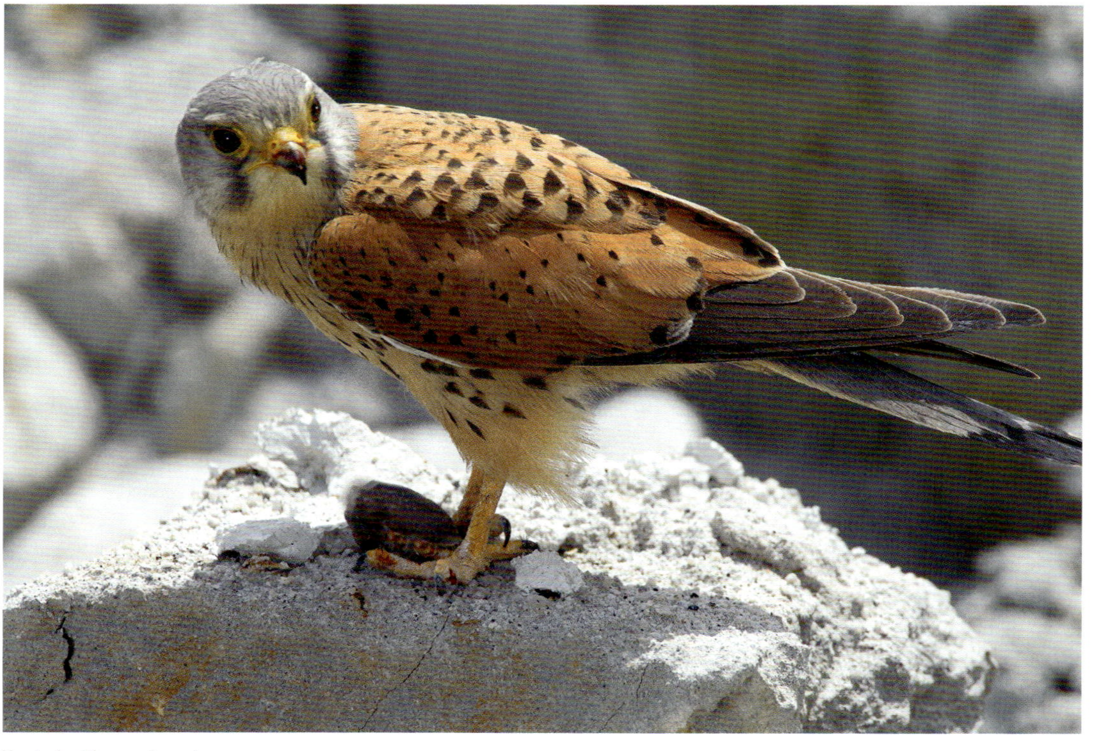

Kestrel with prey in a clay quarry

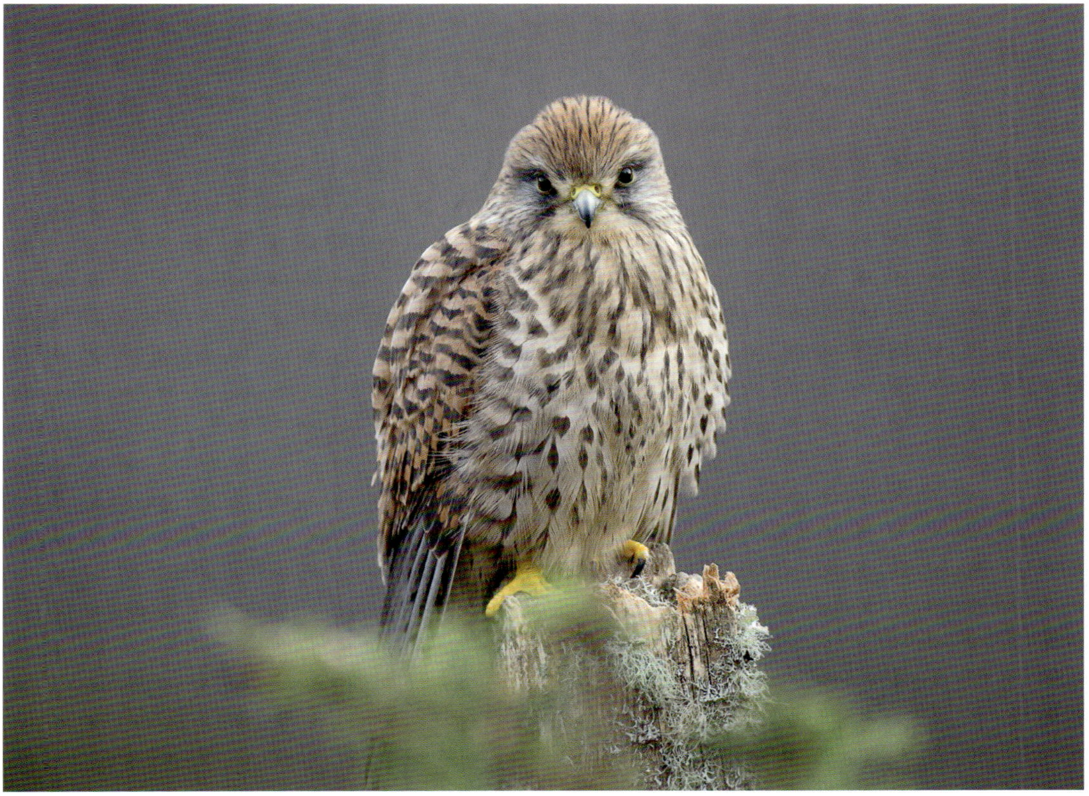

Kestrel (captive bird)

Habitat: Farmland, moorland, sea cliffs, urban areas.

Distribution: Throughout the UK.

Population: 46,000 pairs (RSPB).

Habits

Kestrels hunt by day, hovering above sites where prey might venture. It is thought that they can detect the ultraviolet reflections from rodent urine.

In the field

Photographing Kestrels is made a little easier by the fact that they hover above the ground, often for several minutes at a time, thus advertising their presence.

Kestrels can be found near roads or in urban areas, and word of mouth from photographers or birdwatchers may help you to locate them. Kestrels used to be a common sight hovering above motorways, and although they have declined in recent years, they are still relatively numerous. To be surer of finding them away from urban areas, consult RSPB and nature reserve websites to find which rural areas regularly report their presence. Coastal nature reserves are among the best places to look, especially if the coastline is undulating, with cliffs (to give the birds lift) crossed by valleys or inlets (where the prey live). Kestrels are numerous, for example, near the cliffs of South Devon, which are interspersed with fertile valleys hosting their favourite food, voles. Kestrels can be seen hovering above the cliffs before diving down to the valley floor below. The strong uplift on top of the cliff sometimes allows them to hover without having to flap their wings.

In common with other birds of prey, Kestrels are also attracted to sites with a collection of small birds.

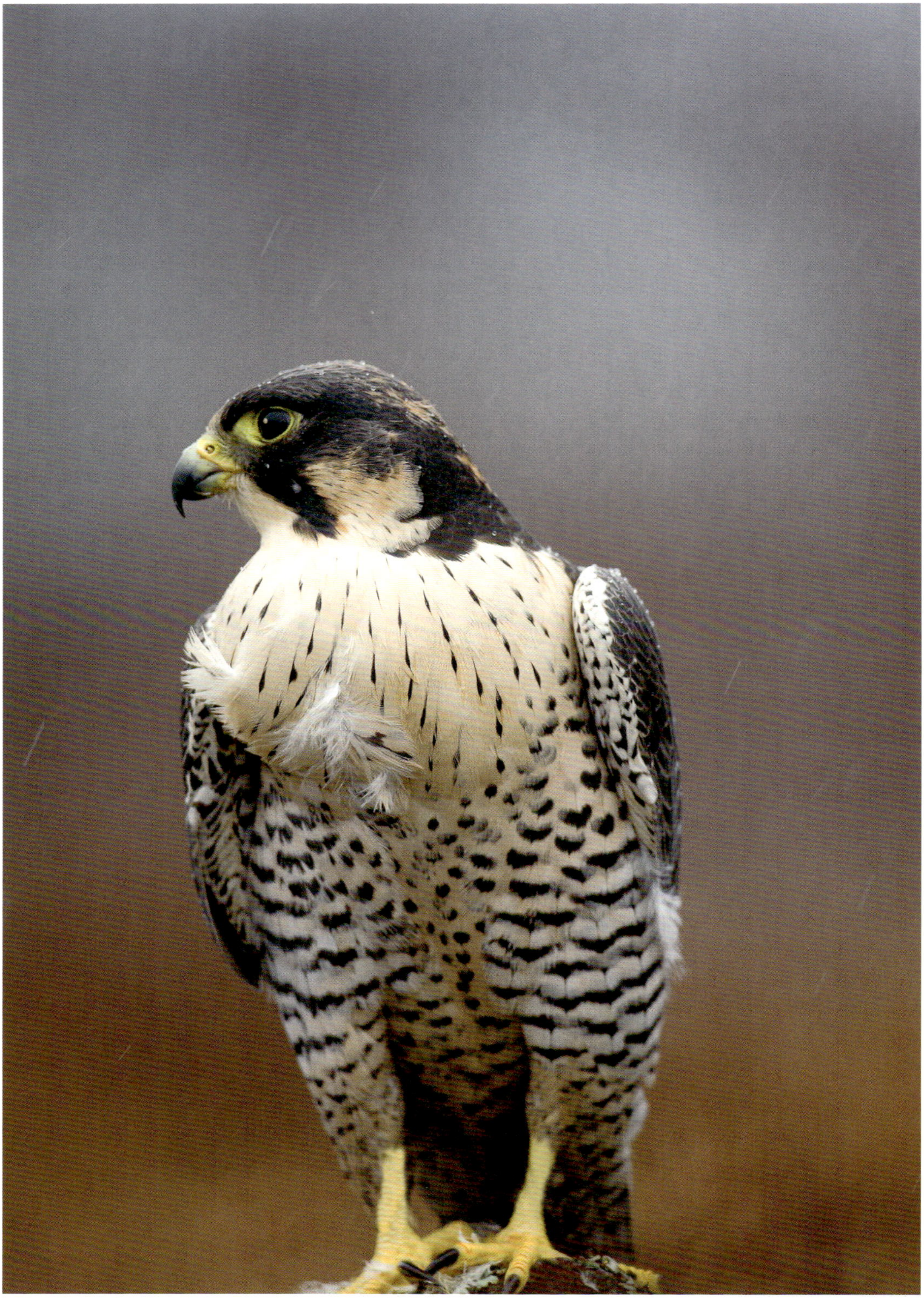

Peregrine (captive bird)

Birds such as Sand Martins, which have communal nesting sites, are likely to attract unwelcome attention from birds of prey. The Kestrel with prey on page 60 is a wild bird that had just raided a Sand Martin nest. I captured this image while sitting in a hide photographing the Sand Martins. I had been in it for some time, and the Kestrel was not aware of my presence. It positioned its plucking post directly opposite the hide. Kestrels will also be found where flocks of small birds commonly feed. Some nature reserves, for example, grow seed-bearing plants to feed finches in winter, and Kestrels, together with other birds of prey, may be seen in the area looking for rodents attracted by the grain, or for the finches themselves.

Peregrine

Basic facts

Description: The Peregrine has a grey back and creamy underparts which are marked with black bars. Body length is about 45 cm, with the female being larger than the male.

Nesting: For nesting, the bird uses a bare or grassy ledge on cliffs and lays three to four eggs from April to May. In urban areas the Peregrine often nests in church towers. Church sites are often reported, and many large towns have a least one Peregrine pair.

Feeding: Pigeons and other birds, and occasionally small mammals.

Pellets: The pellets vary in size, being 2 to 4 cm long and 1 to 2.5 cm in diameter. They come in varying shades of grey, and are similar to those of hawks.

Habitat: Peregrines breed on cliffs, quarries and mountain crags. Cliffs facing the direction of the prevailing wind are preferred, as they give lift.

Distribution: Scotland, Wales and southwest England.

Population: 1,750 pairs in the UK (BTO). The Peregrine is one of the less common birds of prey.

Habits

The Peregrine is regarded as the fastest bird in the world. It dives down on its prey in a 'stoop' which can be over 500 m long, and its prey may be killed and knocked to the ground in one blow. They are probably easiest to spot on coastal cliffs, where they hunt seabirds.

In the field

In the 1950s, the Peregrine was almost wiped out by pesticides such as DDT (the falcons eat small birds that have ingested insects which may have fed on pesticide-ridden vegetation), and although numbers have recovered, they still face persecution. Peregrines, and other birds of prey, are still illegally poisoned today, so you may find it difficult to locate them from reports, as those in the know are often wary of giving out information. However, several frequently used nest sites have viewing points with round-the-clock protection. Here you may be able to photograph the birds at the nest, although they will be some distance away and you will probably need a 500 mm lens.

The Brecon Beacons in Wales are a favoured site for Peregrines. This is because there are many hills with steep, rocky faces (good for nesting), facing the direction of the prevailing wind (good for lift), interspersed with fertile, sparsely inhabited valleys where their avian prey are easy to spot from above. This combination is also ideal for other birds of prey including Buzzard, Kestrel and Red Kite, although the Red Kite is more of a scavenger than a hunter.

As I was unfamiliar with the area round the Brecon Beacons, I hired a guide for a day to help me find bird of prey locations. The best spot we found was a Peregrine site in a rocky quarry not far from a public footpath. The birds were well used to people walking along the footpath and showed no sign of being disturbed – and as Peregrines are Schedule 1 birds, we had to be sure that this was the case. The pair had chosen to nest in the quarry, despite the number of regular walkers on the footpath, and had produced three young which had fledged when I visited. The young were very well camouflaged, and most visitors were not aware of their presence.

It was possible to stand some distance from the nest site and photograph the young birds scrambling about on the quarry sides and learning to fly. When passers-by asked what we were photographing (as they always do), we made some vague comment about just waiting to see what came by.

Local people who knew of the birds' presence were very wary about giving away their location, and one bystander, protective of the birds, interrogated us for some time – and only left when my guide made it clear he knew about the Peregrines and would ensure we did not disturb them.

Without a guide, you may not find it easy to locate Peregrines. However, nature reserves often state whether Peregrines are to be found on their sites, although an exact location will not be given. Forming good relationships with reserve rangers will help to overcome the issue. Rangers are generally very passionate about wildlife on their reserves, and will gladly help those photographers who have proved they are ethical with regard to wildlife, and who respect the rules that apply to Schedule 1 species.

Osprey

Ospreys are spectacular migratory birds. They stopped breeding in the UK in the early 1900s, but returned naturally in the 1950s, with the site at Loch Garten in the Cairngorms serving as home to them since 1959.

Basic facts

Description: Ospreys are large birds, dark brown in colour with a white chest. They have a noticeable brown eye stripe and hooked beaks. Wingspan is around 1.5 m, with the females being larger.

Nesting: Nests made from sticks are frequently built at the top of large conifers, but the birds also use human-made nest platforms. Breeding takes place in late spring, when the female lays up to three eggs, which are incubated for five to six weeks. Birds often return to the same nest site for years.

Feeding: Fish. Both birds feed the fledglings.

Pellets: Ospreys produce very few pellets, suggesting fish bones are mainly digested.

Habitat: Conifer forests near waterbodies or rivers. The birds also use cliffs and have been known to build nests on electricity pylons.

Distribution: Predominantly in Scotland with a few sites in other parts of the UK. Many Wildlife Trusts have built nest platforms in the hope of attracting the birds.

Population: 250–300 breeding pairs in the UK.

Habits

UK Ospreys migrate from Africa, with the first males arriving in March, and the female some days later. They leave in late summer, although timings vary according to weather and breeding success. The adults leave before the young.

As they feed almost exclusively on fish, they nest near waterbodies – either lakes (lochs in Scotland), rivers (for example the wide rivers in the Cairngorms) or coastal sites.

In the field

There are Osprey sites with viewing hides at several nest sites in the UK, with details on the Wildlife Trusts and RSPB websites. Examples include Loch Garten in the Cairngorms, Cors Dyfi Nature Reserve, just north of Aberystwyth, and Rutland Water Nature Reserve. The hides are some distance from the nests, to protect the birds from disturbance, so a 500 mm lens is a minimum requirement.

Of more interest to photographers are hides near fishing sites, such as those found at Rothiemurchus in the Cairngorms. Many of the fishing Osprey images seen in the media come from this hide. This and other similar hides charge £60 or more to book a place.

However, with up to 300 breeding pairs in the UK (mainly in Scotland), there are obviously more

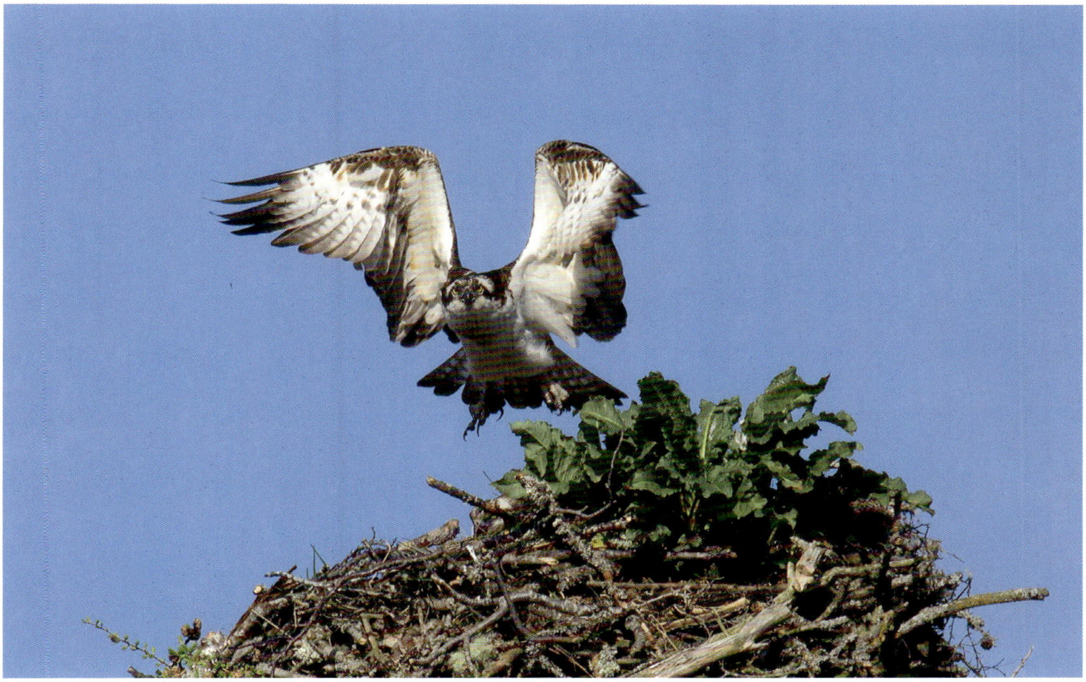

Osprey at nest at a Cairngorms site

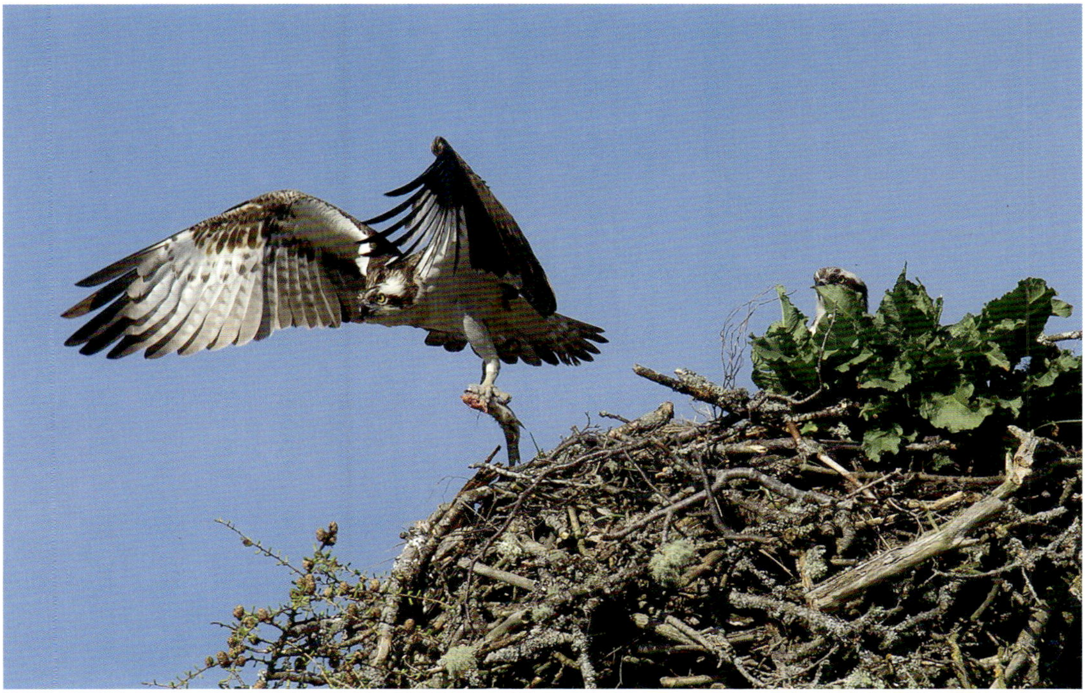

Male Osprey with fish. The female is on the right in the nest (Cairngorms).

NAME	SIZE	FEEDING	HABITAT	NESTING	POPULATION
RED KITE Wales is the stronghold, but they are spreading to other parts of the UK and becoming more common after extensive reintroduction projects.	Length: 60–70 cm Wingspan: 150 cm	Carrion and small mammals	Woodland	Treetops	4,600 pairs
HOBBY Spring and summer visitor. May be seen in the New Forest on heathland, or Lakenheath in the Cotswolds.	Length: 30–35 cm Wingspan: 68–85 cm	Insects and small birds on the wing	Woods and heathland	Old crow nests	2,800 pairs
MERLIN A resident, but moves south in winter. Fast-moving and hard to spot. Easier to see in winter, for example at Martin Mere in Lancashire and Elmley Marshes in Kent.	Length: 25–33 cm Wingspan: 50–60 cm	Catches birds on the wing	Open moorland in summer, coasts in winter	Nests on ground	1,330 pairs
HEN HARRIER A migratory bird, found in spring and summer, mainly in northern Scotland and Orkney. Also the Isle of Man.	Length: 45–55 cm Wingspan: 110 cm	Small mammals and birds on the wing	Moorland	Nests on high moorland	700 pairs
GOLDEN EAGLE Mainly in the Scottish Highlands. Consult RSPB sites for sightings.	Length: 80–90 cm Wingspan: 185–200 cm	Larger mammals and carrion	Mountains and upland moorland	Large nests on cliff edges	440 pairs
GOSHAWK Rarely seen, especially as it hunts in dense woodland. Consult birding sites for recent sightings.	Length: 50–65 cm Wingspan: 90–120 cm	Ambushes pigeons and small mammals	Woodland	Large nests in woodland	410 pairs
WHITE-TAILED EAGLE Mainly found in the west of Scotland after reintroduction, but can be found on other UK coasts.	Length: 75–90 cm Wingspan: 200–40 cm	Mainly fish	Near water, especially marine	Trees or cliffs	160 pairs

Table 1.2 Rare birds of prey

Ospreys about – finding them is the problem! During a recent trip to the Cairngorms, I saw two Osprey pairs at nests and one single Osprey. One Osprey pair was at the RSPB Loch Garten Centre. I had a 400 mm lens with me, but the nest was too far away to get anything other than a very small bird in the frame. Watching the Ospreys on the viewing monitor, however, made the visit worthwhile.

The single Osprey was a bonus seen while we were looking for Golden Eagles. We stopped near a loch and saw an Osprey in the water being mobbed by a gull. The Osprey ignored the seagull and sat on the water like a duck and preened itself, which was amusing to watch. Eventually the gull flew off and the Osprey rose from the water with a large fish in its talons. Obviously it had been holding the fish underwater all the time, and was just waiting for the gull to leave. The bird was a bit far away for a worthwhile photograph, but the encounter demonstrated that Ospreys can be seen anywhere near a waterbody in 'Osprey country'.

The final pair were found due to a tip from a friend who lived in Aviemore. The nest was on top of a tree on an island in the middle of a loch. In this case, the nest could be seen from the side of the loch while standing under another tree.

As the Osprey is a Schedule 1 bird and it is an offence to cause disturbance at the nest, I had to be sure that photographing the bird did not cause any harm. Fortunately, the nest was far enough away, and the 'hide' tree gave sufficient coverage, that the birds paid no attention to me and carried on adjusting their hideaway and mating. My Osprey photographs were taken at this site. They have been heavily cropped as the birds were distant, so I was glad I had a full-frame camera.

Other birds of prey are harder to find and photograph, although the Red Kite is becoming more common and can be seen frequently in Wales. Table 1.2 lists the rarer birds of prey to be found in the UK.

Shortcuts to finding birds to photograph

If you wish to shortcut the photography of birds, especially birds of prey, there are several methods you may find useful.

1. Set up a feeding station

These are made from logs around 1.5 to 2.5 m tall and with a diameter of 10 to 20 cm. They can be fixed by several methods, including digging a hole and inserting a drainpipe into the ground, putting the log into the drainpipe, and if necessary, packing it with small pieces of wood; or hammering a post into the ground and tying the log to it using cable ties (this second approach is shown over).

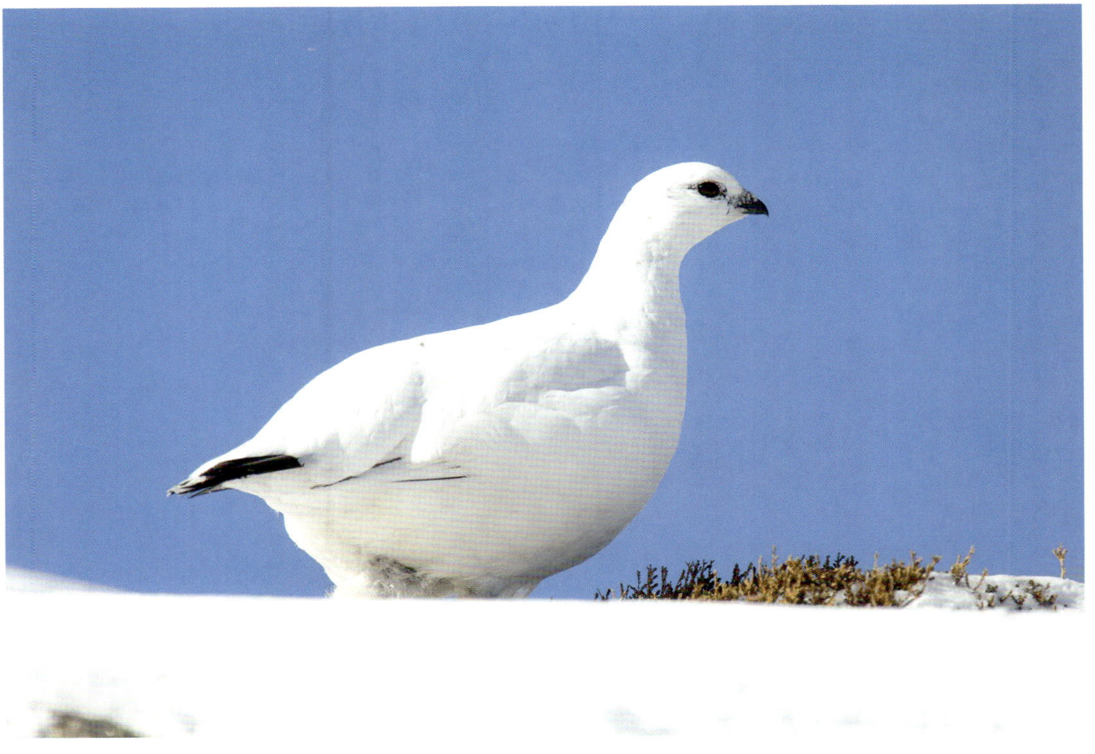

Ptarmigan high in the Cairngorms in winter snow

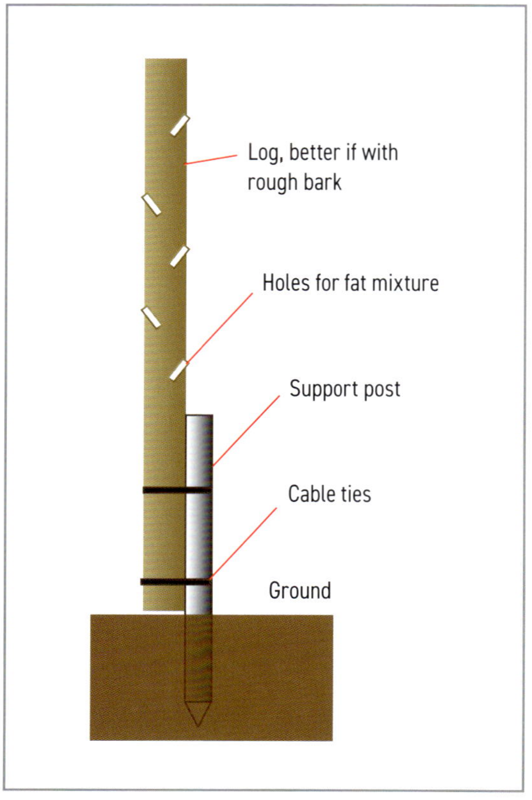

A log feeder

Next, drill holes at an angle into the log. The holes, of about 0.5 to 1 cm in diameter, can be filled with a fat/nut mixture, made as follows:

- Melt a packet of lard in a pan.
- Grind up an equal weight of peanuts.
- Add the ground peanuts to the pan and stir.
- Pour the mixture into an ice cream carton to cool.
- Spread small quantities of the mixture into the holes.

Knobbly wood such as conifer is easier for the bird to perch on than smooth wood. As well as Great Spotted Woodpeckers, other birds including Nuthatches and Long-tailed Tits will make use of the feeders. Jays will appear if whole nuts are placed in some holes or on top. Usually I find the birds get the whole nuts before Grey Squirrels, but your experience may be different.

2. Visit bird of prey centres

Select those which give flying displays of birds of prey. The majority of bird of prey pictures you will see in books and magazines have been taken in this way, so there is no shame in it. This will allow you to appreciate fully the beauty of these birds. It will also enable you to practise your skills in capturing birds in flight. There is nothing to beat the thrill of photographing wild birds of prey, and if you have honed your technique in a captive setting, you will find it easier to get good shots when you do encounter wild birds. Birds of prey generally move very quickly, so you need to be ready.

3. Visit a Red Kite centre

These centres feed the birds, but they are still wild animals, attracted by the food, and so this is a comfortable halfway house between captive birds and birds in the wild. Most centres are in Wales, which is a stronghold of Red Kites. There is a well-known centre at Gigrin Farm, in mid Wales, but the smaller and more remote Red Kite centre at Llanddeusant in the Brecons is excellent. The birds can be seen from a long way off, coming across the flat moorland, and make a dramatic and awe-inspiring sight. There are fewer birds here than at Gigrin Farm, which makes photography much easier. If you are in the area for an hour or more beforehand, you will see the birds circling before feeding, giving the opportunity for some truly wild shots.

4. Use hides in established bird areas

Dawlish Warren in Devon is one of many established bird areas. There is an excellent hide there on the estuary of the River Exe, which attracts a large variety of birds. Most nature reserves have a bird hide, and the larger reserves have several. In popular areas, it is usually a good idea to arrive early before the crowds, as a surprisingly large number of people are unaware of hide etiquette, such as being quiet and keeping still. In tidal areas, it is important to arrive when the tide is in a suitable position. In

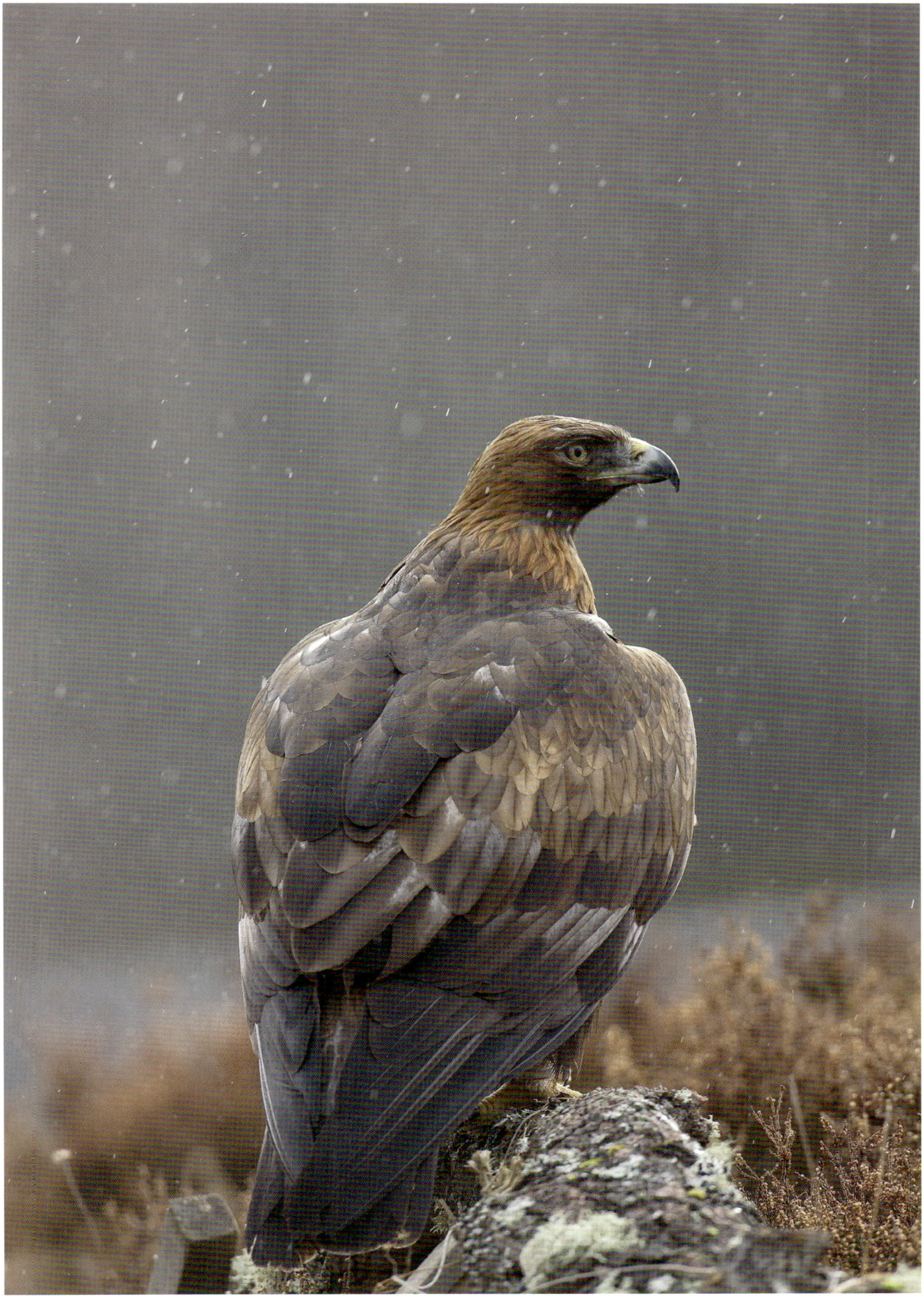

Golcen Eagle in the rain (captive bird)

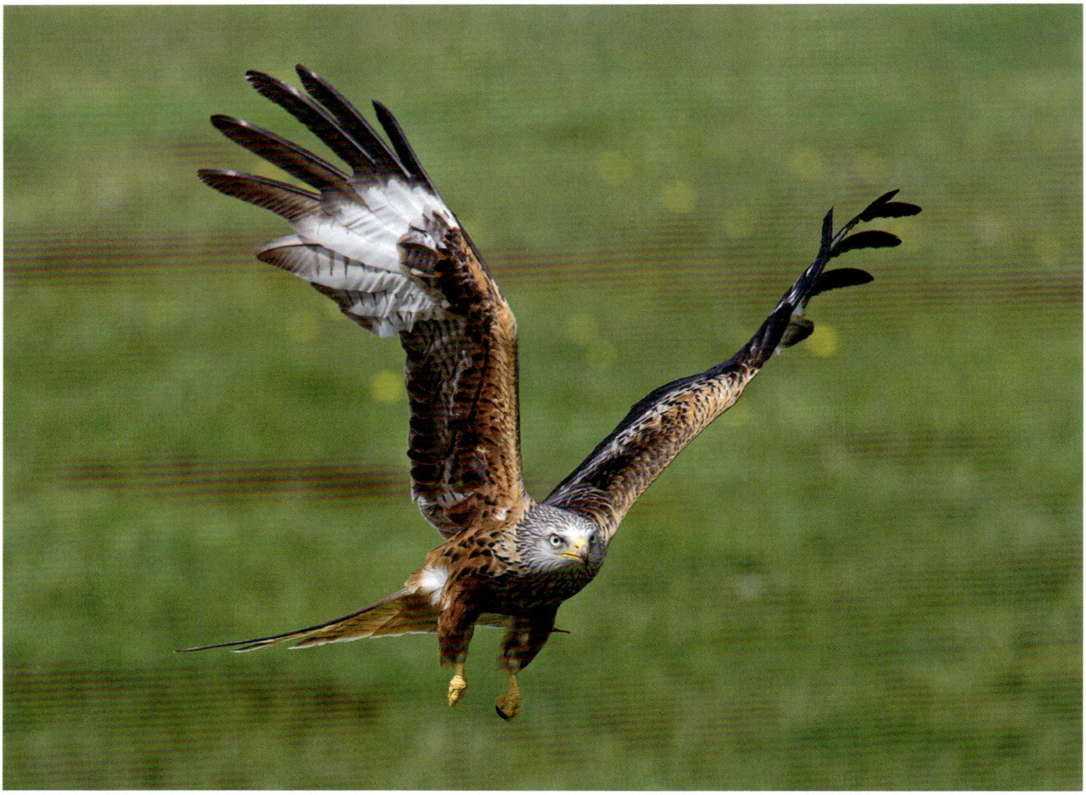

Red Kite at Gigrin Farm

most cases, arriving an hour before high tide and leaving an hour after high tide is the best timing, as the birds are close but still have an area to wade in. Avoid times of exceptionally high tides, as the birds may roost elsewhere. At low tide, they are often too far from the hide.

The Redshank shown on page 72 was very close to the hide and posed artistically next to some rocks.

5. Attend a guided workshop

The Ptarmigan in on page 75 was photographed on a guided trip in the Cairngorms. Only someone familiar with the area would know where to find Ptarmigan. The day this photograph was taken was one of those rare days in the Scottish mountains: two feet of snow had fallen the night before, but the day was one with bright sun, a brilliant blue sky and not a cloud to be seen. Rarest of all was the complete lack of wind on the mountaintops. We sat for hours watching and photographing these beautiful birds, which are full of character. They are quite comical in nature, with large hairy feet. Every now and then they would break through the snow crust and list to one side, then carry on unperturbed.

Most professional wildlife photographers use guides to help them find wildlife in unfamiliar areas. It can take years to become really familiar with a large site, and using a guide is the only cost-effective way for those who consider it their day job.

There is a big difference between a workshop with a group of photographers, and one-to-one guiding. Although the latter is more expensive per day, it can work out cheaper in the long run, as not only will the guide deliver exactly what you want, but it is also much more concentrated. If a sociable gathering is what you prefer, a workshop would probably suit you best, but if your only aim is to photograph a particular species, I would recommend the one-to-one approach. Further information can be found in the Appendix.

6. Attract birds

There are several ways to attract birds, other than the use of bird feeders, and these can create opportunities for natural shots with interesting backgrounds.

Flowers

A rough patch with wildflowers can attract a range of birds, especially seed eaters. If you have space in your garden, leaving a portion untended so that thistles and other seed-bearing weeds grow will offer many photographic rewards. Large thistles and teasels are two of the best wildflowers to appeal to seed-eating birds.

If you prefer something 'tidier', growing Dwarf Sunflowers is a good idea. Sunflower seeds are a major constituent of birdseed mixes, and are a great favourite with a number of bird species. I have often seen birds sitting on my feeders sorting through and discarding food until they find a sunflower seed. Fortunately ground feeders such as Dunnocks and Pheasants are grateful for the throwaways. Planting Sunflowers is therefore a great way to attract a range of birds. The dwarf varieties are best, as the seed head is at a convenient height for taking photographs. Plant the seeds in May with 25 cm between each (and allow a few extra for non-germination). If the plants are spread out, the flower head and hence seed heads are much bigger, even four of five times larger than those on plants that are close together. Dwarf Sunflowers are also best because they do not need support.

Blue Tits, Great Tits, Greenfinches and Goldfinches are attracted to the seed and will often cling to the flower head and peck away, giving an opportune moment for attractive shots. If there is a large clump of the flowers, flies and pollinating insects are also attracted, which in turn may attract the Spotted Flycatcher. Ground-feeding birds will pick up any seed that has fallen. I regularly grow Sunflowers for this purpose and have often seen a large number of birds fly out as I walk past.

Ponds

It's no secret that birds are attracted to ponds. However, the shape of the pond and the vegetation growing in it can affect the type of birds lured in. Barn Swallows, for example, drink by swooping down and gathering water with an open beak before continuing the upward arc. Ponds which are long and rectangular will give them an easier flight path than smaller round ponds. Vegetation such as water lilies and pond weed should be cleared from a portion of the water to guide the birds along a narrow path. This will make the difficult task of capturing the bird in flight that little bit less onerous. If you are fortunate enough to have bats coming to drink at your pond, they also will follow a line of clear water.

Bird baths

Bathing birds provide interesting photographic opportunities. If you do not have space for a pond, a small bird bath may be an alternative option. They can be built with stones cemented together to leave a hollow in the middle. A combination of cement (ready-mixed mortar will do) in the hollow, painted liberally with plastic pond paint, will make it waterproof. The water should only be a few inches deep, and a flat stone should be placed in the middle for smaller birds. Even birds that do not use feeders will be attracted to the bath, especially in dry weather.

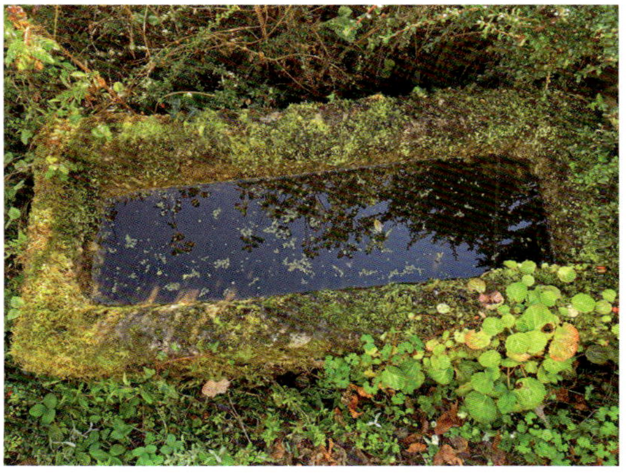

A small bird bath

The photograph on the previous page shows an old stone trough which is ideal for a bird bath, as long as there is gravel and/or stones in the bottom to keep the water level low. The weathered appearance makes an attractive background for bird photography, too.

General fieldcraft for birds

Research

- Find out where your bird of choice is likely to be through reading and Internet research. See the Appendix for a list of suitable books and websites.
- If you visit a reserve or National Park, ask the rangers for their help in locating birds. Initially, however, they will be unlikely to give out the location of birds of prey in order to protect them from persecution. Building good relationships with rangers is important and the time spent will reap many rewards. Join conservation work parties on reserves if you can, as that is the best way to get to know a site and its rangers.
- Study all available information on nature reserves, especially via their websites. These may not tell you exactly where protected species are, but usually the websites give lists of regular visitors.
- Read guidebooks on your chosen area and on the preferences and habits of different species, as this will help you to narrow down the search.

Visit

- Pay several early morning visits to your chosen area, taking note of what you see, where and when you see it.
- Trail cameras are not generally as useful for birds, as it is difficult to predict their location, but they may be worth considering for ground feeders.

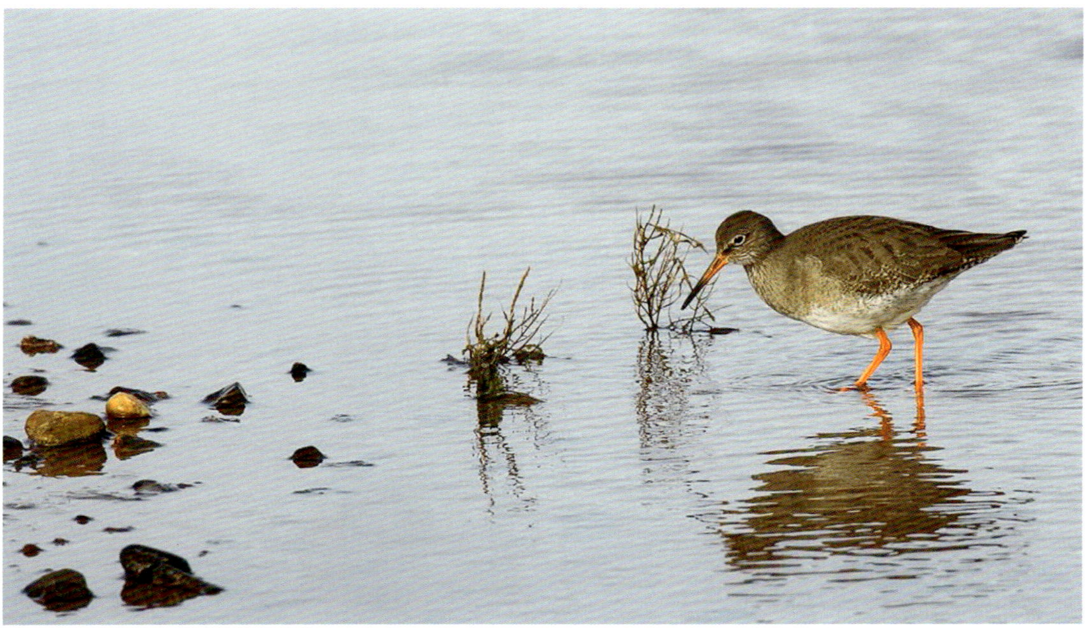

Redshank at Dawlish Warren, Devon

- Choose a good position with natural cover, select an appropriate spot for a portable hide, or use fixed hides if they exist. For reserves without hides, you should ask permission to put up yours. Using a camouflage net and sitting on a stool, however, is all that is required for many birds, with the exception of birds of prey who will spot you from a long way off. However, they may even ignore you if **a**) you are far enough away and **b**) they are busy hunting.
- Full camouflage clothing is not necessary, but it makes sense to wear greens and browns (or white in snow).
- Birds are likely to visit ponds in dry weather, so positioning a hide near a pond may be fruitful.
- Arrive before dawn (not easy in summer) and settle into position, trying to keep still and quiet.
- Wait and be quiet, still and patient.
- If no luck, analyse the cause: is it bad luck, bad weather, too many people about, the wrong position?
- Try again on another day. Remember (again!) to keep still and quiet.
- Persevere. If after three or four visits you have no success, do not give up if you know the birds do come to that spot. That fifth visit is likely to be the successful one.
- Once you have a successful day, it will all seem worthwhile.

Stalking

At the beginning of this book I said that fieldcraft was not just about creeping around in bushes. I am not a fan of stalking, partly because it does not work well with most birds, and partly because it generally means handheld images, which are usually inferior to those taken with a tripod. Also, for many of us, it is very difficult if not impossible to handhold a 500 mm lens. However, there are species for which stalking is the only option – but even then, there are usually ways of avoiding handholding.

The Ptarmigan, for example, is such a bird. It is found high on the slopes of the Scottish Highlands, and can only be photographed using stalking. The steps taken in the field are very similar to those for other large birds:

- Find out the most likely areas. Birders are the best source of this information, together with local photographers.
- Use the bird facts to determine the best time to see them. With the Ptarmigan, winter and snow are ideal.
- Scan the land in front of you with binoculars at regular intervals to spot where the birds are.
- Approach very slowly and quietly, using the slope of a hill, if possible, to shield you from the birds. Ideally wear white in snow, or at least neutral browns and greens.
- As you get closer, hide behind rocks or trees, carefully and slowly balance your camera on your rucksack or beanbag, and wait.
- Gradually creep closer, freezing in position each time the bird looks your way, and hiding behind rocks or trees whenever possible.
- Take images at each stage so you have something if they move off. Use a quiet shutter setting if you have it, and do not use burst mode.
- Stay in position for as long as you can, as this way the birds are less likely to be disturbed. Any sudden movement or noise will cause them to fly off.
- Make sure you have several layers of warm clothing with well-padded knees. Avoid going into the Scottish Highlands in anything but good weather, as temperatures can quickly become like those of the Arctic. The Cairngorms are a good bet as there are good, well-worn tracks, but avoid skiing areas and do not go on your own. Always tell someone where you are going.

Stalking waterbirds is a little easier, especially if they dive for food. You can move rapidly whilst they are underwater. Practise doing this so that you can quickly slide the tripod forward and drag your seat and camouflage cloth with you, without tripping up (which is not as easy as it sounds). Be aware that they often surface in places you might not expect.

In order to get close to wading birds, you can choose between wriggling towards them on your stomach, or sitting in a sheltered position covered with a net and waiting for the birds to come to you. Portable hides are not satisfactory on beaches, as sand does not hold tent pegs and it is often windy. A flapping hide will scare everything off.

Remember, it is illegal to photograph close to the nests of Schedule 1 birds without a licence, if in doing so you disturb them. See the Appendix for a list of these protected species.

Photographic equipment and techniques for birds

Lenses

If you are on the move, take a lighter-weight zoom or prime lens. A 100 to 400 mm zoom lens (or similar) is very useful as it is flexible and relatively lightweight, although image quality will not be as good as with a prime telephoto lens. If you are sitting waiting for birds, take the longest and best lens you can afford and are able to carry. A 500 mm lens is a good choice, if pricey. An extender is often essential. Extender values vary with lens manufacturer, but for Canon a 1.4× extender will give a 500 mm lens the reach of a 700 mm lens. Be aware that some lenses will not accept extenders, and with others, automatic focusing is affected.

Aperture and shutter speed

Use aperture priority and choose your setting wisely. A very large aperture gives faster shutter speeds and can blur the background nicely, but it can also blur the subject. An aperture of f/5.6 often works well when used with a 500 mm lens, but for closer subjects, select an aperture that separates the subject from the background. The actual aperture value will depend on how close the subject is to the background, and on the focal length of the lens. For a bird against the sky, smaller apertures can be used; for a bird close to vegetation, or taken with a short focal-length lens, a larger aperture may be required. Be aware that cameras with smaller sensors have greater depth of field, so it may be difficult to blur the background with subjects that are close. Each camera/lens combination is different, so you should test various mixtures of camera, lens and aperture before going into the field. That way you will grow to know the correct combination without thinking about it.

Aim for as high a shutter speed as you can, as even slight movements of the subject can reduce image sharpness. For small birds in flight you will need to aim for shutter speeds of 1/1,000 s and preferably even faster than this, as they fly very quickly. Larger birds are slower, but the fastest shutter speed possible should always be aimed for nonetheless.

Exposure and focusing

Manual focusing may be required if the bird is surrounded by vegetation, otherwise the autofocus will ‘hunt’ for the focus point. First position the image roughly using autofocus, then switch to manual. Manual focus is often the best method for birds in flight, but it needs a great deal of practice.

If photographing against the sky, you may have to add one or two exposure values to expose the subject correctly. Blue sky or dark clouds give the best results, but a hazy white sky is very difficult to expose for, as the birds will almost always look dark. Always test for the best exposure before seeing the bird, and be aware that on days with variable amounts of cloud, the settings required will change.

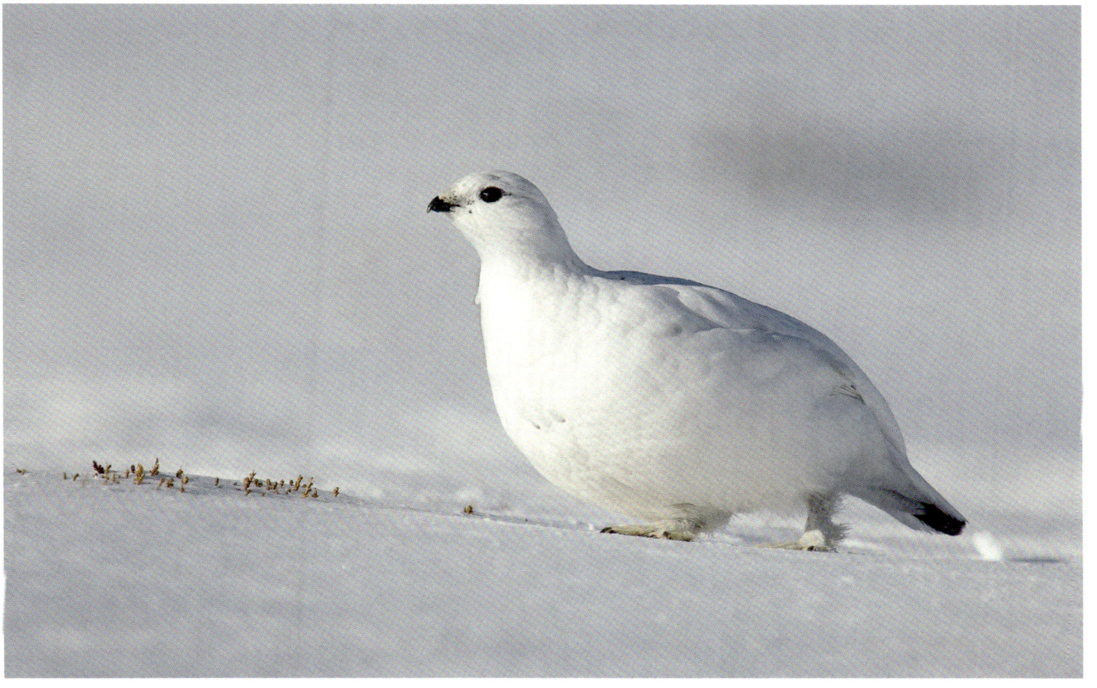

Ptarmigan high in the Cairngorms. Note the large feathered feet.

ISO

In order to get fast shutter speeds, and in poor light, a high ISO may be required. This can give rise to noise problems, although newer cameras have ways of mitigating this.

Techniques

Use a good-quality tripod whenever possible. Hold a telephoto lens firmly to avoid camera shift, as even slight movements are very noticeable with a long lens. Press the shutter slowly or use a remote release cable. Try to take single images rather than bursts if possible as this gives more control over focusing, especially since birds rarely sit still in one position for long. Bursts may be required for fast-moving objects, although the technique, in my opinion, is overused.

Camouflage

Wear neutral clothing and if not using a hide, use a camouflage cloth or net. Take a fold-up stool to sit on. Wrap camouflage tape round your lens, especially if the lens is white.

Be patient

For every good day there are probably three or four unsuccessful ones. Treat them as learning experiences. If your chosen subject is nowhere to be found, be prepared to take photographs of other available wildlife.

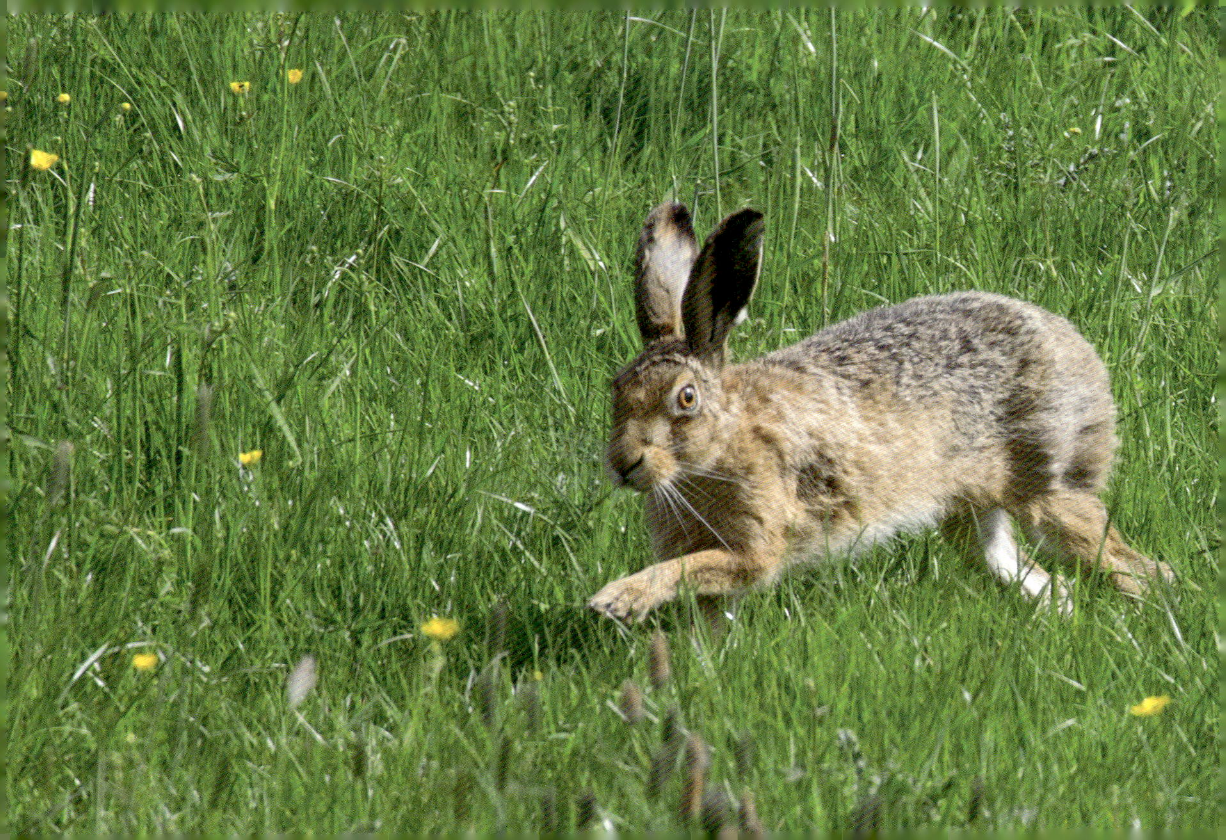

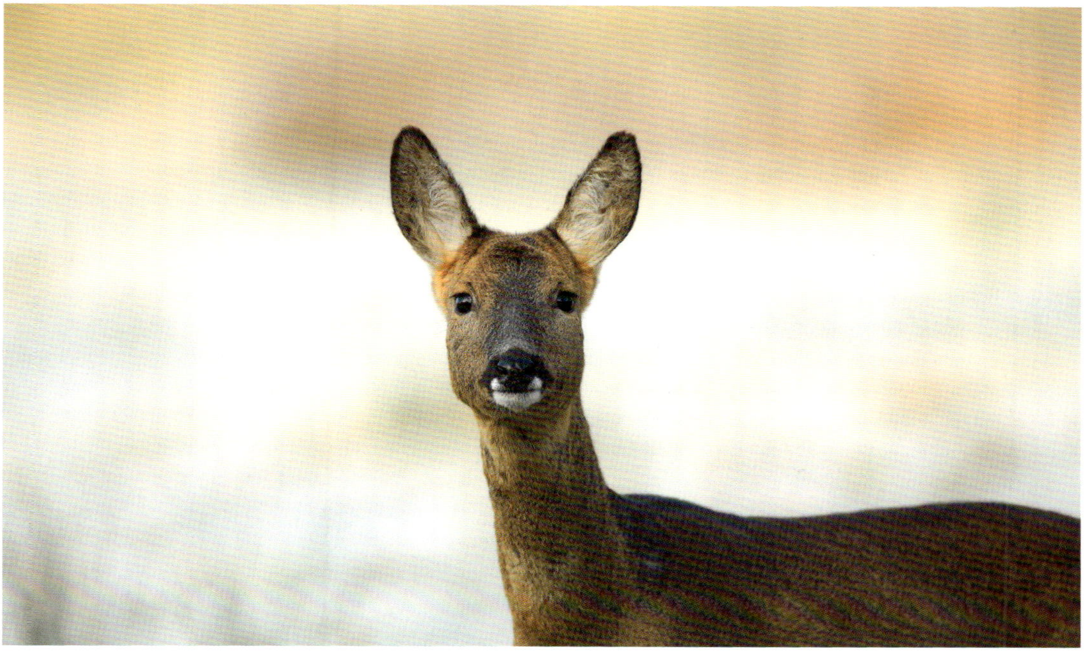

Young Roe Deer in a Devon field

Introduction

There are relatively few mammal species in the UK, and the structure of this chapter is, as a result, rather different from the previous one on birds. The commoner mammals are described in detail, with particular attention being shown to tracks and signs, where appropriate. The use of a trail camera is explored, as this is a helpful, if not essential, tool for finding mammals.

As a result of the destructive action of man, many species of mammals which used to inhabit the UK are now extinct here. There have been attempts to reintroduce rare or extinct species such as the Water Vole and Beaver, but other species such as the Scottish Wildcat are fast approaching extinction. Most mammals in the wild are either nocturnal or very nervous of man, so gathering as much knowledge as possible before going out in the field is essential. As each mammal is very different, I have given photographic advice for each main species rather than generalising for all.

Deer

Successfully photographing wild deer can be quite a challenge, and requires a good knowledge of their habits, tracks and signs.

It is a good idea to practise adapting lens size, aperture, ISO and shutter speed with tamer deer, such as those found in a deer park, so that when you come across deer in the wild, you can react quickly with the correct settings. The three main deer types found in the UK are described below. It is important to be able to distinguish their signs, as their behaviours and appearances are quite different. The mating season for most species of deer is at a fixed time of the year. The males generally compete for the females, sometimes fighting to gain supremacy. The rut, as this is called, serves to ensure survival of the fittest. Muntjac breed at any time of the year, however, and Roe Deer, being solitary, are much less likely to compete for females.

CASE STUDY: Roe Deer

Roe Deer can be very difficult to find even if you live in a rural area as they are generally solitary and nervous. Early morning forays are required. This was a subject I had wanted to photograph for some time, but was put off by the effort necessary. However, I was keen to take a series of Roe Deer photographs for a book, and this gave me the motivation to carry on.

Much of the information I have collected about deer was a result of many failed attempts in the past; I had seen Roe deer bounding off on many occasions and realised how much effort would be required to get close enough to photograph them. I think it important to realise that even with knowledge and good research, some targets require great perseverence. Do not let that put you off, as success is very sweet indeed, and those photographs can be very valuable to you.

Basic facts

Description: Roe Deer have reddish-brown coats in summer, which darken in winter. A typical height to the shoulder is 65 cm. The antlers on the male are short and spiky, and unlike those of other deer, are cast in October and grow in winter. Roe can be distinguished from other deer by an inverted heart-shaped white rump, with a tail that is hard to see, being only 2 to 4 cm long. They have a black nose and a conspicuous white chin. *It is essential to be aware of the basic facts for the other deer species as well, as it is easy to confuse them until experienced.*

Weight: The buck weighs about 24 kg, with the female being closer to 23 kg. *The weight of the animals makes tracks clear.*

Feeding: Roe Deer are browsers, and will nibble at a wide range of foods, mainly brambles, herbs, ferns and the new growth of trees and shrubs. Because they tend to be solitary or in small family groups, they cause much less damage to the landscape than those deer that gather and feed in herds. *Being solitary nibblers, they are much more difficult to find than a herd of Fallow or Red Deer.*

Breeding: Twins are commonly born between May and June.

Habitat: Roe Deer are found in a diverse range of habitats, such as coniferous or broad-leaved woodland and farmland; however, they are more frequently to be found where there is a mix of wood and field. Woodland with a thick level of undergrowth supplies a greater variety of food, and is favoured. They are also found in urban and suburban areas where there is sufficient cover. *This narrowed my search to fields at the edge of woodland.*

Distribution: Roe can be found throughout most of mainland Scotland, northern and southern England, and they are spreading to parts of Wales and the Midlands. The Roe is a native species of deer. *Devon was as good an area to search as any other.*

Population: Around 500,000 in the wild. Despite being the most numerous of the deer species, they are much less often seen due to their secretive nature. They are not usually kept in deer parks as they are not gregarious creatures. *This means they are around, even if hard to see, so worth persevering for.*

Tracks and signs

Hoof tracks

Deer leave characteristic tracks and signs, and it is essential to get to know these in order to locate different types. Often there can be more than one species of deer in an area and, because their behaviour is different, it is important to know which is which. Deer tracks are most easily seen in wet sand or mud, which can also smear out the tracks.

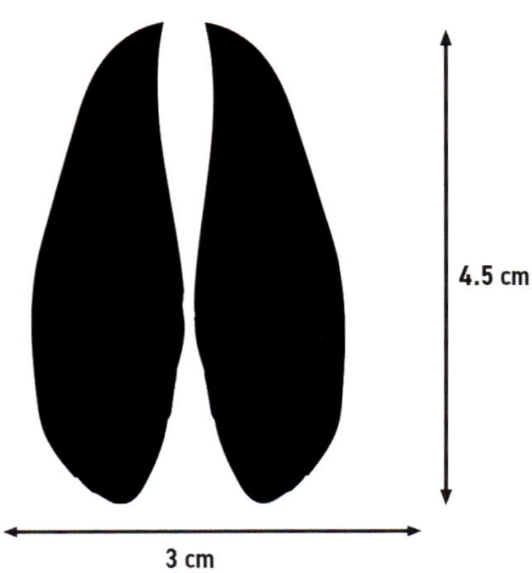

Roe Deer tracks

Roe tracks are relatively small compared to those of Fallow and Red Deer. When the deer is moving at speed, the tracks are splayed out to the sides and dew claws may be seen as two small marks. *Good in theory, but still hard to distinguish between species in practice.*

Droppings

Roe droppings consist of small cylinders, pointed at one end and flattened at the other. They are black and shiny when fresh. In terms of size they are about 1.2 cm long and 0.9 cm in diameter. In summer they may be connected together into furrowed lumps. *This is a clear indication of the presence of deer.*

Unnatural tree growth

When deer browse they often eat shoot tips. This can lead to unnatural tree growth. The next image shows what should be a single-stem tree, but instead there is a group of smaller stems round the main one, where deer have eaten the new growth. The lower part of the stem has been protected by the tree protector.

Browse lines

This is one of the best indicators of deer, assuming there are no domesticated browsers such as cattle nearby. Deer love the new growth on shrubs and trees and will browse on it up to a height they can reach, roughly 1 m for Roe Deer and 1.5 to 2 m for Fallow Deer. This gives a distinct browse line, most noticeable along a woodland edge where it borders a field. *The height of the browse line is a reasonable indicator of the deer species present, but less of an indicator if more than one type of deer is using the area.*

In the first photograph overleaf, an untidy tree has a geometrically flat bottom where it overhangs the hedge and deer have browsed to their maximum height.

Frays and scrapes

When trees are frayed, bark is rubbed off the trunk, usually in spring when Roebucks are removing velvet from their antlers.

Roe Deer may also scrape away twigs and branches with their hooves before lying down. The next photograph shows both flattening and scraping. The bracken round the outside of the image has been flattened, and much of the central part has also been scraped. This not only makes the area more comfortable, but being amidst bracken, a Roe Deer would be invisible when lying down. The size

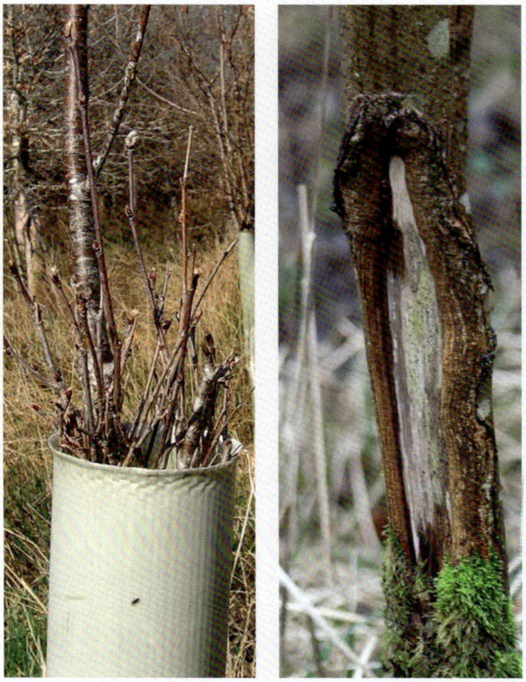

Damage from browsing (on the left) and fraying (on the right)

of the scrape here is too small for Fallow Deer, although it is possible it was a young deer from that year's births.

I took this photograph in the early morning when dew was thick on the bracken. I noticed that the central area was completely dry, so it was possible the deer had left soon before I arrived. I know the area well and it is a favoured place for the local Fallow and Roe Deer species.

Questions

What is the best time of day to see Roe Deer? Dawn and dusk are the times you are most likely to find Roe Deer. They often emerge from woodland cover and feed in open fields at dusk. If it has been wet, they may emerge from woodland earlier in the afternoon, and when the young are first active, around September, they may be seen more often during the day. If you are looking for deer in early summer, you may possibly come upon a young fawn curled up in the grass. Keep well away if you do, as the mother may abandon it if she suspects that a human has been too close. *I had to be prepared for some early mornings.*

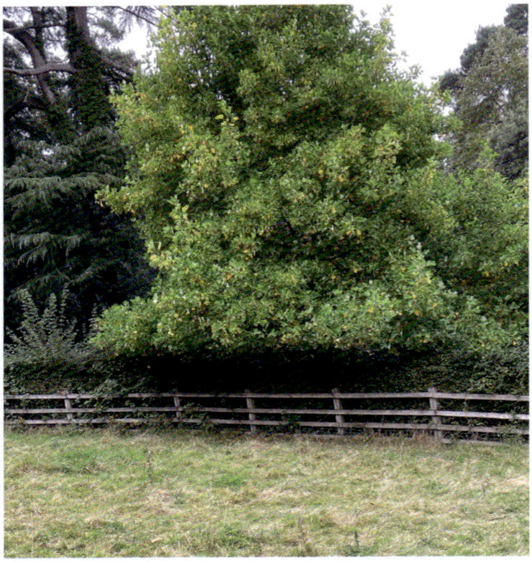

Browse line clearly shown under the centre tree

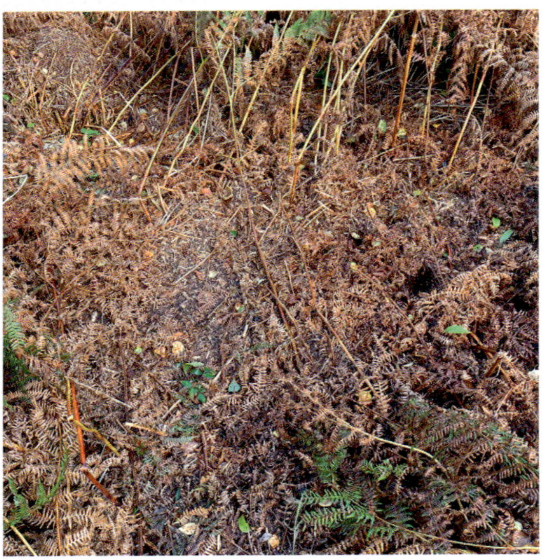

A scrape made by deer

How good are their senses? Roe Deer have good hearing and an excellent sense of smell. Their sight is poor, but they are sensitive to movement. *This means keeping very still when taking photographs, and approaching downwind.*

Equipment

The most useful item for finding deer is the trail camera, although it would be unwise to take it with you if there is any likelihood of it being stolen. A 500 mm lens is useful when taking photographs as it allows you to position yourself a reasonable distance away, but a shorter focal-length lens may be suitable if you can get close. *In my case, trail cameras were out of the question as time was short.*

Habits

Finding and interpreting tracks and signs will indicate Roe Deer are present, but knowledge of their habits is also required in order to increase your chance of finding them. Roe Deer can be active at any time of day or night, but their main feeding times are dusk, when they emerge from the cover of trees to graze in fields, and dawn, before they return to cover. They are much less active in winter. Unlike other deer, the Roe Deer rut is in July/August, but as Roe have their own territories, fighting is rare, and the rut will generally pass off unnoticed. The fertilised egg is held in suspended development for several months before growth starts, ensuring that the young are born at the optimum time of year. Fawns are born in April/May and lie inactive in long grass for several weeks. In late summer, the young can be seen with the doe, and may stay in a family group until the next spring.

The deer do not have a specific home, but will range over an area, the distance being determined by factors such as group size, area of woodland cover, food available and degree of disturbance – the latter being mainly by man and his dog. The secretive nature of Roe Deer, and the fact that they do not collect in herds, means that they can be found in urban areas where there is sufficient cover, such as parks, golf courses and even cemeteries.

Roebucks will 'bark', especially when disturbed, and this is most likely a sign that you have been spotted.

In the field

Knowledge gathered from previous, unsuccessful searches is described below.

To illustrate how earlier information gathered helped my final success, in this section I initially describe here the facts I had gathered, and whether or not they helped on this occasion. Once you have discovered by word of mouth or by Internet search where Roe Deer are likely to be present, set up a trail camera, if possible. This will confirm the presence of deer and will give an indication of when they are most likely to be active. Many wildlife reserves have Roe Deer, and the rangers will tell you if they are around, and may even divulge a favoured spot, if it exists. Walk through the area looking for signs and tracks, and in particular in fields bordered by woodland. *In my case, time was short and I could not scope out areas with a trail camera.*

A good time of year to look for Roe Deer is late summer when the young are first exploring. At this point they are still being fed by the doe, who will be close by, but are often out exploring during the day. *In this case, I was looking in very early spring, but hoped that I might see an overwintering family group.* It is possible to stalk the deer, or to let them come to you; I have found that the sit-and-wait method gives a higher quality of image. Approach a likely area in the early morning around dawn, ensuring that the wind is blowing towards you. *This was the approach I used here.*

If you have to walk through woodland, take care to travel very slowly as it is very difficult to traverse this terrain quietly. The deer may be lying behind tree trunks and will easily see you, even if you do not see them, so if possible avoid woodland if there are suitable fields around. Fields surrounded by woods are very popular with deer as they provide several escape routes. *This knowledge helped to narrow down areas to look.*

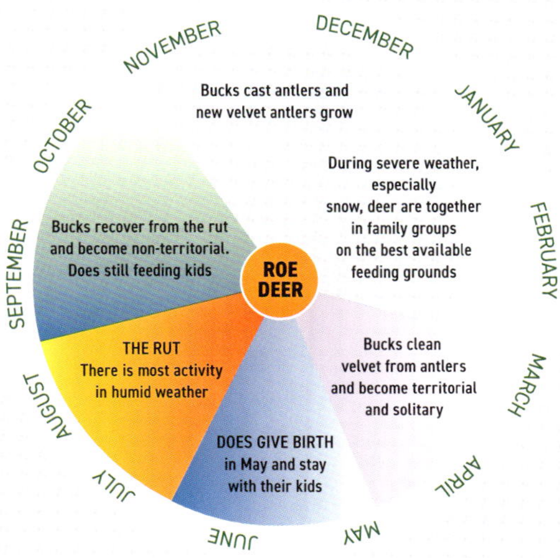

Roe Deer calendar

A good place to stand (or sit) and wait is under a tree, or on the edge of a field bordered by woodland. Cover your tripod, camera and yourself with a camouflage cloth and be prepared to wait for some time. If there is no sign of deer, return in the early evening and repeat the whole process over the next few days. *I did not return in the evening as the days were short when I was searching and I do not like walking around unfamiliar areas in the dark.*

On average I would say it can take four or five visits before being in a position to get high-quality images. Although Roe Deer have their own territory, it may be quite large, and it will be impossible to predict exactly where they will be at any given time. *This had put me off in the past, but on this search I was motivated to persevere.*

Although Roe Deer have poor eyesight, their sense of smell is very good. They lick the tips of their noses to improve scenting. Their hearing is also very sharp, and the sound of a shutter is likely to disturb them if you are too close – so avoid burst mode unless the deer is already running off. *Fortunately this information stood me in good stead.*

My successful search is now described.

My first step had been to ascertain where Roe Deer were likely to be by a study of maps of the local area. I settled on several meadows surrounded by conifer woodland and edged with deciduous trees, close to where I was told Roe Deer had been seen. An experienced deer stalker had given me advice on how to approach deer in general, and armed with research on Roe signs and habits, I paid several visits to the chosen area. I was visiting in eary March, which was not an ideal time of year as it can be cold and wet, but as the Roe Deer calendar shows, family groups can be seen around this time.

To my delight, there were signs of Roe Deer in the meadows and the woodland: fresh droppings of a suitable size, hoof prints and the fraying of tree stems. Early one misty morning, I saw several Roe Deer from a distance, but the only way to approach them was through woodland littered with branches. It was almost impossible to walk quietly, and not only that but the wind was blowing from me to them, so it was no surprise that they ran off before I could get close.

That early meeting, however, had highlighted a favoured site, and I made the decision to approach them next from the other side of the field, and to sit and wait. Two early mornings were unsuccessful, but on the third, I positioned myself on the side of a stream bank behind a fence, covered tripod, camera and myself with camouflage cloth, and waited. The wind was blowing towards me, and the stream bank, being lower than the meadow I was watching, offered the advantage of cover, with only my head and the camera lens protruding above the fence.

It was very cold and frosty and my feet gradually became numb, although the sun was shining. Just when I was thinking of leaving, two Roe Deer literally leaped out of the wood close to me, followed by their two young from the previous year. I spent some time photographing the buck and doe together with their youngsters. Initially they had no idea I was there and did not seem disturbed by the sound of the shutter, which was on quiet mode. The two youngsters came closer until I could only get a head in the camera frame. Eventually they came so close that they heard the shutter and probably smelled me, so they bounded off.

In all it took five visits before I got pictures I was happy with. Perseverance is necessary even when the approximate location of wildlife is known, but success is worth the effort. In this case perseverance really paid off, as I was able to get very close, and the frosty ground gave beautifully toned images.

A year or two after this success, Roe Deer became seen more often in and around my rural garden, and a buck and doe visited us frequently. In summer the doe often wandered across my neighbour's field early in the evening. The series of images I took in early summer led me to believe that the doe was pregnant, as she appeared fatter than on previous occasions. She disappeared for several months, although the buck was often present, and in early September she reappeared followed by two young fawns. The group were often seen over a period of several months, with copious droppings showing just how frequently they visited. This was very exciting, but somehow the photographs I took did not have the same value to me as those I had previously worked so hard to obtain.It is possible that by creating appealing habitats, the best encounters can be on your own doorstep. You may not be able to attract deer, as I was fortunate to do, if you live in the middle of a large town, but there can be a surprising amount of wildlife even in cities.

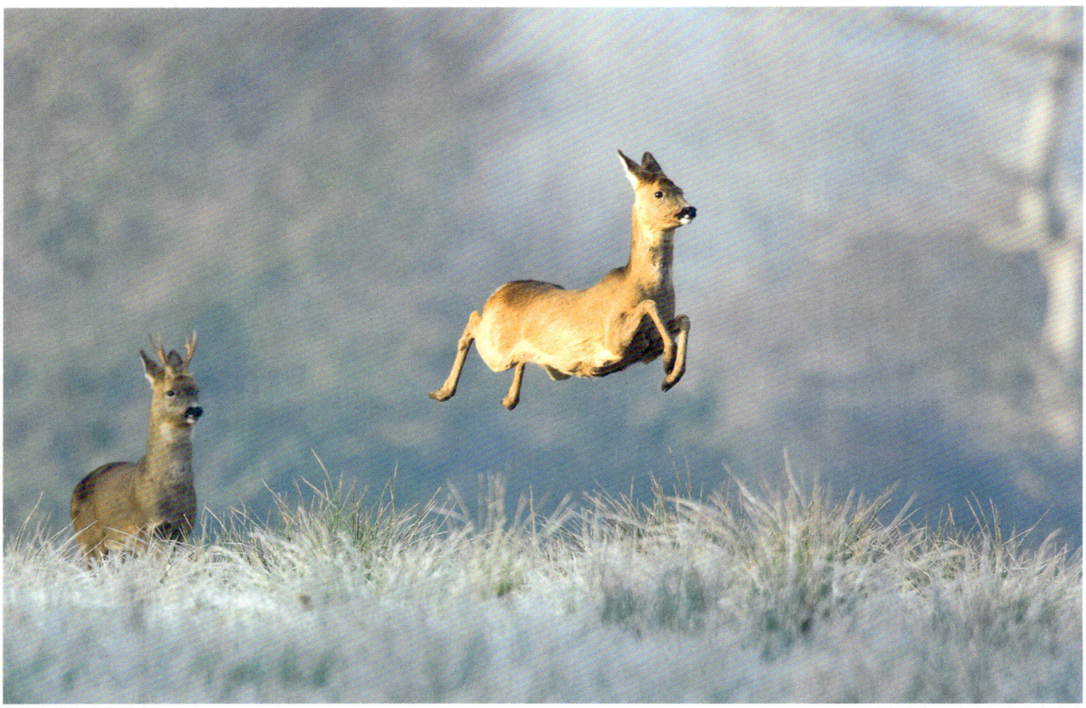

Young Roe Deer jumping

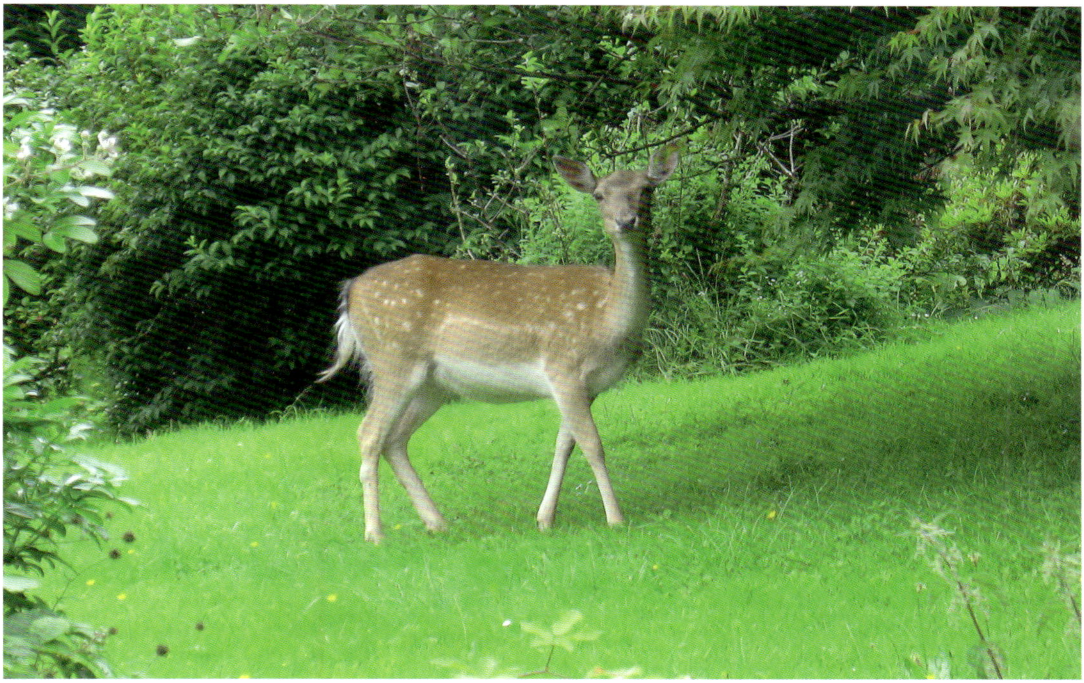

Fallow doe in the garden

Fallow Deer

A strain of Fallow Deer is believed to have been present in Britain before the last ice age, but later became extinct. Fallow Deer in the UK today are not this native species, but were introduced to Britain in the eleventh century by the Normans, for the purpose of hunting. This deer is a favourite for deer parks, due to its attractive spotted coat and its gregarious nature, but it can also be found in the wild. They browse as a herd, and can be very destructive to woodland. A visit to a deer park presents excellent opportunities for photographic practice.

Basic facts

Description: The Fallow is taller than the Roe, having a height at the shoulder of 80 to 90 cm. The coat is a fawn colour with white spots in summer, and darkens in winter. There are also paler and darker strains, including black.

The antlers are broad and flattened with short spikes, and are cast in spring. The white rump has black horseshoe-shaped edges and the colouring can be used to distinguish the Fallow from other types of deer. The tail is black on the top surface and white underneath, and is 18 to 21 cm long. The tail is often raised when the alarmed deer runs off.

Weight: The weight of a wild adult fallow buck is about 50 kg, and that of a doe about 35 kg.

Feeding: Fallow Deer are grazers, and will tend to work their way through a patch of grass or other vegetation rather than browse and nibble like Roe Deer. Because they keep together in herds, they can be very destructive,especially if they stray into field crops.

Breeding: A single fawn is born June to July.

Habitat: Fallow Deer prefer mature woodland, either deciduous or coniferous, for shelter. They feed on open grasslands and farmlands, especially in spring and summer.

Distribution: Found in much of England and Wales, but much less widespread in Scotland.

Population: 100,000 in the wild, but large numbers are kept in deer parks.

Tracks and signs

The hoof marks left by Fallow Deer appear long and narrow compared to those of Roe Deer.

Droppings are similar in appearance to those of Roe, but are larger, at approximately 2 cm long and 1.5 cm in diameter.

Fraying and browse damage to trees is similar to that of Roe, but as Fallow Deer are taller, the damage is likely to be higher up the trunk. Tree guards have to be taller if Fallow Deer are present. The browsing line on woodland edges is higher than for Roe Deer.

Antlers that have been cast may be found, their flattened shape in Fallow Deer being very distinctive. Antlers are cast from April to June, and the new ones grow until August. However, discarded antlers are soon eaten by deer, squirrels and other rodents, so they are only likely to be found soon after casting.

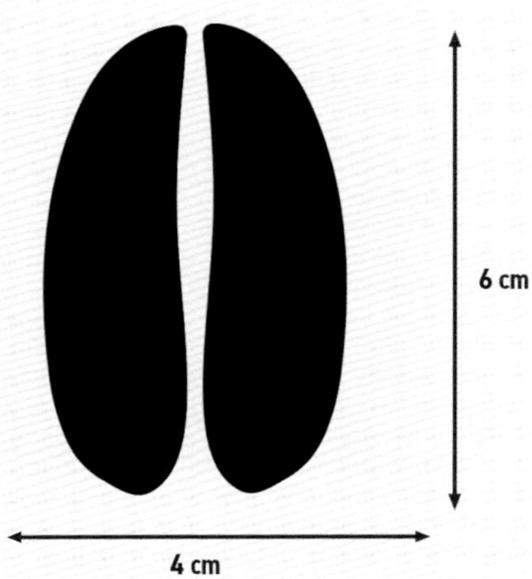

Fallow Deer tracks

Questions

What is the best time to view Fallow Deer? The rut is the best time, especially as the adult males advertise their presence, and there are more likely to be large gatherings.

How good are their senses? In common with other deer, Fallow Deer have acute hearing and sense of smell. They have poor eyesight, but will quickly detect movement.

What are the best locations? The New Forest in Hampshire, Haldon Forest in Devon, and the Forest of Dean in Gloucester have good populations. Haldon Forest deer are suspected to be outcasts from ancient deeer parks, as they are predominantly black. Reserve rangers may hold deer walks in October, but a large group of people is only likely to encounter the sight of deer running off, or of deer moving in a dark forest.

Equipment

Trail cameras can be useful, but as Fallow Deer are more likely to be found in large woods, protecting them from theft may be a problem. A tripod and camouflage cloth are recommended for photography.

Habits

The behaviour of Fallow Deer in the wild is very different from that in deer parks, where they are relatively tame. They are most likely to be found in larger woods, as human disturbance tends to move them away from smaller areas, especially if near habitation. They collect in herds, and thus are easy to see when found– but they also have sentries, so it is more difficult to stalk Fallow Deer than Roe Deer. They rely on woods for cover, and at dusk can be seen moving out into feeding areas, with very open areas being used more at night. They return to cover at dawn. Males and females tend to be separated except during the rutting season, and female groups may be led by a dominant doe.

The Fallow Deer rut takes place in October, but is affected by the weather and by human disturbance. In Haldon Woods, a Forestry Commission site in Devon, the rutting season is affected by weather, and mild, wet autumns can delay the process. The

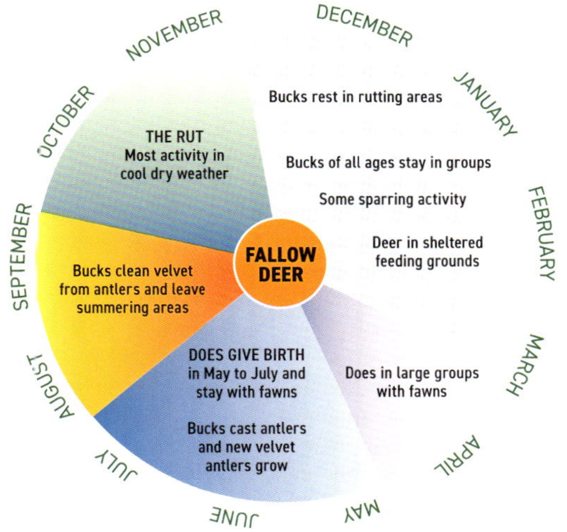

Fallow Deer calendar

presence of humans (often to observe the rut) has tended to push the deer into deeper cover. As a result of this combination of factors, there appear to be fewer large Fallow gatherings than in the past.

Because Fallow Deer stay in groups, browsing damage can be severe. A lack of thick understorey, especially of tree seedlings due to deer browsing, can reduce cover and edible plants and have a negative effect on other animal life.

In the field

As I mentioned earlier, stalking Fallow Deer is more difficult than stalking Roe Deer, due in part to the fact that Fallow Deer post sentries. I recall one morning when a small group of us sat quietly for some time on the edge of a potential rutting ground, wondering where the deer were, unaware that all the time we were being watched by a very handsome buck. The deer are much easier to see when moving out of cover into rutting areas, but as this tends to take place just before dawn, it can be too dark for photography, especially as flash cannot be used (it would soon frighten them off).

Provided that you are very careful and quiet, and approach with the wind blowing towards you, it is possible to surprise small groups of deer – but you must have your camera at the ready, as you will only have a brief time to get the shots before they depart at speed. For the best images, it is advisable to arrive very early before dawn and set up position near to likely rutting grounds. Be careful with wind direction and take care to walk quietly. Be aware of the possibility that deer may approach from behind and smell you, so if possible, sit with a slope at your back. Repeat this for several mornings and you are much more likely to be successful.

As the deer will often cross tracks within the woods, a car can be used very successfully as a hide, providing that a) it is possible to drive into the wood and b) the deer are used to the sight of cars.

Red Deer

Basic facts

Description: Red Deer are so called because of their red-brown coat, which becomes greyish in winter. The rump is paler, and the tail is ginger in colour, being 12 to 20 cm long. The Red is the largest deer, with height at the shoulder at 100 to 120 cm. The antlers are large and branched when mature.

Weight: The weight of an adult stag varies between 60 and 100 kg, with hinds being about 20% lighter.

Feeding: Red Deer feed predominantly on grasses in summer, but also on heather and tree shoots.

Breeding: A single fawn is born from May to July.

Habitat: The deer prefer mature woodland, either deciduous or coniferous, but large numbers are to be found on Scottish moorland.

Distribution: Widespread in Scotland, but also found in parts of England, especially Exmoor, Cumbria and the New Forest.

Population: 350,000, with 75% of this figure being in the Scottish Highlands.

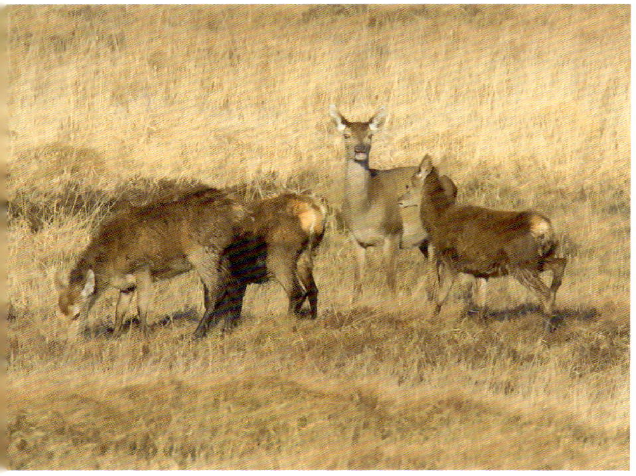

Red Deer on Mull. In the wild, this species is usually only seen from a distance.

Tracks and signs

Tracks and signs for Red Deer are similar to Roe and Fallow. Hoof tracks are larger and broader, being 9 cm long and 7 cm wide.

Droppings are also larger, with individual cylinders being 3 cm long and 1.5 cm wide.

Browsing lines can be up 180 cm high, as the deer may rear up on its back legs to eat tree vegetation.

Antlers may also be found soon after casting in April/May.

Habits

The rut is the favoured time for watching Red Deer. This can take place from mid-September until November. Stags can be very aggressive at this time and each year people have to be rescued after being threatened by them, so great care is required. The Red Deer rut is seen frequently on television as it makes good viewing, and because it is possible to get good clear shots of moorland deer. In practice, the rut is not quite as dramatic as this footage would suggest. During the rut much of a stag's time is spent in sizing up other stags, and trying to intimidate them with its size and by its roaring. Much less time is spent actually fighting.

Red Deer are active throughout the day, and in the Scottish Highlands will tend to move from higher to lower levels at dusk, and vice versa at dawn. In woodland areas, they will move to open grasslands, this being more usual at night.

Red Deer generally stay in herds of females (hinds) and young, led by a dominant female, and only meet up with males in the rutting season.

In the field

Many of the reserves which are strongholds of Red Deer hold guided events to watch the rut, and this is a safer way to get photographs. For example, Galloway Forest Park in Newton Stewart, south-west Scotland, takes parties to a hide for watching the deer, and other reserves throughout the UK offer guided walks especially to see the rut. This is probably the best way to locate the deer, and you can always return on your own, provided of course that you are careful to keep your distance. At other times of year, the hinds form groups with other females and young, with the stags forming smaller groups.

Do not assume you will observe many stags fighting during the rut, as seen on TV. As mentioned

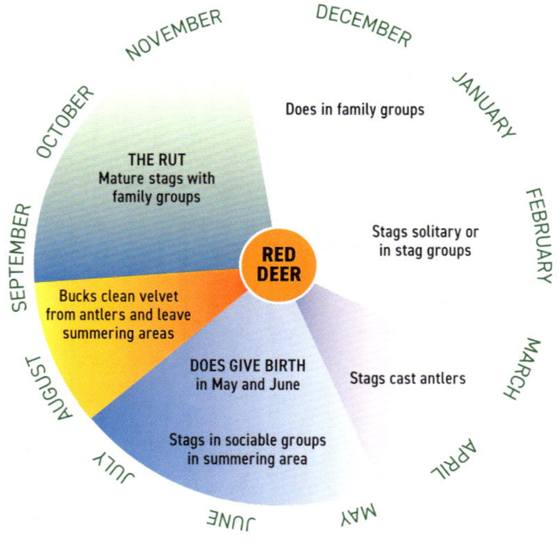

Red Deer calendar

DEER TYPE	SIZE TO SHOULDER (cm)	HOOF PRINT (mm length × width)	DROPPING LENGTH (cm)	POPULATION	DISTRIBUTION
RED DEER	100–120	90 × 70	3.0	350,000	Mainly in Scotland
FALLOW DEER	80–90	60 × 40	2.0	100,000	Mainly southern England
SIKA DEER	70–80	80 × 50	1.5	20,000	Scotland, southern England
ROE DEER	60–70	45 × 30	1.2	500,000	Widespread in UK
CHINESE WATER DEER	50–60	40 × 30	1.0	1,500	Southern England
MUNTJAC	40–50	30 × 20	1.0	52,000	South-eastern England

Table 2.1 Species of deer in the UK

above, they spend most of their time assessing one another, and for every hour of fighting there are days without a single skirmish.

Lack of fighting, however, does not mean you should get close to them – if you do, you may find yourself in danger from a testosterone-fuelled stag.

General fieldcraft for the main deer species

- Find areas of suitable habitat: woodland and adjacent fields or moorland. Make sure the landowner does not object to your presence.
- If possible, ask locals if and where deer can be seen. This will be most successful on nature reserves such as those owned by Wildlife Trusts or the Forestry Commission, as they usually have rangers on site familiar with the local wildlife. However, some nature reserves are busy, and if there are regular visitors, deer will most likely be found in areas where human access is more difficult.
- Look for deer signs: hoof prints, droppings, feeding marks and flattened grass, as described above. Signs and habits are similar for all deer, and distinguishing between species will depend mainly on hoof track size, dropping size and height of browsing line, together with knowledge of the expected distribution.
- If possible, attach a trail camera in what appears to be a suitable area. Take care with your choice of location as cameras are likely to be stolen if in an obvious position. Check the camera each day and move it if necessary. This will give an indication of the time the deer are around.
- Camouflage clothing is very helpful if stalking, and useful, if not essential, at other times.
- Approach likely areas just before dawn. Walk slowly and quietly in a direction such that the wind does not blow from behind. If a deer looks in your direction, freeze in position. Provided they cannot smell you, they may ignore you, as it is movement that catches their eye. In woods walk very slowly, stopping at regular intervals to look around. Be aware that it is almost impossible to walk quietly

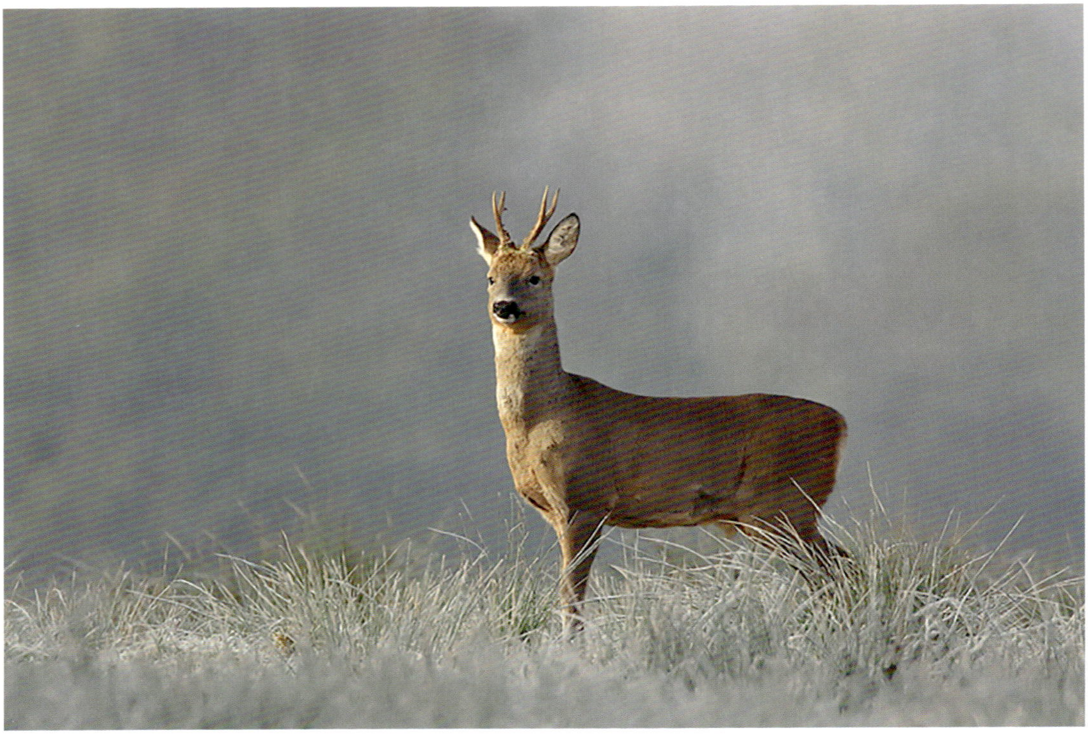

Roebuck

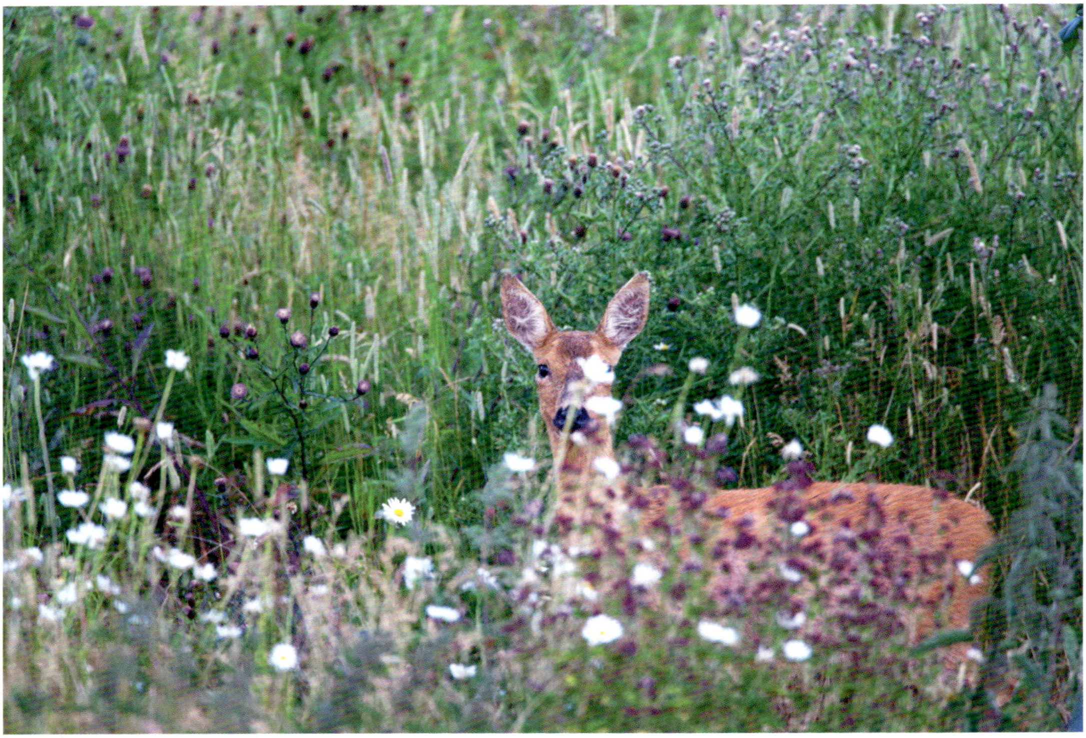

Roe doe

in a wood and deer will hear every crack of a broken twig.

- Find a suitable hidden spot and wait. This is likely to give better-quality images than stalking.
- If no deer are seen, repeat in the evening . Deer often emerge from the cover of trees after rain, as the rain may have prevented them from feeding.
- Repeat this over a period of time. Be aware that deer do not have specific 'homes' but will wander around a territory.
- In spring, when the young are born, they will lie in the grass for several weeks and are easier to photograph, provided you do not get near enough to frighten them. Under no circumstances should you get close enough to touch the young, as the mother may then abandon it.

The easiest time to see Red Deer and Fallow Deer is autumn, during the rut. Deer often have 'traditional' rutting grounds and it is easier to lie in wait for them. Be aware that the stags can be very aggressive at this time.

Photographic equipment and techniques for the main deer species

There are two main ways of photographing deer:

- stalking them using a handheld camera and a shorter focal length;
- finding a suitable position and waiting for them to come to you.

Stalking

This approach is more suitable for Red Deer on moorland, or for various types of deer in woodland. Stalking deer is difficult enough without carrying heavy camera gear. Fortunately, as deer are relatively large, a shorter focal length lens may be successful. A zoom lens (say 100 to 400 mm) will be easier to handle than a heavy 500 mm lens, for example. Handholding is the most practical method when stalking. In woodland there will usually be branches between you and the deer which makes focusing difficult. It is easier to see deer from a distance and in the open on misty mornings, but difficult to get close.

Personally, I think stalking is less likely to give good-quality photographs. Light levels in woods are low, and it is very difficult to creep up on deer unseen on open moorland. Once a place becomes known for deer, photographers and naturalists come in droves. The deer become more sensitive and tend to move deeper into the forest to escape humans. There are, of course, tamer deer in parks, but there is little photographic challenge here and less likelihood of seeing natural behaviour.

Waiting for them to come to you

This method depends on good preparation beforehand. Knowing where the deer are likely to be and waiting for them to appear may be time consuming, but will, I believe, be more rewarding. A long lens, such as a 500 mm, is practical as you will not be walking around, and a tripod can be used. As you are likely to be waiting at dawn or dusk, light levels will be lower. This means lower shutter speeds, hence the need for a tripod. It is not always necessary to photograph deer in detail and a silhouette can be very effective, especially if rim lighting or a sunrise/sunset background is available.

It is a good idea to practise adjusting lens size, aperture, ISO and shutter speed with tamer deer, for example in a deer park. The disadvantage of this is that some parks are not open at dawn and dusk, so although you can practise some aspects, lighting out in the wild is likely to be very different. However, once you have honed your skills, you will be able to take shots 'on the hoof' with more confidence, and will become proficient in getting the right aperture/ISO combination.

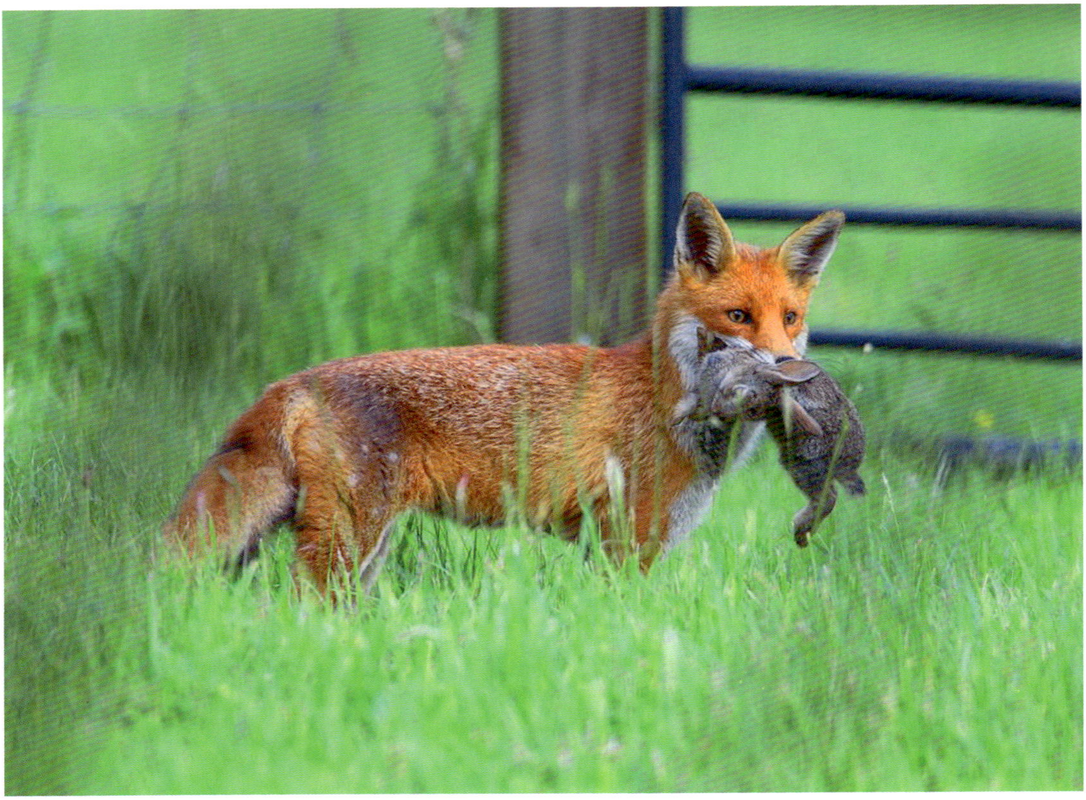

Fox with Rabbit near a Devon wood

Red Foxes

The Fox is much maligned, but is a beautiful animal with the strongest of survival instincts. Its service in keeping down the rabbit population is not always fully appreciated.

Basic facts

Description: The Red Fox, to give it its full name, is reddish brown with a white chest and often with black socks and ears as well as usually the characteristic white 'brush' at the tip of the tail. The colour varies in intensity, with urban Foxes being much less red, possibly because of a difference in diet. Males are 65 cm long, with the tail being about a further 40 cm long. Females are slightly smaller.

Weight: On average a dog Fox weighs 6.5 kg, and a vixen 5.5 kg.

Feeding: The Fox has a very varied diet , and it will consume almost anything (molluscs, for instance, are an important food source for young foxes). Foxes are opportunistic feeders, and their adaptability with regard to diet is one reason for their success in urban areas.

Breeding: An average litter of four is born, mainly in March.

Habitat: Foxes are found in a range of environments, including urban areas. Although very adaptable to habitat, they are most abundant in those of a diverse nature as this offers the potential for a greater variety of prey.

Distribution: Most of the UK, with the exception of offshore islands in Scotland.

Population: 225,000

Tracks and signs

Tracks

Fox tracks are similar to those of a small dog, being about 4 cm wide and 5 cm long. They are narrower than those of a dog and often show marks left by the hairs between the pads. They are probably easiest to see when in soft mud, for example on the sides of ponds or rivers. A trail camera in situ will confirm if and when Foxes are present.

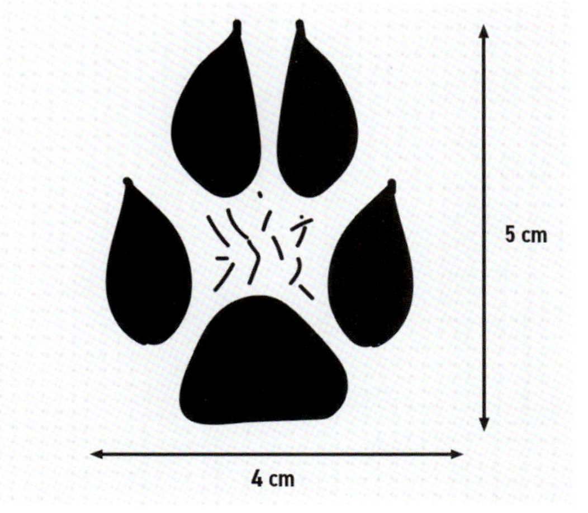

Fox tracks

Droppings

These are similar to those of a small- to medium-sized dog, but often have bones or seeds visible.

Evidence of kills

When eating pigeons or other birds, Foxes bite the feathers off, leaving the ends broken and flattened. This distinguishes their kills from those of a bird of prey, as the latter pull out the feathers and leave the point intact. The feathers plucked by a bird of prey are also likely to be spread over a larger area as the wind catches them.

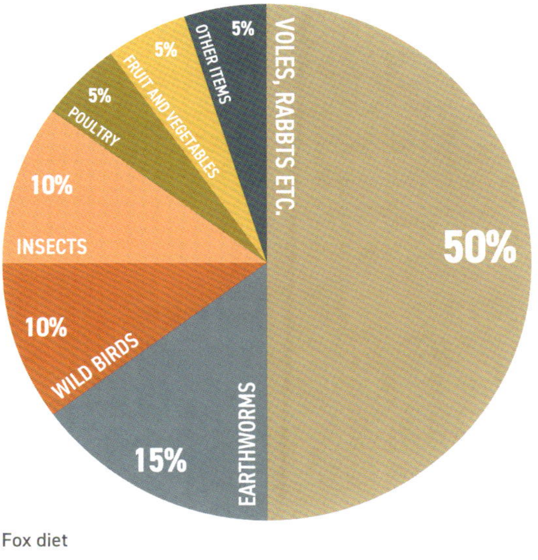

Fox diet

Dens

Foxes use dens, or earths as they are officially called, mainly for breeding. At other times, earths are only used in bad weather. Earths take numerous forms depending on the habitat, but in rural areas are often old Badger setts, or enlarged rabbit burrows. Vixens usually have more than one earth, and will move cubs if at all disturbed by man or dog. In urban areas, earths are often under sheds, in overgrown gardens or in wasteland.

Questions

What is the significance of a vixen having several earths for cubs? It is tempting for the photographer to try to get close to a Fox den if cubs are present, but this may simply result in the vixen moving them elsewhere. It is better to wait some distance away so that the den is not disturbed. In any case, the cubs will start to explore after a few weeks and are likely to come closer to you.

How keen are Fox senses? Unlike deer, Foxes have good eyesight, required for catching prey. They are believed to see monochromatically, which enhances their sensitivity to movement. Their hearing and sense of smell are also acute. If stalking or waiting for Foxes, ensure that the wind is blowing towards you and keep very quiet.

Equipment

Trail cameras are an extremely useful tool for confirming the presence of Foxes and their likely timing.

Habits

Foxes are mainly nocturnal, but can be seen leaving the den at dusk to go hunting, or at dawn returning. The cubs are born mainly in March, with four or five being regarded as a typical number, although not all may survive. A neighbour of mine filmed a vixen with 8 cubs recently, but we assumed she was baby sitting. Young cubs are brown and look like puppies, with the characteristic red coat not appearing until they are eight weeks old. Cubs become completely independent by September, but a vixen may stay within the family group to help with the next year's cubs. Territories for the family group may be around one square kilometre in size, depending on the availability of food.

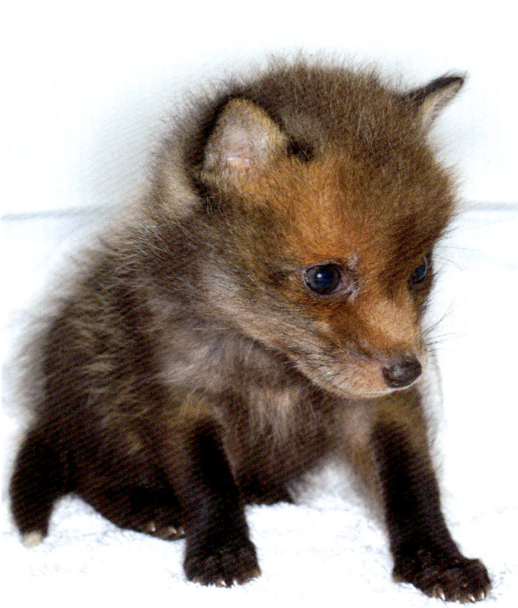

Baby Fox in a wildlife hospital

In the field

Foxes are probably present in most areas of fields and woods in the UK, and in a wood their den may be part of an old Badger sett. Waiting close to a field at the edge of woodland in the early morning may offer the sight of Foxes returning home. The best times to see an 'early evening' Fox is when the young are a few weeks old and eating meat. The adults have to work hard to supply meat for the cubs as well as themselves, and are often to be seen out during the day, trying to keep the growing family well nourished. The cubs born in the spring start to become independent and to explore their territory any time from May to August, and are likely to be seen frequently in the early evening and, as they explore further, at other times of the day. If, however, you want to increase the odds of finding a Fox, the best way is to look for Fox signs. I always know when the young are striking out by the sudden increase in the number of droppings. The young are less wary than adults, and it is possible to get quite close, provided that you are downwind of the animal, and you make very little noise and keep still.

The best place to wait is in an area where you have seen signs of Fox: tracks, droppings or animal kill. In the evening, Foxes are likely to be coming out of woodland into fields to hunt, although this will not always be the case. If safe from theft, set up a trail camera and move it every few days until you capture a Fox on camera. Position yourself in the area you captured the images, set up your camera with as long a lens as you can, and wait. Use a tripod, a large aperture and as high an ISO as possible without ruinous noise, so that you can achieve a reasonably high shutter speed to freeze-frame any movement.

In urban areas, Foxes can be found almost anywhere, depending on food sources. Word of mouth is possibly the best method to locate them, and parks with a good rabbit population are likely to be a popular habitat.

Walking the streets at dusk with an expensive camera and lens is not always advisable in some urban areas, so a group outing may be a safer option.

CASE STUDY: Red Fox

This case study is rather different from the previous examples, as I discovered a family of Foxes close to me almost by accident, and was in the lucky position of being able to photograph them with very little additional research as they were literally in my own back yard – albeit this is a rural garden surrounded by fields.

I offer this example to demonstrate that luck often plays a part, and it is important always to be ready for action, making use of information you have previously gathered. In other words, do not leave research to the last minute, just when you want to photograph a particular animal, but carry out research on wildlife you aim to photograph, even if you have no immediate plans to do so. This means that if a lucky chance comes your way, you are already prepared. It also demonstrates that looking for one animal can put another your way.

It might be a useful exercise to check the research above to see which parts I used in this case.

I had laid out peanuts in the wood for my local Badger as usual, one May evening, and had set up a trail camera to check at what time the Badger would come. Next day, on checking the camera, I noted a Fox was present, a little before the Badger. I put the camera out the next night and found not only the Fox but also three very small cubs. There is a field next to the wood, which has another section of forest on the other side, and as I had seen Foxes there the previous year, I thought it a good place for an evening watch.

The first evening at about 6 pm I set up my camera, tripod and camouflage cloth behind a low hedge, making sure that the wind was blowing towards me. I expected to wait for a couple of hours, but after fifteen minutes a vixen appeared, carrying a rabbit. She trotted off towards the top of the field and into the small wood which bordered it, indicating the likely position of the den.

The next night I saw three small cubs emerging from the wood near the top of the field, and moving in the direction that the vixen had headed the night before. At this stage it would have been very easy to move closer to the den area to get some close-up shots of the cubs, but I resisted for two reasons. First, I did not want to disturb the group, and because Foxes have a very keen sense of smell, they would likely be disturbed by a human anywhere nearby. As a result, the vixen would probably have removed the cubs to another area. Secondly, I knew that the cubs would start exploring when they were older, so waiting a few weeks would mean the opportunity for many more shots without disturbing the family group.

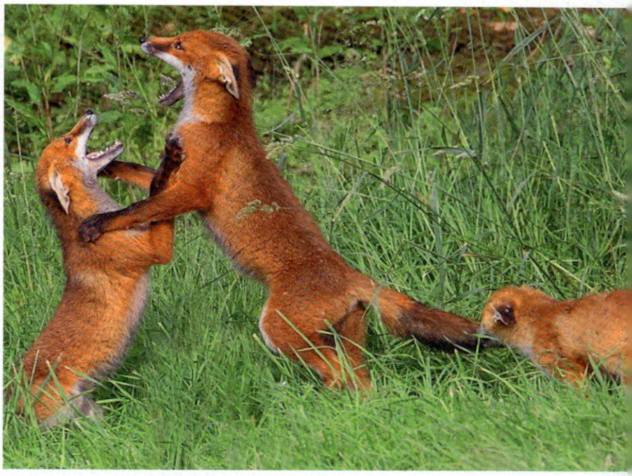

Sibling Fox cubs at play

I watched the group over the next few weeks, usually between 6 and 8 pm, and saw many instances of the cubs playing and of the parents bringing them rabbits. Each time I had to be careful of the wind direction, as a slight whiff of human sent them running off. By mid June, the cubs had started moving further from the den and I got many shots of them sleeping in the long grass, walking along a stone wall and play-fighting. They were most frequently seen when it was sunny, and were often out at 5 pm and at other times during the day. Once September arrived, they were spotted less often, but one cub stayed and was often caught on the trail camera in the early evening.

There was obviously a hierarchy within the group, as the three cubs were of different sizes, with the dominant male being the largest – probably because he had first go at any food brought to them. The image above highlights the size difference, with the smallest cub appearing to bite the tail of the largest!

Badgers

Badgers are a protected species and it is an offence to disturb them in their sett, or damage the sett in any way.

Basic facts

Description: Badgers have coarse, dark grey fur and a characteristic black-and-white striped face. The body length of the male is about 75 cm, with the female being around 72 cm on average. The tail is short and hairy and about 15 cm long.

Weight: The male is around 11.5 kg, with the female on average around 10 kg.

Feeding: Badgers are omnivorous foragers, eating earthworms, insects, carrion, cereals, fruit, small mammals, slugs and fungi. Typical percentages of each diet element are shown in the pie chart, although these are very variable depending on what is available. Badgers are often accused of 'hunting' Hedgehogs, but it is more likely a case of them finding one by chance, as they are foragers rather than hunters.

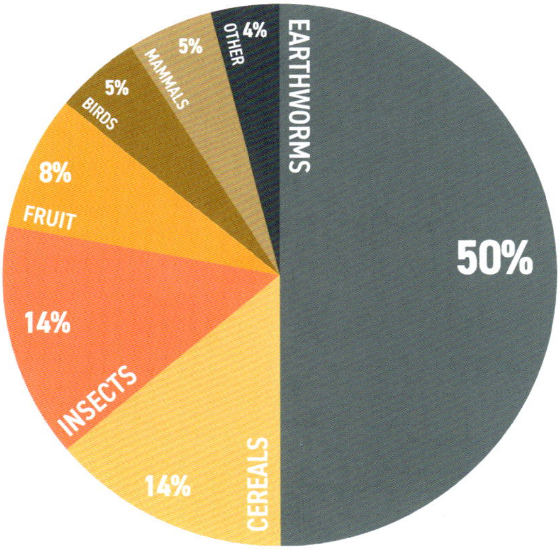

Badger diet

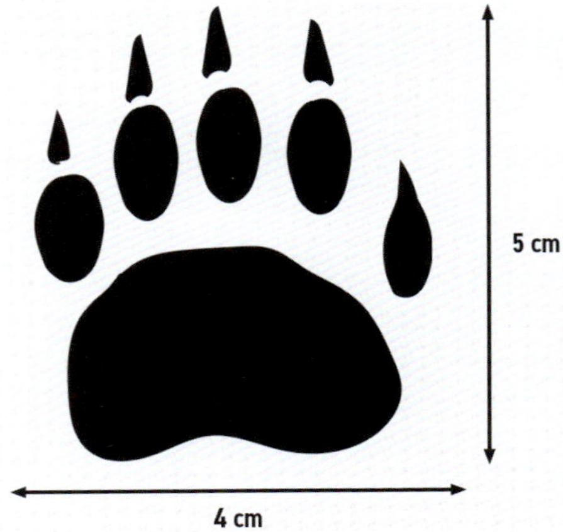

Badger front track

Breeding: Up to five cubs are born in February, although usually only those from dominant females in a social group survive.

Habitat: Badgers inhabit deciduous woodland near moist pasture land. They are particularly fond of south-facing limestone hillsides because the slope and the orientation assist with sett drainage. In addition, limestone is often broken up rather than in a solid mass of rock and is thus easier to dig out, as well as being well drained. Badgers are also found in suburban areas, for example in parks and large cemeteries.

Distribution: They are found in most of Britain at levels below 500 m, particularly in the south and west.

Population: Approximately 350,000 in the UK.

Tracks and signs

Tracks

Badger tracks are unmistakable, and they can be seen in soft mud, sand or snow. Front-paw tracks can be about 5 cm long and 4 cm wide, but Badger size is variable. The marks from the long front claws are often clearly visible, making them simple to identify. They are easily distinguished from dog tracks, for example, as Badgers have five toes.

Setts

Although the large holes of a Badger sett entrance are very distinctive, they are not necessarily active entrances. If you find one large hole, look around, as an active sett will have several others. Freshly dug holes have heaps of loose soil at the entrance, and the entry will be clear of leaves and twigs. Sometimes, especially if it has been wet, the entrance tunnel will be worn smooth by the Badger's body.

The sett in the next photograph had been recently dug as winter quarters. As well as piles of loose soil, and well-worn tracks, there was a distinctive musty smell of Badger.

Latrines and paths

Badgers dig holes in which they deposit faeces. These are usually found at the boundaries of their territory and a fresh latrine is the best indication that Badgers are present. There will also be well-worn paths and signs of digging as if left by a rotovator.

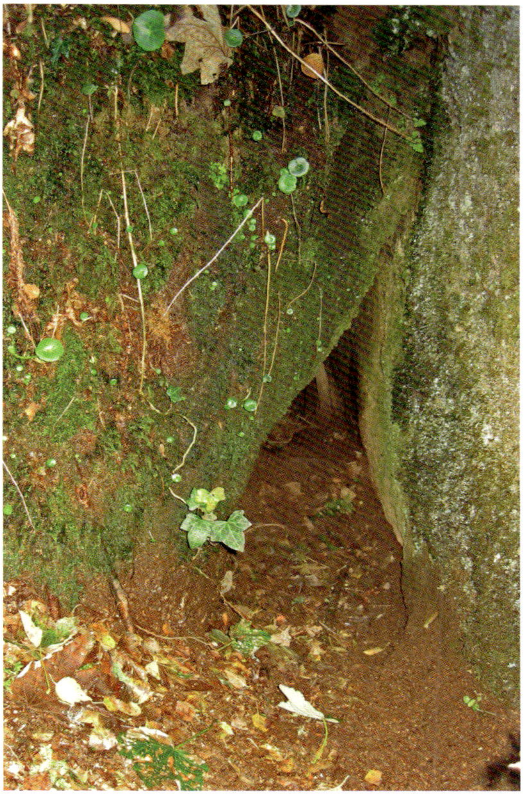

Badger sett entrance located on a rocky hillside near Dartmoor

Questions

How sharp are Badger senses? Badgers have a keen sense of smell, which is useful when digging up earthworms in the dark. Take care to be perfume-free in their presence. They have excellent hearing, but their sight is poor. Provided you have the wind blowing from the Badger to you, they can come very close. However, although sight is poor, they detect movement easily, so any camera waving may spook them.

Equipment

If you can manage it, fixed lights are best to provide illumination for photography, as Badgers quickly become accustomed to them. Flash can be used, although this is likely to disturb them.

Habits

Badgers are of course nocturnal mammals, living in social groups in underground passageways and chambers called setts. Badger setts consist of a large number of entrance holes, often in a south-facing slope, connected with underground tunnels. Not all entrances are active, and setts can extend for some distance. Territories vary in size according to food available, but there may be up to ten Badgers per square kilometre.

Badgers can mate at almost any time, but delay implantation until December. This means that the fertilised egg is held in suspended animation and does not fix to the uterus and start growing immediately. As a result, births are synchronised and most young are born in February when food sources are at their optimum. In April, Badgers often come above ground before it is dark, so this is a good time to spot them. This is also when the cubs first emerge, although they are not weaned for several months. In May the cubs start to explore, so are more commonly seen. By June, most cubs are fully weaned and starting to forage. Adventurous

Badgers can often be attracted with a few peanuts

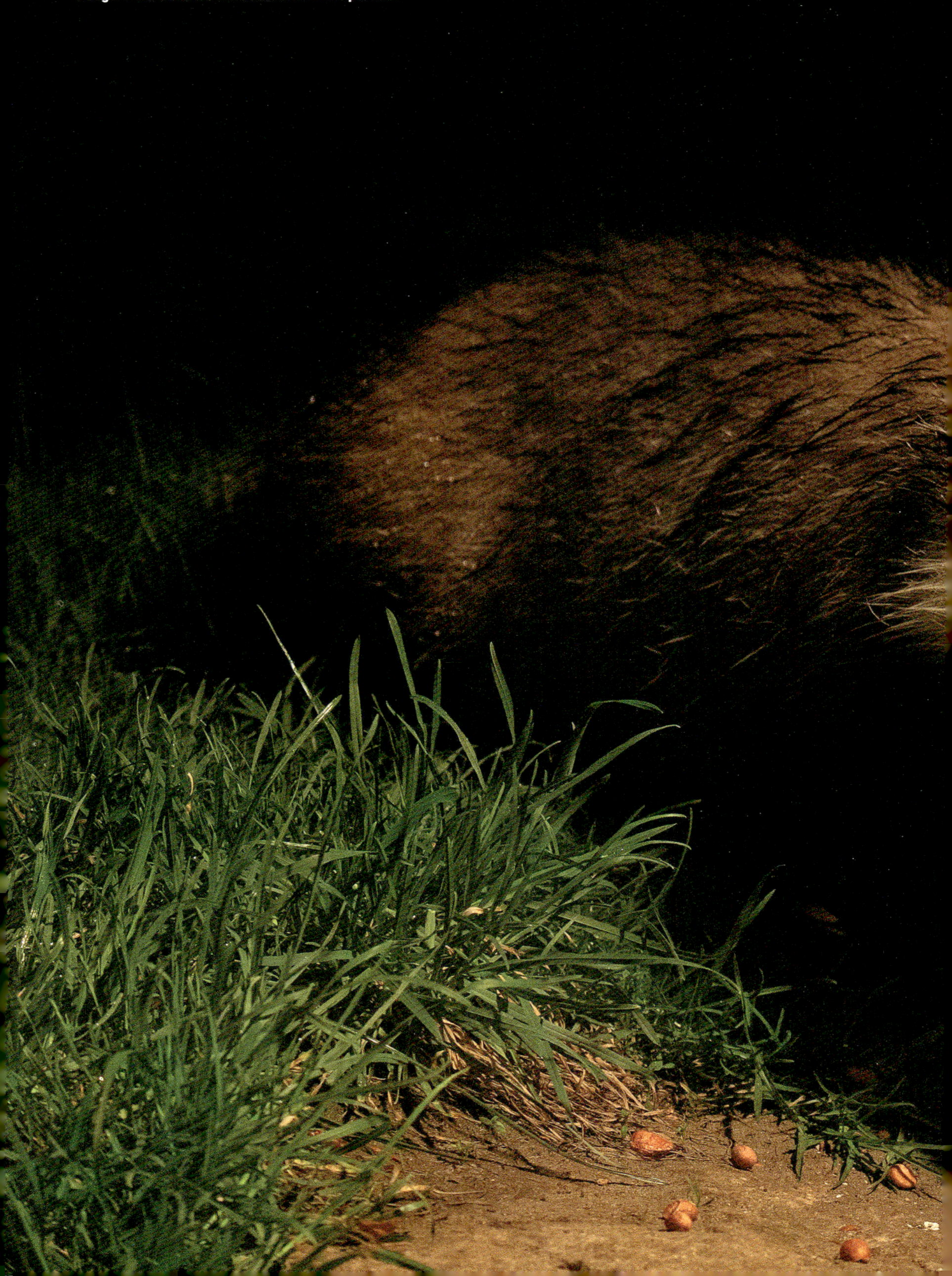

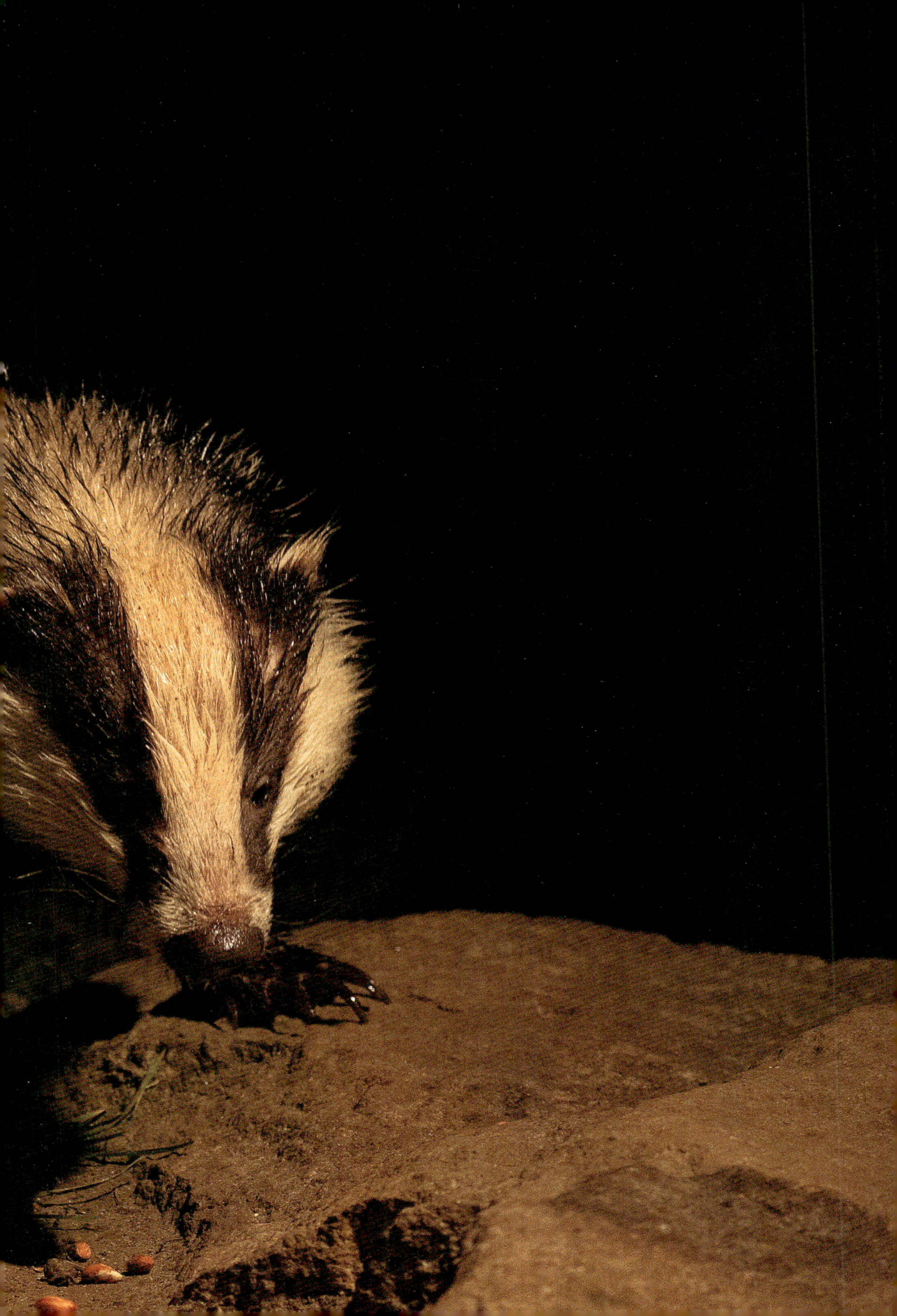

cubs often emerge during the afternoon, creating the opportunity for photography in daylight.

Badgers do not hibernate, but sleep much more in winter. They emerge less often from November to January, so this is not likely to be a productive time to Badger-watch.

Although they live in social groups with anything from two to twenty-two members, they tend to forage individually, which can give the impression that there are fewer Badgers in a group than in reality. I captured a short video showing what happened when a male strayed into the favoured feeding place of the regular female. There was a great deal of shoving, pushing and jockeying for position, but no real aggression.

Badger claws are important for digging, either tunnels in the sett or for food, and have to be kept in good condition. Tree stems are used to sharpen claws, with elder apparently being a favoured scratching post. Badgers are very strong and one only has to watch them moving large rocks to appreciate their vigour and persistence when looking for food.

In the field

Badger signs are unmistakable, so discovering their location is not difficult. Most deciduous woodlands will have Badger setts, especially if they have south-facing slopes. The problem for the photographer is that Badgers are nocturnal and live underground during the day. However, they can be tempted out earlier in the evening with a regular supply of peanuts. If it is not your land, make sure you have permission first from the landowner. Be aware that many farmers and landowners are not well disposed towards Badgers, as they have been led to believe that they are responsible for the increase of TB in cattle (the science does not agree). So it is best to ensure first that the landowner is not anti-Badger.

Nature reserves are generally well disposed to all wildlife, but may not be so keen on trails of peanuts. Make sure the nuts are covered with stones, or they will be stolen by Foxes, Jays and squirrels. I put a metal dog dish upside down over nuts, then place a piece of breeze block on top. Initially you will have to put some nuts outside the rock until the Badgers learn where they are. The Badgers have no trouble moving the block, but other wildlife cannot.

Once you have detected the position of a sett, and have found that the peanuts are disappearing regularly, trail cameras are invaluable for showing where and particularly when the Badgers are to be found. If you lay a trail of nuts to your chosen position on a regular basis, the trail camera may show them coming earlier each evening.

Only a small quantity of nuts should be given and they should be laid in the vicinity of the Badger sett, but a short distance away. Encouraging them to come close to houses is not a good idea, especially if there are roads nearby. About half an hour before the earliest time the Badgers arrive, according to the trail camera, position yourself several metres from the peanuts, ideally in a hide, and wait. Keep downwind of them and avoid trampling the site too much beforehand. Badgers have poor sight, although they will detect movement, but they have a keen sense of smell. Quiet is also essential. It is only when sitting waiting for wildlife in fading light that you can appreciate just how noiseless one has to be. Even the slightest movement can cause rustling that is noticeable to human ears, so must be extremely loud to the sensitive hearing of a Badger.

Many photographers believe that flash is essential to photograph Badgers and use two or more flashes to get better images. The Badgers, however, may not always enjoy the experience, and my local one shot off at great speed when I first used flash. I have found that using fixed lights disturbs them less, as they tend to ignore them. The great advantage of fixed lights is that it is easy to focus without resorting to using a torch in the dark. If you have a camera with low noise at high ISO, flash can be dispensed with altogether, when lights are used, as long as the Badger is relatively stationary.

Spend several nights watching the Badgers before taking photographs. Even if you are downwind, some human smell is likely to be detected, so waiting will give the Badgers time to get used to it. It is very important to keep quiet. If the Badgers appear undisturbed by your presence, take one or two images, but no more if you are using flash, as the well-being of the animal should always take precedence. If you are using battery-powered LED lights or mains-powered floodlights, it will be possible to photograph for much longer. LED lights are very varied, but are easy to obtain over the Internet. Check carefully how long the light lasts, as some only give out light for a short period before the battery runs out. Rechargeable batteries are a must.

My local Badger had been visiting for several weeks at the regular time of 9.30 pm in summer for her evening snack of peanuts. I had a hide set up close to the trail, by now well marked. I heard the Badger before I saw her, as the sound of peanuts being munched was very loud in the quiet of the evening. When she was close to the hide she looked up and I took this shot. Immediately she turned and ran with a speed I had not thought Badgers capable of. After that I started using LED lights to light up the scene so that I could just about get away with not using flash. The sett is passed regularly by dogs and people, so the Badgers are very wary. Badgers in areas further from human activity may be less sensitive, and flash may be a reliable option.

I often use a trail camera and take short videos of the Badgers. Badgers form social groups, but I have recorded a maximum of six, consisting of four cubs and two adults.

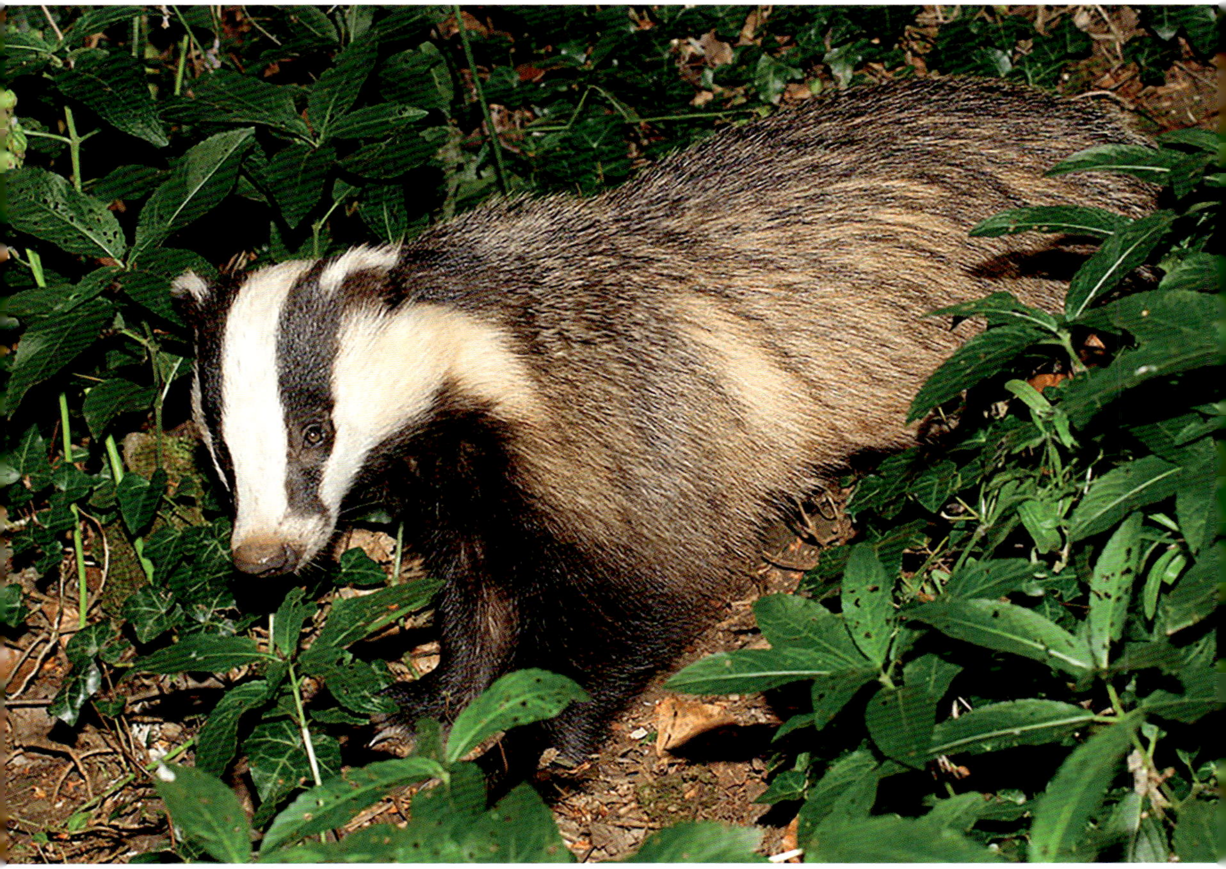

The local Badger

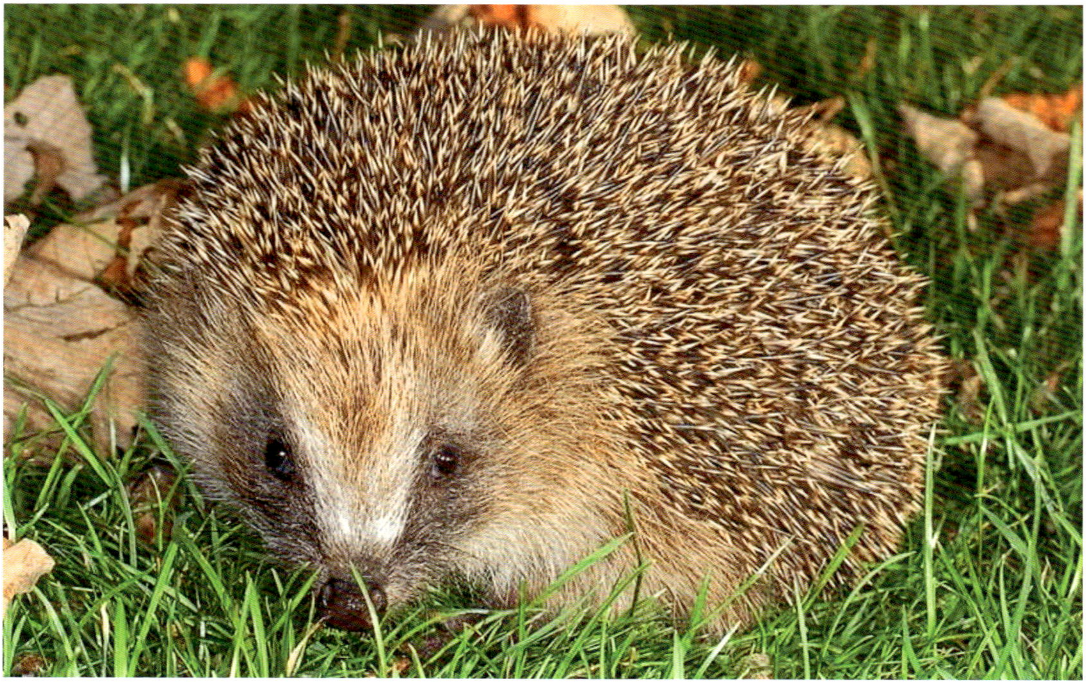

Hedgehog

Hedgehogs

At one time Hedgehogs were commonly seen, especially in suburban gardens, but now their numbers are decreasing rapidly. Recents reports have suggested that more than 150,000 are killed in road traffic accidents annually, according to the People's Trust for Endangered Species (PTES).

Basic facts

Description: The body is covered in brown and cream spines with coarse hair underneath. The head and body length is 23 cm for males and 22 cm for females. The tail length is about 2.5 cm, although it is hard to see, as a rule.

Weight: The male is heavier, weighing 900–1,200 g, and the female is lighter at 800–1,025 g.

Feeding: The Hedgehog diet includes beetles and other insects, caterpillars and earthworms. They do eat slugs, but as a minor part of their food intake.

Breeding: A litter of four to five on average is born from May to July or in September.

Habitat: The favoured habitats are the edge of woodland, and hedgerows close to grassland. Hedgehogs are at their most numerous in suburban areas, such as parks, golf courses and gardens.

Distribution: Most of lowland Britain.

Population: Estimated at 1.5 million in the UK, but numbers are decreasing.

Tracks and signs

Hedgehog tracks show five toes, but the fifth, smaller toe may be hard to see. The tracks are easy to see in snow and soft mud, but not otherwise.

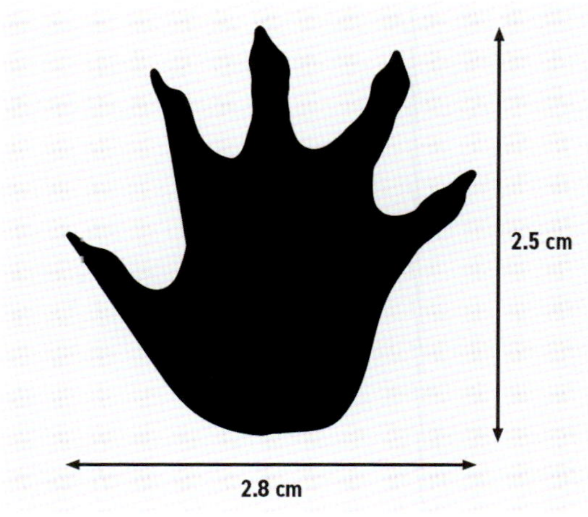

Hedgehog front track

They are about 2.5 cm long and 2.8 cm wide. Hedgehogs are relatively heavy for their track size, so the prints are likely to be relatively deep.

Questions

How keen are Hedgehog senses? Hedgehogs have an acute sense of smell and good hearing, although their vision is weak. They do not seem particularly sensitive to humans, so sitting in wait in a garden that they habitually use is likely to be successful, especially if your camera has a quiet shutter.

Equipment

It is possible to get quite close, so a focal length of anything from 50 to 300 mm may be suitable. A quiet shutter is advisable as they react to noise, but flash can be used in moderation as they are less affected by it, in my experience.

Habits

Hedgehogs are nocturnal, and are most likely to be seen at dawn and dusk. They create nests in summer for daytime refuge, and often move from one to the other. Hedgehogs hibernate from October to March or April, and create large winter nests for this purpose. Favoured nesting positions in the garden are under sheds, under log piles or in grassy plants, with Pampas grass being a well-recorded preference. Generally quiet, they make snuffling sounds when foraging, and rather louder grunts and squeals when mating.

In the field

Hedgehogs are very endearing, especially when very young, but successful photography in the wild can often depend on who you know. Hedgehogs are nocturnal, and difficult to find in the wild, but many people have them in their garden – so if you're not one of these lucky people, it would be worth trying to find someone who is. If you are a fan of social media, that is a good place to ask who has Hedgehogs in their garden, and whether you can photograph them.

If you cannot find Hedgehogs by word of mouth, you might like to carry out Hedgehog surveys. The easiest way is to walk along hedgerows in the evening with a torch, but the method suggested

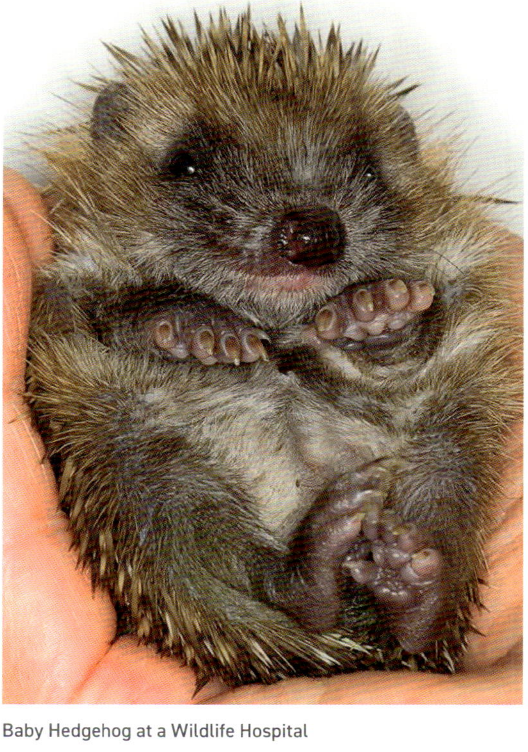

Baby Hedgehog at a Wildlife Hospital

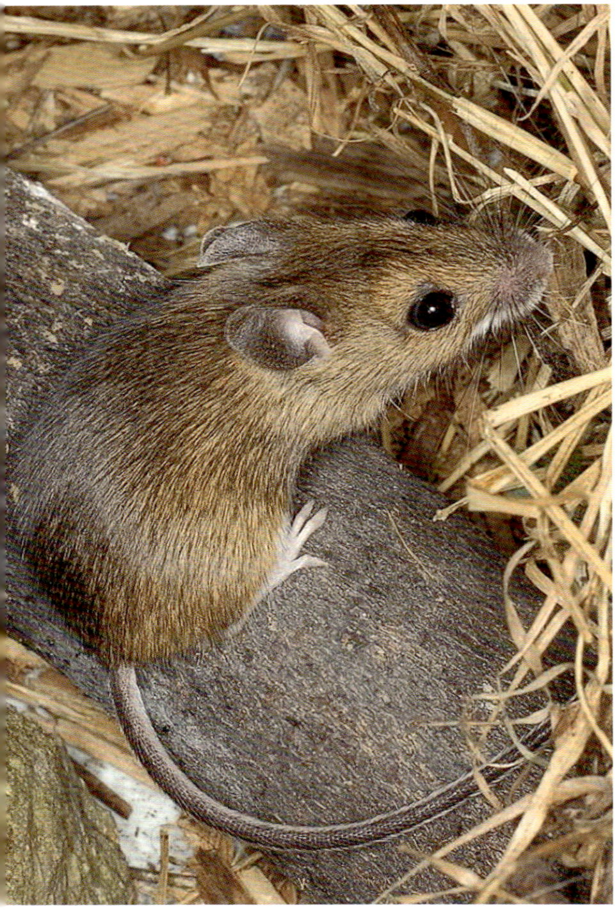

Wood Mouse

by the PTES is to use footprint tunnels. These are cheap to buy and easy to use. The PTES website also has details of how to make and use these tunnels, which can alternatively be purchased from ecology supply companies. Using a trail camera will minimise time spent looking. Provided it is not overused, and you only take a few photographs at a time, flash will not harm the Hedgehogs, who, in my experience, are more likely to be disturbed by a loud shutter.

Hedgehogs seem to be particularly damaged by the presence of humans, and not only by cars. A visit to a hedgehog hospital shows that Hedgehogs get caught in nets, stuck in tin cans and attacked by dogs, to name a few causes of injury.

Mice and voles

The commonest small mammals are the Wood Mouse (also known as the Field Mouse) and the vole (Bank Vole and Field Vole), the latter being the favoured food of a wide range of predators. The Wood Mouse is the easiest to find and identify, in my experience, so I have included its details below.

Wood Mouse

Basic facts

Identification: The Wood Mouse is reddish-brown with large, slightly protruding eyes and very large ears. The head and body length is 9.5 cm on average, with females a little smaller than males. Tail length is only slightly less than body length. The tail is slightly hairy and is the best way to distinguish the Wood Mouse from other mice and voles, which have shorter tails.

Weight: The average weight of the Wood Mouse is 19 g for the male and 18g for the female.

Feeding: Seeds, grain and nuts, especially hazelnuts, and insects.

Breeding: The Wood Mouse can have several litters a year with about five in each. The young can breed when several months old.

Habitat: The Wood Mouse prefers deciduous woodland, but is also found in grassland, dry-stone walls and hedgerows.

Distribution: Throughout the UK.

Population: 38 million pre-breeding in spring, 100 million after breeding in autumn.

Tracks and signs

The footprints of the Wood Mouse are very small and hard to distinguish, with other signs being clearer. Caches of nuts are commonly found, either in appropriated nest boxes, or half buried in the ground. Mouse droppings are narrow, black and slightly greasy, being about 5 mm in length, although it is almost impossible to determine what type of mouse they belong to without other evidence. Nests are made from brown leaves and moss and are often found in bird boxes and Dormouse boxes.

Nuts, seeds and particularly hazelnuts are eaten in a characteristic way, and can be used to confirm Wood Mouse presence. The cut edge has vertical gnaw marks, rather like the edge of a coin, and there are often indentations too on the outer surface of the nut.

In contrast, nuts eaten by squirrels are broken open and have jagged uneven edges, nuts chewed by voles are less likely to have gnaw marks on the outside, whereas Dormouse-chewed nuts only have bites on the outside and have a smooth surface on the cut edge.

Equipment

If you can manage to tempt Wood Mice out in daytime with a little food, a lens of focal length between 50 and 180 mm will be suitable.

Habits

Wood Mice are mainly nocturnal, making use of keen eyesight and acute senses of hearing and smell. The Wood Mouse is preyed upon by a large number of mammals and birds of prey, and rarely survives much more than a year. They are found in barns and other buildings in winter, especially in cold weather, and can often be seen on or near bird feeders looking for an easy meal.

In the field

Mice and voles are the favourite food of a wide range of animals, and have evolved to reproduce in large numbers. The mouse population is well over 100 million in the UK in autumn. Although Wood Mice are mainly nocturnal, they are relatively easy to find.

There are two main methods for the photography of these subjects, which are found in most environments, including suitable urban gardens. The first makes use of their dependence on shelter, and the second their attraction to easy food sources:

- If you put down either corrugated sheets or carpet tiles, mice and voles often build nests underneath them. If you lift up the sheet with your camera ready (easier if you have someone to help), you will have a short time to photograph them before they run off. Check the best camera

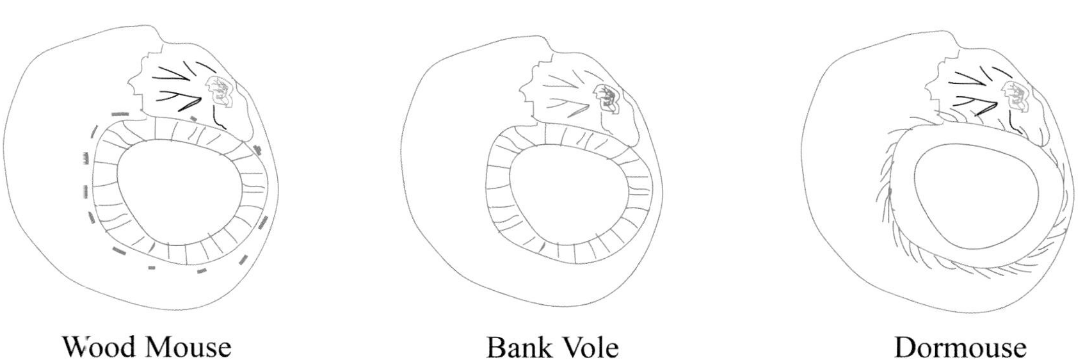

Comparison of feeding signs on hazelnuts

NAME	DESCRIPTION	SIZE	FOOD	HABITAT	POPULATION
FIELD VOLE	Greyish-brown, small ears and eyes, blunt nose, short tail	Length 11 cm Weight 21 g	Leaves, grass stems, moss	Rough grassland. Vole holes easy to see	75 million pre-breeding
BANK VOLE	Chestnut brown, small ears and eyes, blunt nose, longer tail	Length 9.5 cm, tail 4.5 cm Weight 18 g	Green leaves, seeds	Woodlands and grasslands	23 million pre-breeding
HARVEST MOUSE	Reddish-brown, small hairy ears, blunt nose, long prehensile tail	Length 6 cm Weight 6 g	Grain and invertebrates	Tall dense grasses or rushes. Summer nests above the ground	1.5 million but declining

Table 2.2 Details of other mice and voles

settings for exposure first, and pre-focus, as you will not have long to take the shot. Use a macro lens and flash for the sharpest images. You may even be able to photograph a nest of babies.

- Mice are very fond of birdseed, especially black sunflower seed. If you put birdseed on a log, with long grass or similar cover nearby, and set up a trail camera, you will be able to find out when they visit. It is best to put the seed out during the day and remove it at night, otherwise they may just come out when it is dark. Take care to position the food so that the mice have some protection from predators that is, do not put it out in the open. Another technique is to use a hanging bird table and suspend it from a tree. Wood Mice are almost certain to visit at some point. You may even attract a Dormouse. Once you know from the trail camera when they are likely to appear, you can be ready. As long as you stand still, you will not need a hide – but for long waits, a hide is the more comfortable option.

Some well-known wildlife photographers capture mice and voles for the purpose of photography. To my mind, not only is this not true wildlife photography, but it also may harm the animal – and that is not an option as far as I am concerned.

Stoats and weasels

Stoats and weasels live life in the fast lane. They have short lives of only a few years, and seem to spend every minute of it rushing around at great speed, examining every nook and cranny that could hold food. Finding them is difficult, and is very largely a matter of luck. Even if you do see one, taking a photograph before they shoot off is not easy. Stoats and weasels are similar in appearance, so knowing the stoat and weasel 'facts' thoroughly is important.

Questions

How do I tell the difference between Stoats and Weasels? The obvious answer is that Stoats are bigger, but that is only of use if you see them next to each other. There are several ways to distinguish, apart from size:

- Stoats have a long, bushy tail with a black bottom half.
- Weasels have large brown spots under the chin.
- The line between brown back and white chest is straight with Stoats and wavy with Weasels.
- Weasels often have brown marks on the belly.

When are they most likely to be seen? In common with many species, the best time is when the young have first ventured from the den. They often play outside during the day. With Stoats, this is likely to be in May or June. The female is also more likely to be seen during this time as she has to hunt vigorously to feed the growing kits. With Weasels, timing is less certain, but on average early summer is the best time.

Stoat

Basic facts

Description: The Stoat has a long sinuous body, chestnut fur with cream underparts and a bushy tail with a black tip. There is a straight edge between pale and dark fur. In northern parts of the UK, Stoats may turn white in winter, with the tail tip remaining black. The head and body length is 29 cm for males, and 26 cm for females, on average. The tail length is 10 cm for males, and 8.5 cm for females, with black taking up almost half of its length.

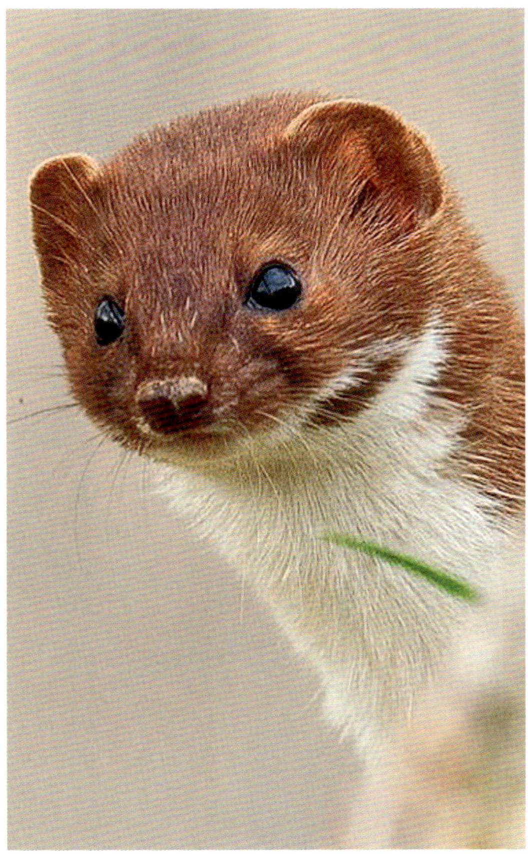

A Weasel returns your gaze

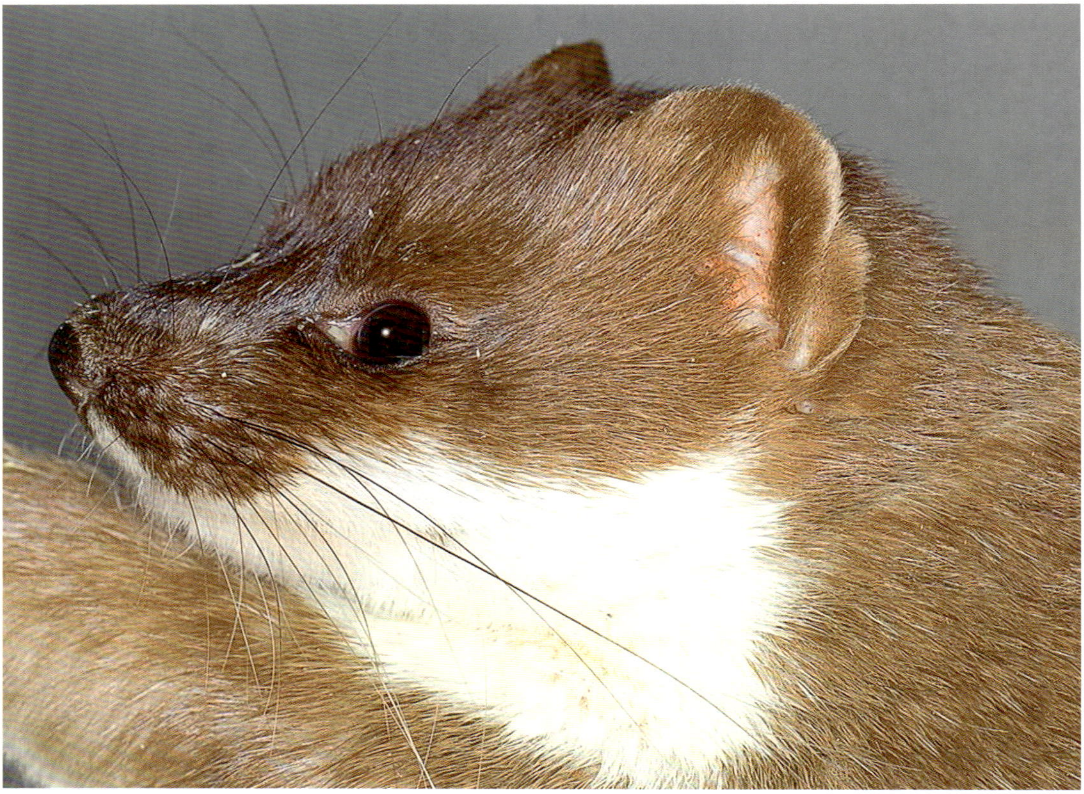

Stoat showing no brown fur under the chin

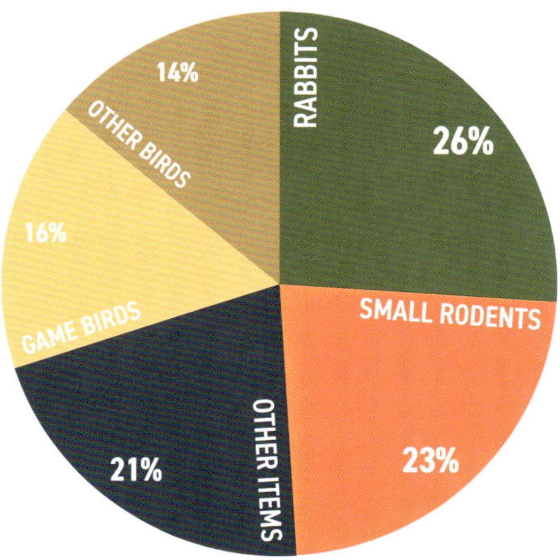

Stoat diet

Weight: The average weight is 365 g for males and 240 g for females.

Feeding: Small rodents, rabbits and birds.

Breeding: Stoats mate in early summer, but delay implantation of the embryo for nine months so that young (six to nine in the litter) are all born in April. As a result, they only have one litter a year.

Habitat: Any environment with sufficient prey and cover. Stoats like areas with hedges, stone walls and ditches, as these offer good hiding places. They are more likely to be found where rabbits and small mammals are plentiful, for example in rough grassland at woodland edges or near piles of logs or brush.

Distribution: Throughout the UK.

Population: Estimated at roughly 440,000 in the UK.

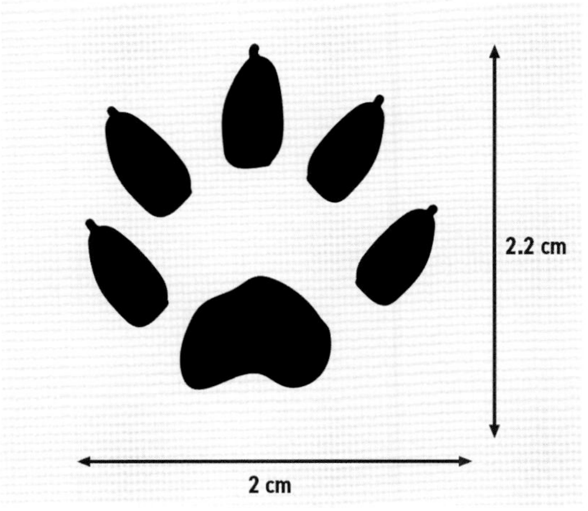

Stoat front track

Tracks and signs

Tracks are most likely found along the line of hedges or dry-stone walls. Those of the front foot are 2.2 cm long and 2 cm wide. Hind tracks are wider.

Droppings are long and thin, being 60 mm or more in length, but only a few millimetres in width. They are likely to be found in the same place as tracks.

Habits

Stoats are mainly nocturnal in winter, but hunt during the day in summer. They are extremely active and move at great speed, especially across open ground. Their dens tend to be the usurped homes of their prey, such as rabbit tunnels which they line with the fur of their victims. Litters of six to nine are produced in April, although the majority do not survive more than a year. Despite the population figures, these animals are rarely seen and have been the subject of few studies, mainly because of the difficulty in finding them.

In the field

Stoats leave very few signs, as their tracks are very small and their droppings, or scats, small and thin. Stoats have dens, usually the former nests of prey such as rabbit, but these are difficult to find. A careful study of hedge lines and the bottom of dry-stone walls may show some indication of Stoats, provided they are in areas where rabbits and small mammals are to be found. Finding Stoats is largely a matter of luck and the trail camera is probably the best method for detecting their presence. When they do venture into the open, they tend to run very quickly to the next piece of cover, so ensure you have a trail camera with a fast response time.

Weasels

Basic facts

Weasels are delightful animals, provided you are not their prey, despite the bad press given by books such as *Wind in the Willows* – not to mention the common perception of Weasels as being sneaky and sly. Knowing some of the relevant facts can help in locating them, but the odds of finding Weasels are small, despite the fact that they are very common.

Description: Weasels have a long, sinuous body, chestnut fur with cream underparts and a short tail. There is an uneven edge between pale and dark fur, and brown spots under the chin. Head and body length is 22 cm for males, and 18 cm for females. Tail length is 5 cm for males, and 4 cm for females, with no black tip.

Weight: Average weight is 125 g for males and 70 g for females.

Feeding: Small rodents, rabbits and birds.

Breeding: Weasels usually mate in February and give birth in March/April, with a litter size of around five. They can have a second litter, if there is sufficient prey, as they do not have delayed implantation like Stoats.

Habitat: Any environment with sufficient prey and cover. Weasels like areas featuring hedges and stone walls, as these give cover, and they are rarely seen in the open. They can be found in urban areas, for example parks with woodland and rough grassland.

Distribution: Throughout the UK.

Population: Roughly estimated at 450,000 in the UK.

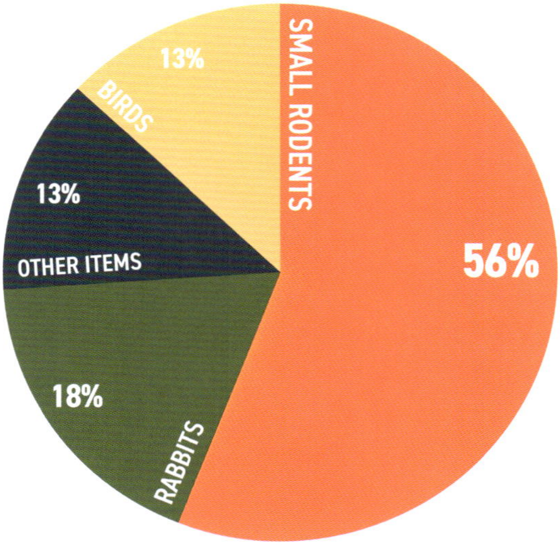

Weasel diet

Tracks and signs

Tracks may be seen in soft mud or snow. They are similar to those of the Stoat, showing five toes, but are smaller at about 1.5 cm long and 1.3 cm wide. The most likely place to find them is along the line of hedges or dry-stone walls, as with Stoats.

Droppings are long and thin, being 45 mm or more in length, but only a few millimetres wide. They are likely to be found in the same places as tracks.

Habits

Weasels hunt during the day, but since much of this time is spent down vole tunnels or in crevices or holes in deep cover, they are rarely seen. Like Stoats, they are extremely active and move at great speed. Litters of about five are produced from April to August, and the young are mature when four months old. They are predated on by Foxes and birds of prey, hence their tendency to hunt only under cover.

In the field

Weasels leave even fewer signs of their presence than Stoats, and they move between various dens, often previously occupied by their prey. Once again the trail camera is probably the best method for detecting them. Weasels are most likely to be seen when the young have first ventured out of the den and play outside it.

Photography of these two species can be summed up in one word: difficult. It is no coincidence that there are few photographs of them around. They are present in almost all parts of the UK where voles and rabbits are found, but are rarely seen and almost impossible to find from tracks and signs. You may see them while you are sitting in a hide waiting for something else, but probably the best approach is to leave out food on a regular basis.

Take account of the fact that Stoats and Weasels like cover, by putting together a few logs near to a hedge or dry-stone wall in an area where there are rabbits and voles. Place the food between the logs in such a way that the Weasel or Stoat will feel relatively safe from predators, but you will still be able to see them arriving. Alternatively, put food under a bush. This technique worked well for me by accident when there was a dead rabbit under a bush in my garden. I saw a Stoat gnawing on the rabbit while I was looking out of the window. A dead mouse from a pet shop will be suitable as bait (they are sold as reptile food), or another option is a (dead) day-old chick. These are used widely

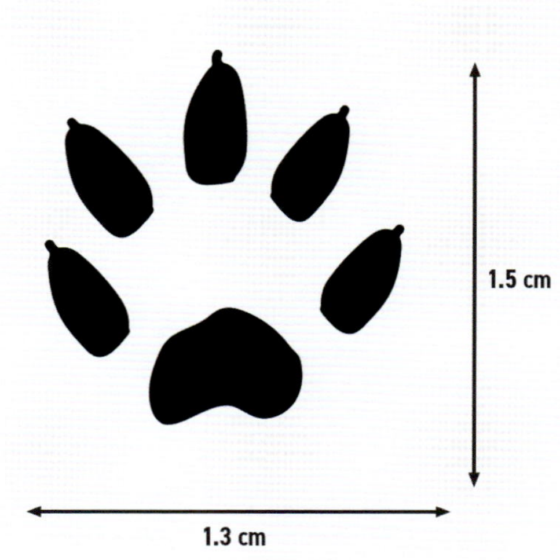

Weasel track

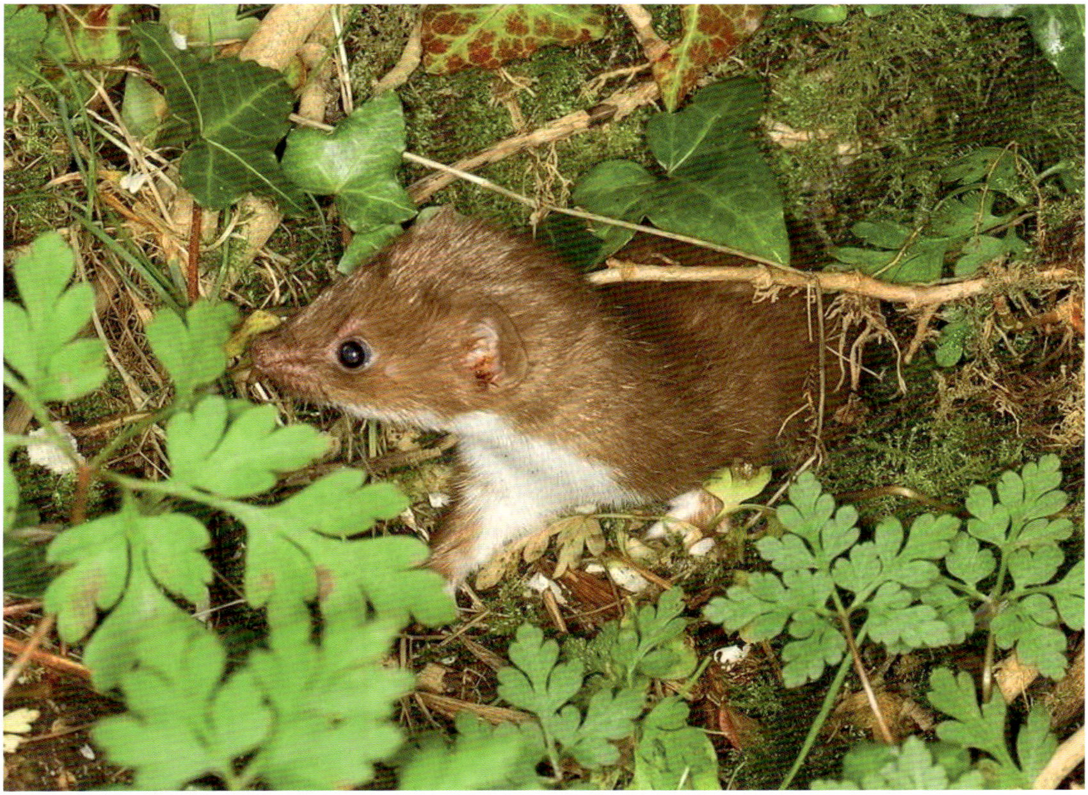

Young Weasel emerging from a vegetation-clad stone wall

as a food source by wildlife centres and zoos, and can be bought frozen in bags of 50 (my advice is to assume this is going to be a long haul). Obviously they should be thawed first. Chopped rabbit is another option if you can find a butcher that sells it.

Set up a trail camera and check it daily. Assuming that Weasels and/or Stoats are in your area, they will get used to food being put out and may start to come more regularly. Once that happens, you can put up a hide near the site, remembering that it will take a few days for them to get used to its presence. When the trail camera shows regular visits, you can sit and wait. Position the hide as far away as you can while still getting a clear image with your longest lens, set up your tripod, settle into a comfortable seat and be patient. I have seen Weasels near bird feeders, but whether they were after the food from the feeder or the birds themselves was uncertain.

As both Stoats and Weasels hunt during the day in summer, the best time for attempting photography is early summer when the young are venturing outside to play. Another method is to walk regularly along tracks or rural lanes, close to hedges or walls in rough grassland near woodland. These animals are very quick, so as fast a shutter speed as possible is advised. Weasels and Stoats are absolutely charming animals and well worth the trouble.

One way to become well known as a photographer (or naturalist) is to specialise in difficult-to-find species. Stoats and Weasels would be an excellent choice, especially as they are abundant.

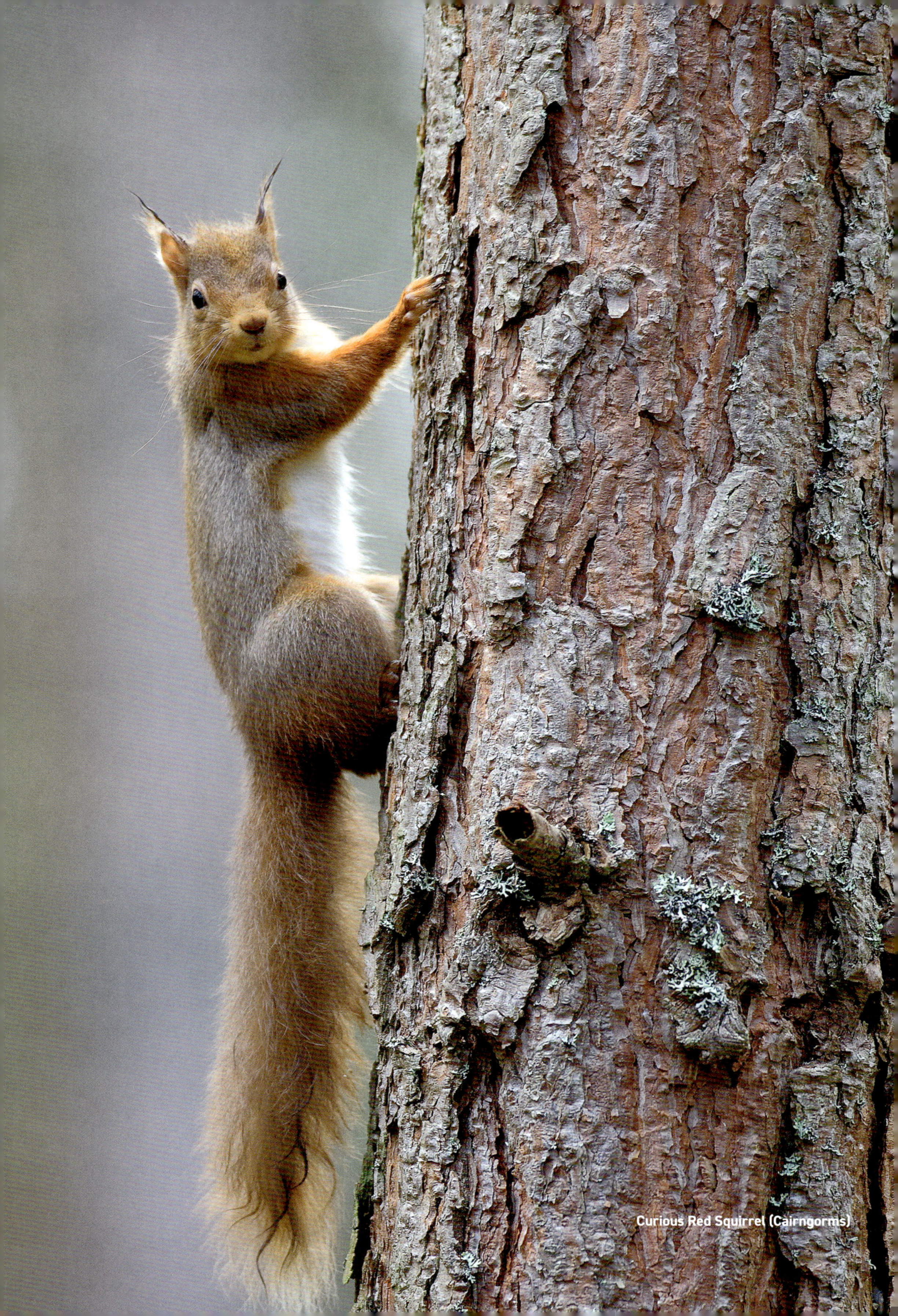

Curious Red Squirrel (Cairngorms)

Red Squirrels

Red Squirrel numbers have declined dramatically in the UK, first because humankind cut down the conifer trees on which the Red Squirrel fed, and then due to the introduction of the Grey Squirrel, which outcompeted the Red for food in broad-leaved woodland. The Grey Squirrel is also resistant to squirrel pox, which is fatal to their red cousins.

Basic facts

Description: Red Squirrels vary in colour from bright chestnut to dark reddish-brown, although they can appear greyish-brown in winter. Conspicuous ear tufts are displayed in winter, but these thin in summer. The head and body length is about 18 to 24 cm. The tail length is almost the same as the body length: about 18 cm long.

Weight: Both male and female Red Squirrels weigh between 250 and 350 g.

Feeding: The Red Squirrel eats nuts and tree seeds including conifer cones, as well as fungi. Only ripe nuts can be digested.

Breeding: There are two peaks of births: spring and summer. Litter size is an average of three.

Habitat: Forests of Scots Pine, Norway Spruce, broad-leaved woodland.

Distribution: There are a few pockets in the Lake District, Dumfries and Galloway, Anglesey, Brownsea Island and the Isle of Wight, but most Red Squirrels are found in Scotland, in areas such as the Cairngorms, where their favoured conifers still grow. More than 75% of the Red Squirrel population lives in Scotland.

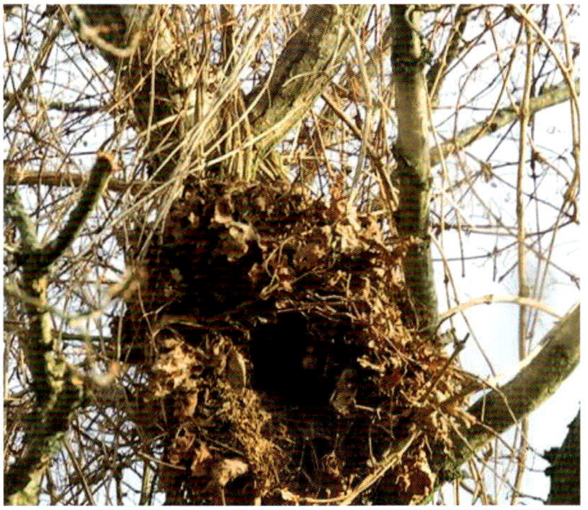

Grey squirrel drey

Population: 287,000 (PTES) and declining rapidly, although there are attempts to stabilise the population with reintroductions.

Tracks and signs

The easiest way to identify the presence of squirrels is by their drey, which is a sphere about 30 cm in diameter built close to the trunk of a tree. Spruce trees are favoured rather than pines, as they are denser. Local knowledge will be required in order to be sure it is a Red Squirrel drey and not that of a Grey Squirrel, although the two are not often in the same locality.

Questions

How sharp are squirrel senses? Squirrels have a very acute sense of smell and good eyesight, although research suggests that they are colourblind. The most successful Red Squirrel photography occurs within hides, and as squirrels have excellent hearing and vision, it is essential to keep very quiet and make limited movements.

Habits

Red Squirrels are shy and reclusive and are very different from Grey Squirrels– although they forage during the day, which makes sighting easier than for some mammals. They are unable to digest unripe nuts, unlike the Grey, and this is put forward as one reason for their decline. The Grey Squirrel also carries squirrel pox, which is fatal to Red Squirrels. Another more recent threat is the adenovirus. It is predicted that Red Squirrels will only survive long-term in conifer patches in Scotland, as that is the only area blessed with their favoured habitat. They may also thrive in other areas if Greys are eradicated.

In the field

It is necessary to travel to Red Squirrel hotspots to see this species in the wild. Most Red Squirrel photography in the wild takes place at feeding stations, where hazelnuts or similar are placed near a hide. Even in a hide it is necessary to wait for some hours, keeping very still and quiet, in order to photograph the squirrels. You may be lucky and see Red Squirrels in other areas, but realistically it would be best to look where there is a hide and feeding station and take a long lens, a beanbag and plenty of patience. If you live near the hotspot islands, such as the Isle of Wight, you may have them visit your garden, but most of us are not so lucky.

Some reserves, such as Brownsea Island, have Red Squirrel walks in October, although you are unlikely to get good clear images with a group of people around. If you return on your own and sit quietly with camouflage cloth over you and your tripod, you may be lucky. The advantage of a place such as Brownsea is that there are a lot of visitors, and as even Red Squirrels do become more tolerant of people with time, this may make them a little bolder than in the large forests in Scotland.

Glenmore Forest Visitor Centre near Aviemore has Red Squirrel feeders in its grounds, around which great views of these animals can be gained. The squirrels are wild, so by sitting quietly in the grounds it is possible to get good photographs.

Autumn is certainly the best time to see them, as they will be busy collecting food for winter, and also there are fewer leaves on the trees, which makes seeing and photographing them less of a challenge. They are captivating subjects and certainly worth spending some time on.

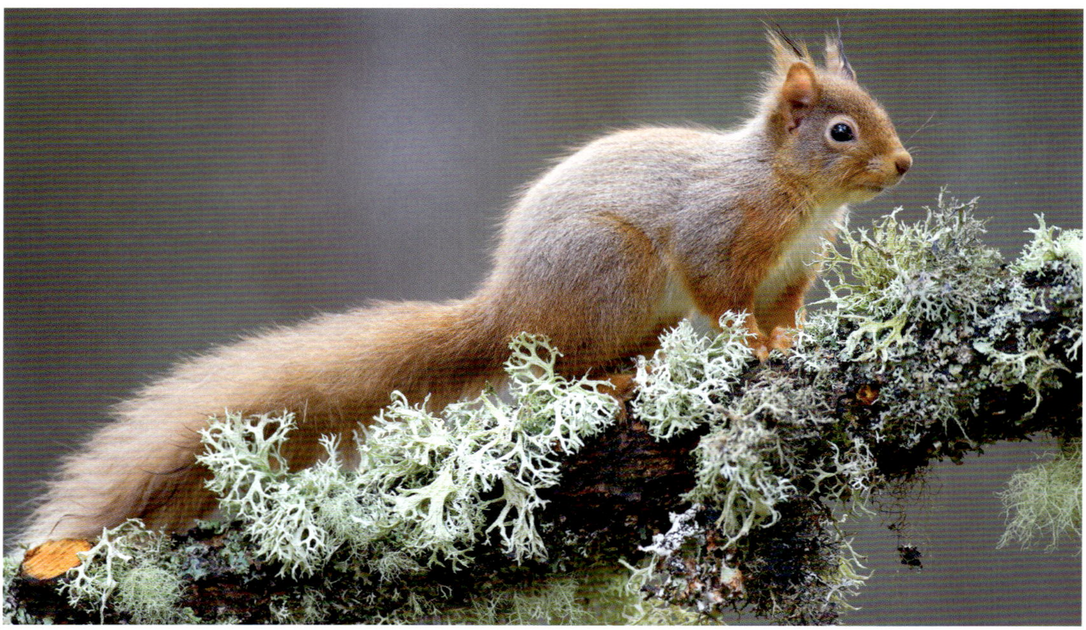

Red Squirrel on a branch, photographed from a hide in a Cairngorms forest

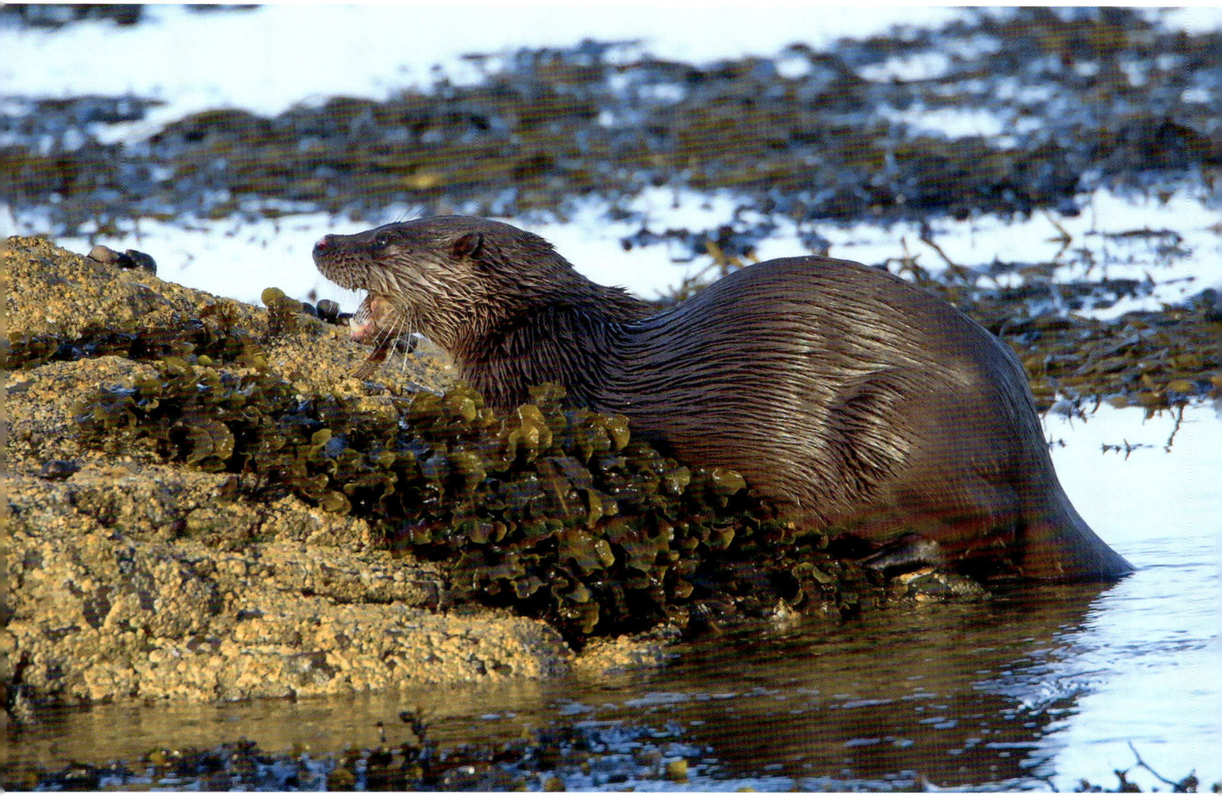

Otter on the Isle of Mull

Otters

Otters are among the most charismatic and elusive mammals. They are a protected species and it is an offence to disturb them in their holts (dens) or resting places.

Basic facts

Description: The fur is a dark reddish-brown with a paler chest. Otters have long sinuous bodies, short legs and a long tail. Take care not to confuse Otters with the smaller, darker Mink, which has a shorter, fluffy tail. The head and body length is about 70 cm, with the female shorter at 65 cm. The tail length is about 40 cm for the male and 38 cm for the female.

Weight: The average weight is 10 kg for the male and 7 kg for the female.

Feeding: Mainly fish.

Breeding: Litters of two or three can be born at any time, although smaller litters are born in northern Scotland and Shetland, where cubs may be born in summer.

Habitat: There are two main habitats: lakes, rivers and streams with fresh water, and coastal areas where fresh water is available to wash salt out from the fur.

Distribution: Scotland and its islands, especially Shetland, Wales, south-west England, and increasing in other areas.

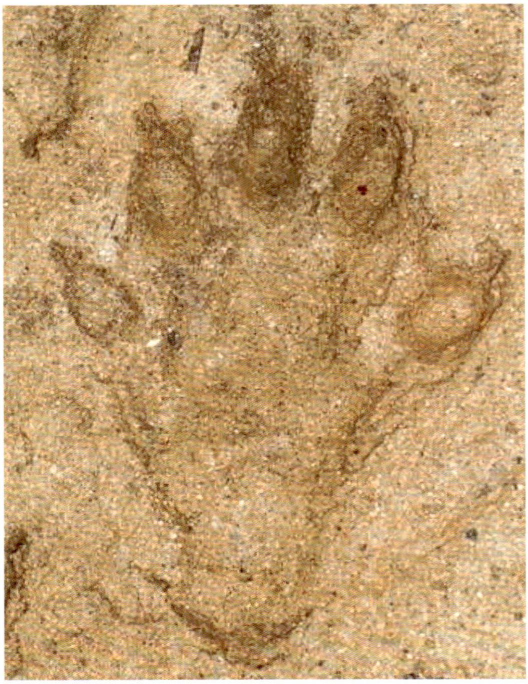

Otter hind track

Population: Believed to be over 10,300 with the majority in Scotland (PTES).

Tracks and signs

Tracks

Otter footprints are very distinctive, being large and deep. The hind foot is about 9 cm long and 6 cm wide. These can be seen very easily in mud or sand on riverbanks, especially if the river is tidal and the ground is kept wet.

If found on riverbanks, they may indicate a good position for a trail camera. If the Otter appears on the camera, then it may be worthwhile setting up a hide. Either stay overnight or arrive very early in spring, and you might be lucky.

Droppings

Otter droppings, or spraints, can be any shade between black and white, depending on what has been eaten. Coastal spraints will be greyish if fish bones and scales are present. They do not have an unpleasant smell, and are often placed in an obvious position on rocks. A fresh spraint is a good indication of recent presence. Older spraints are dry and crumbly.

Holts

Otter dens, or holts, vary depending on location and are often made in natural cavities, such as under trees on riverbanks. In some terrains, such as in Shetland, peat banks come down to the edge of the sea. These are particularly suitable for holts, as soft material is easily dug out and Otters may form tunnels and chambers within.

Habits

Otters have been persecuted by man and his dog for centuries, and are extremely sensitive to the presence of humankind. As they frequent rivers, they can be found in urban areas if the water is clean enough for fish. They have an acute sense of smell and good hearing, although their eyesight is weaker. In fresh water they are mainly nocturnal, and most likely to be seen at dawn or dusk. In coastal areas, feeding is determined by the tides. Some Otters fish on the rising tide, others on the falling tide, and as a result they can be seen during the day. They are superb swimmers, depending on their skills underwater to catch fish, especially in coastal areas, where they prefer sheltered bays and calm water.

In the field

Otters are very charming creatures, and a very popular subject with the wildlife photographer, despite, or perhaps because of, the difficulty in photographing them in the wild. This is mainly due to their shy nature, their acute sense of smell and their extreme sensitivity to the presence of humans. This wariness is not surprising, as they have been persecuted for a large part of their history. They are also nocturnal in inland areas, and even if seen at dusk or dawn, it may be too dark to photograph them successfully – although of course you can be lucky.

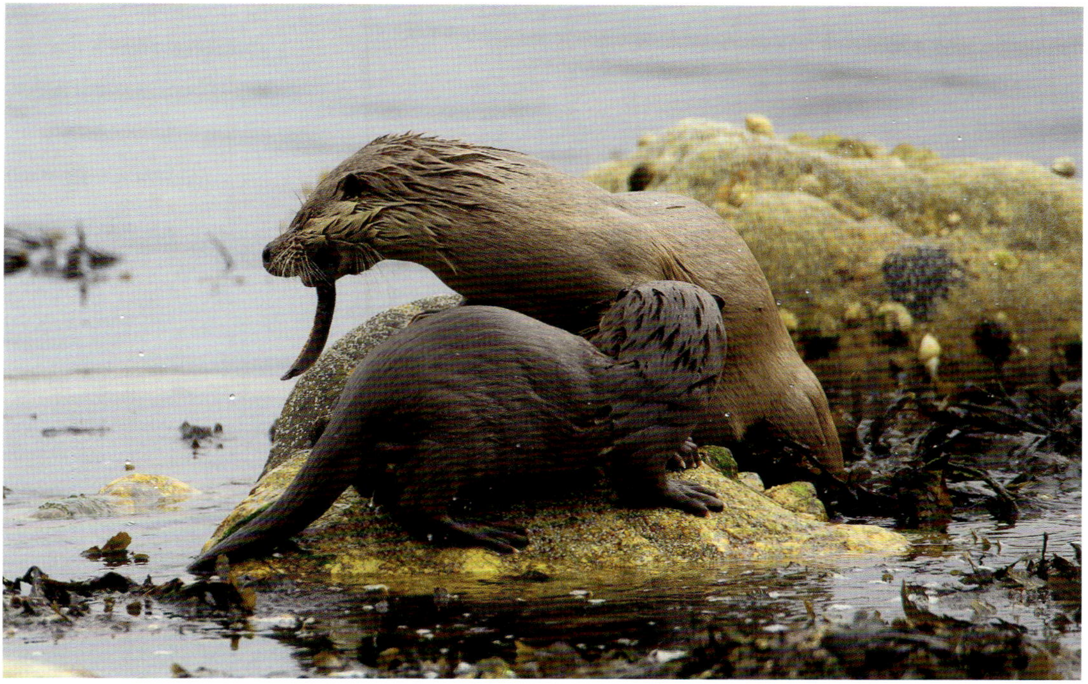

Otter chews on a fish as cub watches

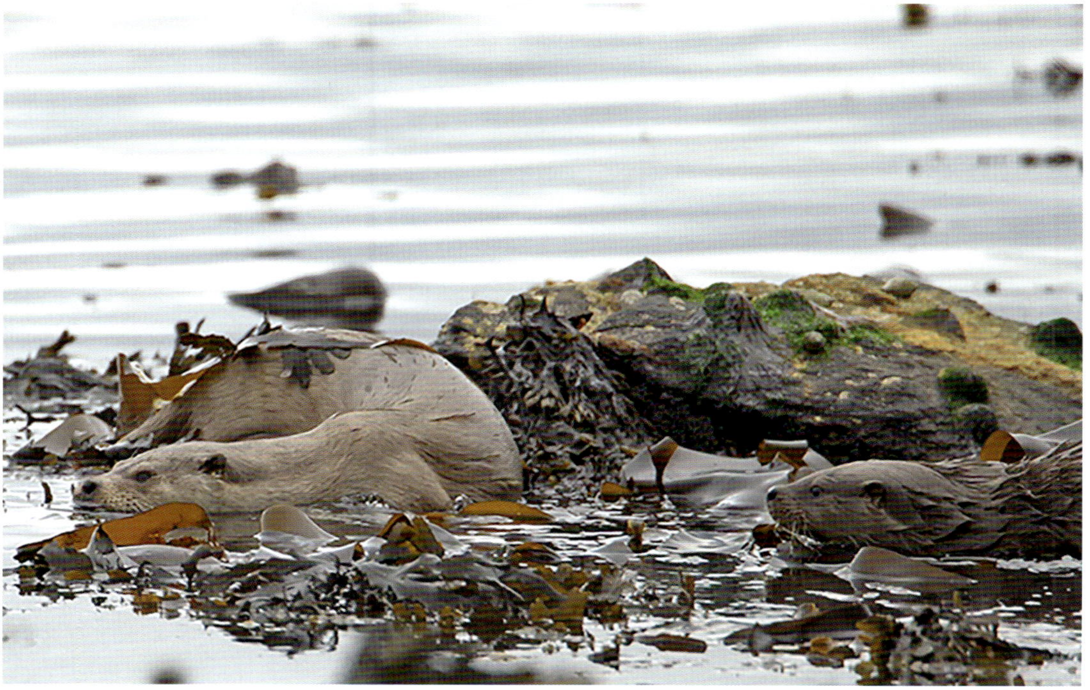

Otter anc cub, Shetland

To photograph Otters inland, first research possible locations. Nature reserves will often state whether Otters are present and are a good place to start. The Wildlife Trusts website has details of where Otters can be seen in their section on 'Where to see wildlife'. Local knowledge is also very useful, as is Internet research on sightings. Pay particular attention to the locations where Otters are most likely to be seen, as shown in the 'Distribution' facts above. Once you have narrowed down the area, and approached the river or lake where they have been spotted, you will need to look carefully for Otter signs. If signs are found, and if they look reasonably fresh, set up a trail camera, as that will confirm if the Otter is still in the area, and will tell you when it moves about.

The next step is to sit and wait at dawn for several weeks, hoping you have the right spot. If possible, set up a portable hide. If you see Otters in poor light, you might be able to use flash, but that is likely to drive them off, and they may not return for some days. My most recent sighting of an inland Otter came about after selecting a suitable spot liberally covered with Otter tracks, and arriving at dawn. I had set up my camera on a tripod next to that area, and almost immediately an Otter appeared on the opposite bank and slid into the water. However, a dark Otter on a shady bank at dawn is almost impossible to focus on, so there was no chance to take a clear picture. Success is possible, but unless you are very lucky, it will take many weeks of keeping unsocial hours. You also have to bear in mind that because of their acute sense of smell, they are likely to avoid areas a human has visited recently – so even setting up a hide in a hotspot may not be successful initially, until they are used to it.

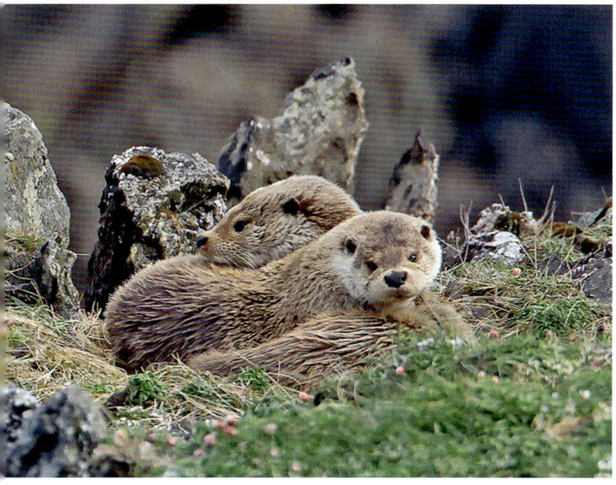

Two Otter cubs on Shetland

But do not despair. There are places where Otters are rumoured to be habituated to humans, such as the Devon Wildlife Trust Cricklepit Mill in Exeter and Bosherston Lakes in Wales. Sightings, however, may be an occasional lucky break, rather than a regular occurrence. Otters can be found in wildlife centres, of course (although they may not be species found in the UK), but wild Otters are easier, or should I say less difficult, to see in coastal districts – however, you may still need a guide to find them. Even some of the best-known wildlife photographers admit defeat when it comes to Otters and take this route, simply because of the time involved in becoming familiar with an area. In coastal areas, Otters fish in the sea, especially in inlets and sheltered bays. They are ruled by the tides and so will come out to hunt and feed during the day, generally at low tide. The Scottish islands, such as Mull and Shetland, are known to be hotspots for Otters, but there are thousands of miles of coast, and putting luck aside, a great deal of dedication plus local knowledge is required for success. A strong belief in ethical photography is important, so that the Otters are unaware of your presence. Life in coastal districts is hard, and hunger in winter a real hazard; if they are disturbed in their favoured fishing locations, they may move to a less suitable position, which could tip the balance between survival and starvation in winter.

The images shown here were taken in Shetland, where there are several guides available, the best being those born and brought up on the islands. Fieldcraft depends on first knowing which of the many bays and inlets to look in, and then choosing a time when the wind is blowing from the sea towards you. The slightest whiff of human and

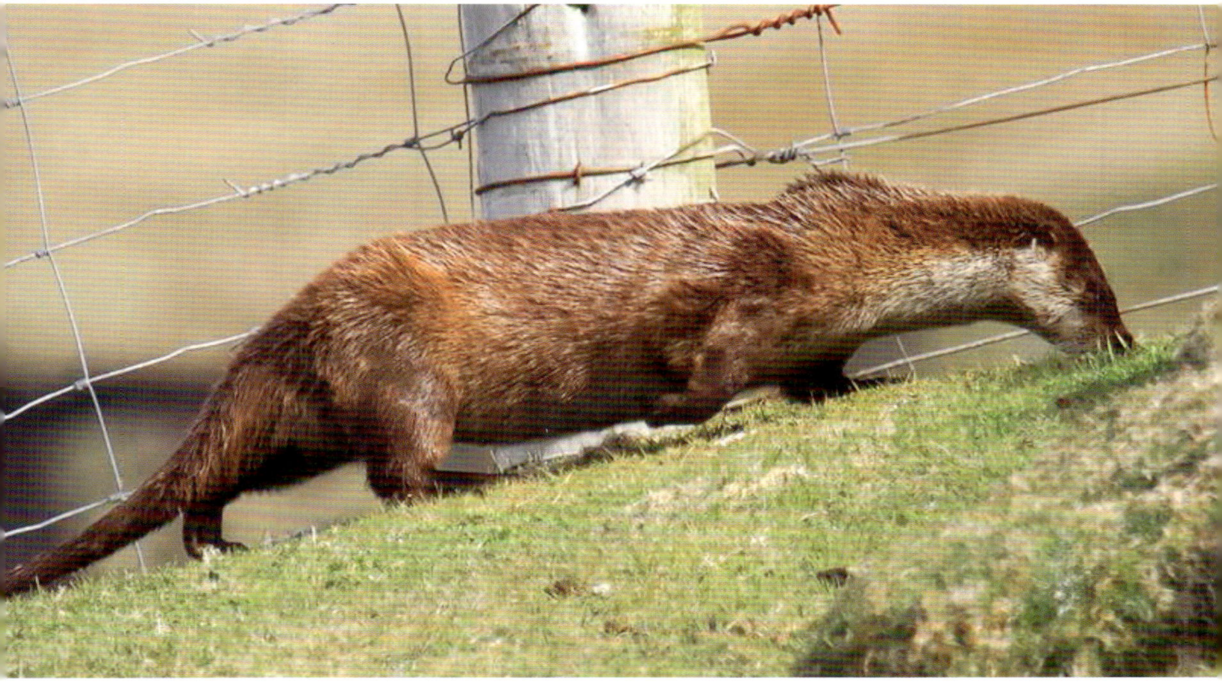

Otter sniffs out its path

the Otters will go elsewhere, and then you would also be guilty of disturbing them. It is necessary to scan both shore and the sea surface continually with binoculars, looking for a tell-tale Otter head (difficult to spot for the inexperienced). Otters will generally come to shore after a spell fishing, or when they have caught a large fish. They also come ashore at regular intervals to bathe in fresh water and wash salt from their fur. At the first signs of an Otter coming ashore, you must move quickly to a suitable spot, hidden from view, and if lucky you may get some photographs. No matter what, it will take time. Most guides reckon on six to eight hours of searching before discovering Otters.

Otters sniff out their route continually along paths, as their eyesight is poor. Not many realise that Otters come from the same family as Stoats, Weasels and Badgers (*Mustelidae*); this photograph highlights the long body and short legs in common with these relatives.

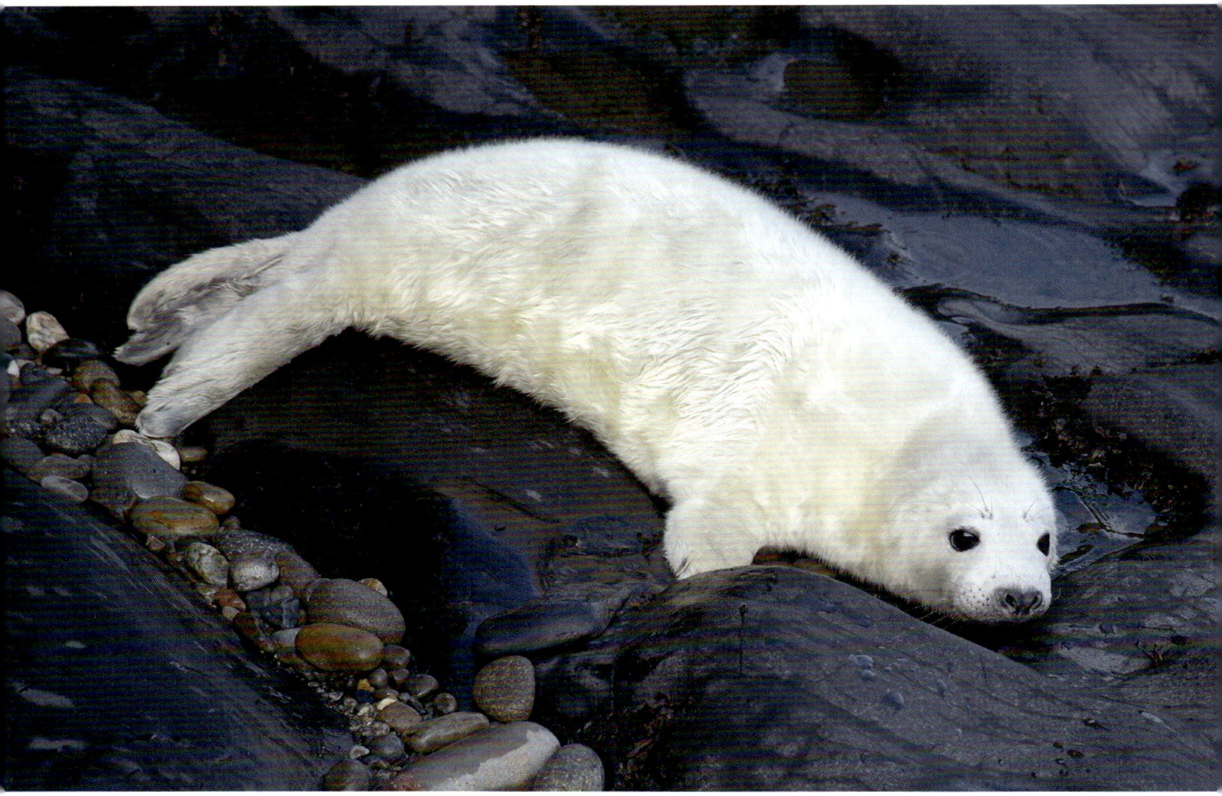

One-week-old Grey Seal pup

Seals

There are two types of seals found in the UK: the Common (or Harbour) Seal and the Grey Seal. Despite the name, Common Seals are much less prevalent than Grey Seals, and tend to be found mainly in the Scottish Hebrides, Orkney and Shetland. I have concentrated on Grey Seals here, as you are much more likely to see them.

Grey Seal

Basic facts

Description: Grey Seals have greyish-brown fur, often coloured in patches, small ears and long noses. Females are about 180 cm long, and males larger at around 200 cm long.

Weight: Females weigh around 150 kg, males 230 kg.

Feeding: Mainly fish.

Breeding: Breeding takes place in autumn, soon after the females have given birth.

Habitat: Rocky beaches and sandy bays.

Distribution: Around rocky coasts of the UK, with the greatest numbers in the west.

Population: Around 110,000.

Habits

Seals spend much of their time at sea, but are frequently seen sprawled out on rocks along the coast. They are easiest to see when pups are born, as the females come to shore to give birth, the pups lie on banks feeding until they can take to the sea, and the males hang around hoping to mate with the females.

In the field

Adult seals are not the most attractive photographic subjects when on land, and most photographers instead want to focus on the newborn pups. Unfortunately not all do this in an ethical manner, and pups and adults can be left distressed. It is important to keep your distance.

Well-known beaches where seal pups can be seen include Donna Nook in Lincolnshire, Blakeney Point in Norfolk and western coastal areas. The popular places are busy and it is difficult to get close without disturbing the seals. The best position to view without interference is from a clifftop overlooking a favoured seal beach, such as those found on the coasts of Cornwall, and Skomer or Ramsey islands off the west coast of Wales.

My photographs were taken on Ramsey Island off the Pembrokeshire coast. Boats frequently visit the island, and many of the seals are used to seeing them and do not seem perturbed. This site also offers the advantage of a raised walkway which goes over one of the pupping beaches. The photographer can thus photograph the seal pups from above without causing distress. As seals are large mammals, a shorter focal length is sufficient.

The pups grow very quickly and can take to the sea at three weeks old. The one-week-old pups are the most photogenic, with fluffy white fur and large dark eyes. At around three weeks they start shedding their baby fur and develop a more waterproof coat. Many of the amusing pictures of seal pups waving or striking anthromorphic poses are due to the fact that their skin is itchy during the fur-shedding process. On Ramsey Island, I saw a mother scratching her pup in a difficult-to-reach spot.

Once the pups are able to take to water the bull seals mate with the females, and they can be seen hanging around just offshore, waiting for the moment to arrive. Not all attempts are welcomed by the females.

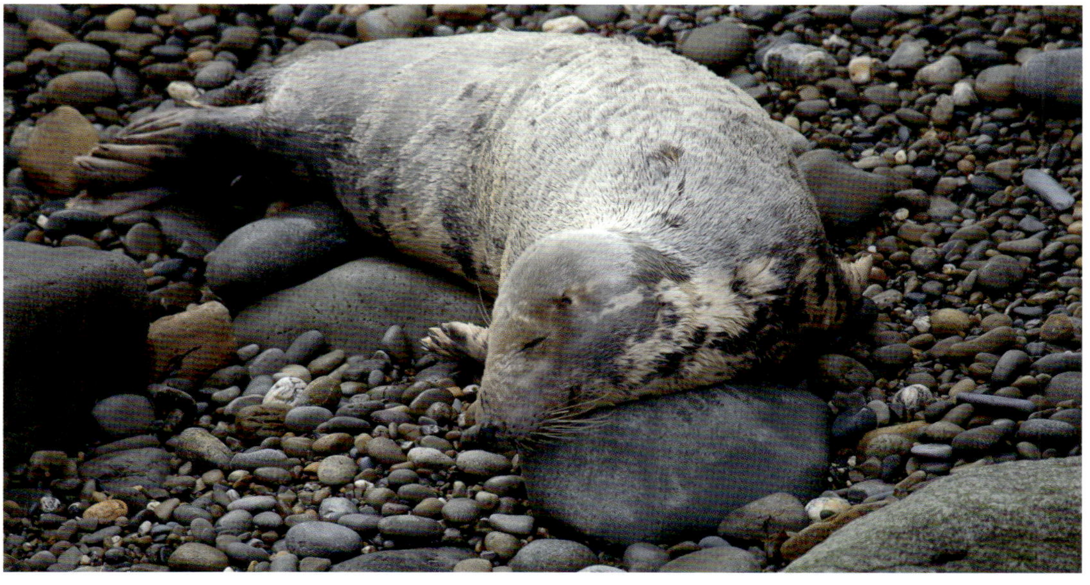

Sleeping female Grey Seal

Shortcuts to finding mammals to photograph

Be aware that a 1 in 5 success rate is about average for locating elusive wildlife – which means for every good day, there will be at least four without any photographs worth keeping. If you are not prepared for a challenge, perhaps these easier forms of encountering wildlife might suit you better. In any case, all of us like an easy day sometimes!

1. Visit a wildlife centre

There are several centres now which feature UK wildlife, rather than non-native species. The British Wildlife Centre, and the Westcountry Wildlife Photography Centre in Devon, specialise in facilities for photography. Although they are basically zoos, wildlife centres have become more aware in recent years of the needs of photographers. Some have special photography days and allow access into some enclosures for natural shots without wire mesh in the way. Such visits can be expensive, but are usually well worth it, if you want a welcome rest from searching for animals in the wild. Such visits may inspire you to persevere longer in the field, and are useful for identification. It is a sad reflection on the state of wildlife in the UK that some species are likely to be seen only in such places.

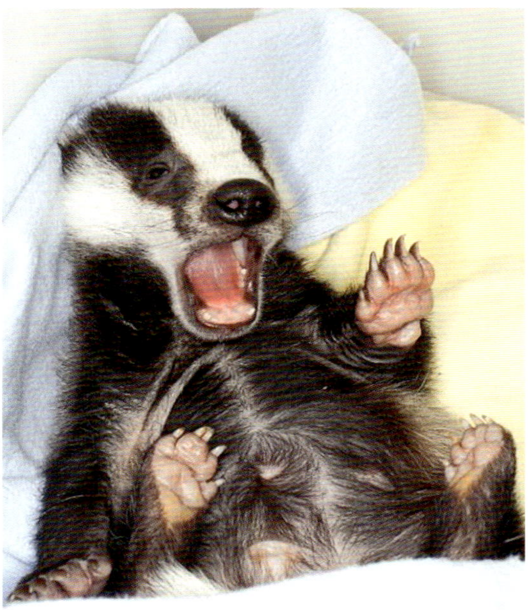

Sleepy Badger cub in a wildlife hospital

2. Create wildlife gardens

If you do not have a garden at all, you will be limited to hanging bird feeders at your window or a window box to attract butterflies, but for those with a garden, it is much easier to attract wildlife. Obviously those with a large garden in a rural area will attract a greater diversity of species than someone with a small urban garden, but even the latter can attract a surprising variety. My own garden is five acres and is surrounded by fields and woods, but wildlife appeared in greater numbers after I had made a conscious effort to plant appropriately. There are several large areas of wildflowers as well as ponds, which attract butterflies, dragonflies, Grass Snakes, Slow Worms, Bank Voles, Wood Mice, Foxes, plus a broad range of bird life. I am lucky enough to have a small wood which is part of a larger forest, and which has Badgers, Roe Deer, Dormice, Stoats and Weasels, and the occasional Hedgehog. Wildflower meadows not only look beautiful, but the dense growth gives excellent cover for young foxes and deer.

The secret is to maintain as many different habitats as possible. Trees, especially oak trees, house very varied insect life, which in turn provide essential sustenance for birds. Conifers, although not as popular with gardeners as they once were, are also valuable as they give cover all year round. Broad-leaved woodland is the best for attracting mammals, but only if there is a good mixture of native species of tree such as oak, ash, holly and hazel, and also a thick layer of ground cover.

3. Get to know a nature reserve well

Even if you live in an urban environment, there will be parks or wild areas where wildlife is present. In fact, there are those who say that urban areas attract

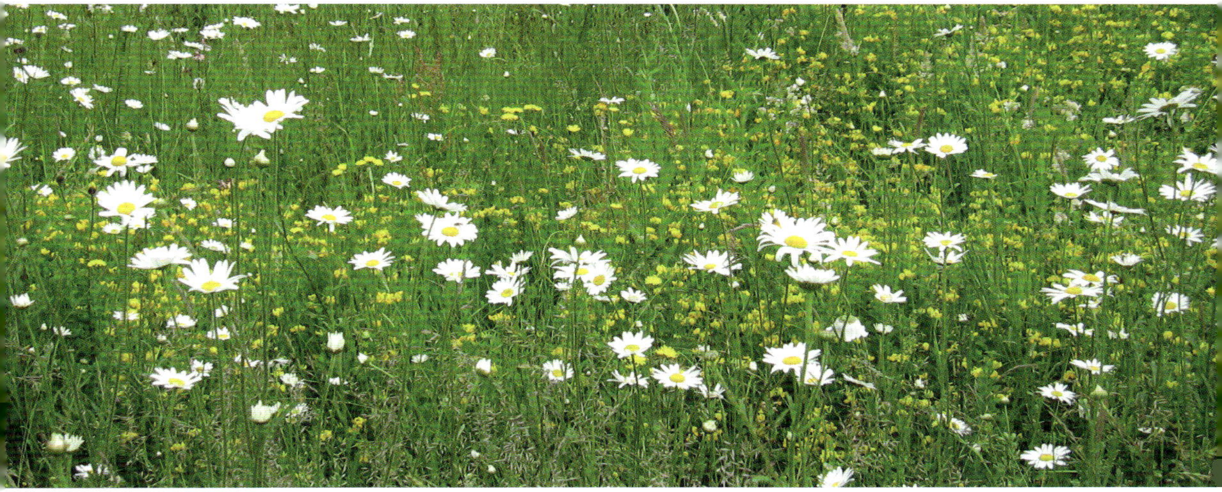

Wildflower meadow in south Devon

more wildlife than monoculture farmland, so do not assume that because you are in a citythere will be no species to see. A trail camera is particularly useful in urban areas, as the wildlife is more likely to be around when people are not. If you can, pay regular visits to a nature reserve, park, green space or even cemetery near you.

Once you get to know a place well, and form good relationships with the reserve rangers, or even the environmental officer on your local council, you will open up great opportunities for wildlife shots. After that it is a matter of persistence, which is easier to maintain if you know the animals are definitely around somewhere. Many nature reserves have volunteer groups which help with maintaining the reserve, and by joining such a group you will make useful contacts with those who know what can be found where. Offering to volunteer with Dormouse box checking or bat surveys also may allow access to protected species.

4. Use a guide for the rarer species

The purpose of this book is to give you the knowledge and confidence to look for wildlife independently – but the rarer species, such as Red Squirrels and Otters, are so difficult for most of us to find that a guide may be required, initially at least. This is not the cheapest method, but can save many days, weeks and months of frustration.

5. Buy a small woodland

This is obviously not a method everyone can afford, at £10,000+ for an acre of mature broad-leaved woodland, but even an acre or two can vastly increase your chances of locating good subjects. The advantage of having your own land is that you can set up hides and cameras where you wish, and can manage the land purely for wildlife. If buying your own land is out of the question, there are wildlife groups which have small parcels of land for the use of their members, so this is worth pursuing.

6. Take wildlife courses

The constant theme of this book is that to be able to photograph UK wildlife successfully, a great deal of knowledge is required. Many universities and colleges offer modular courses which will allow you to gain this expertise and also meet like-minded people. There are courses available by distance learning if you are not near a college. The best value is possibly to be found at field centres, such as the Field Studies Council which gives short courses on specific species

DRAGONFLIES and BUTTERFLIES

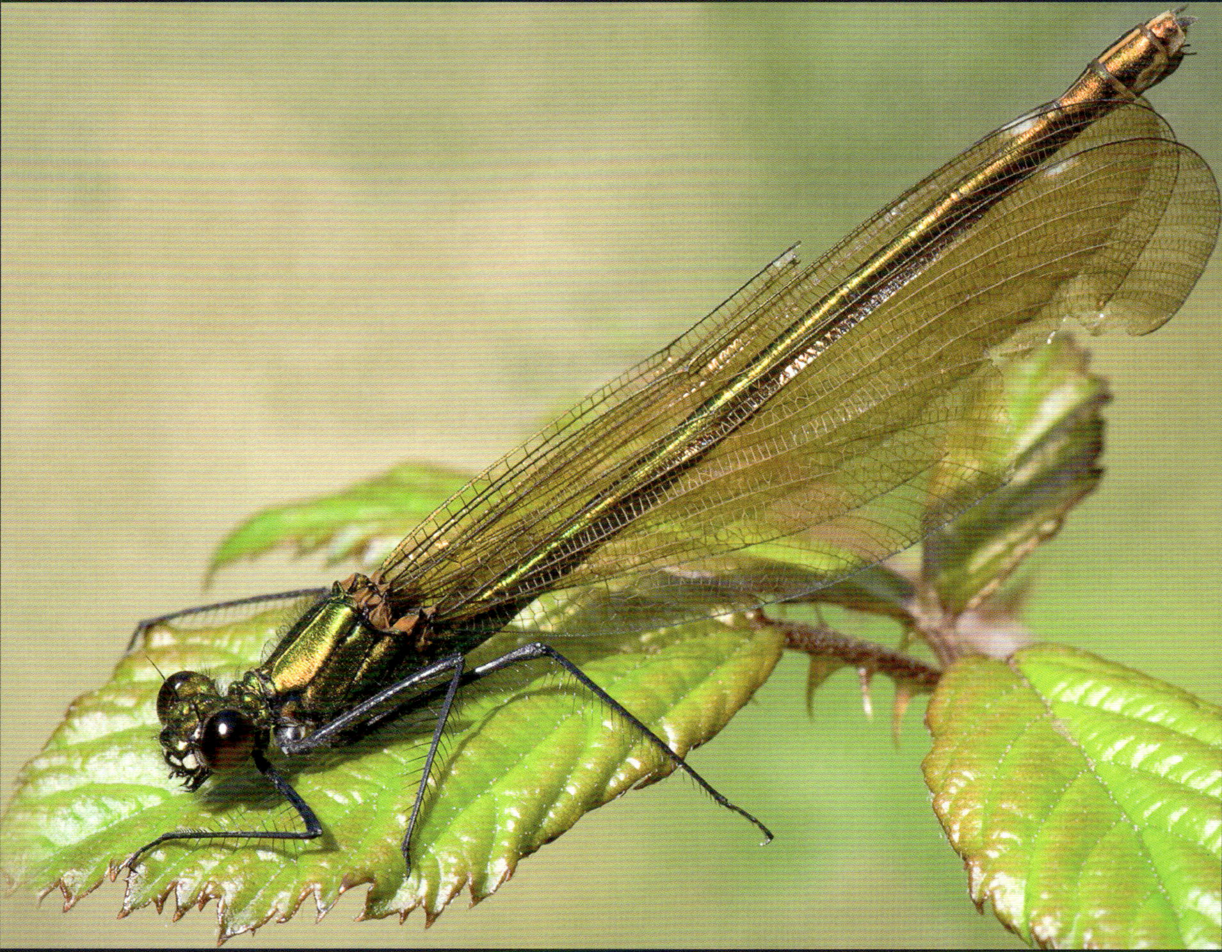

Beautiful Demoiselle female

Here I do not discuss any insects other than dragonflies, damselflies and butterflies, as finding invertebrates can often be a matter of luck, and photographing such creatures requires specialised photographic techniques rather than an emphasis on fieldcraft. Dragonflies and butterflies can be photographed with or without flash, depending on the light levels and the effect you are seeking.

Dragonflies

The broad category of dragonflies also includes the damselflies. Damselflies can often be distinguished by the way they hold their wings when perched: frequently, they are folded along the length of the body, or held at a 45-degree angle in the case of emerald damselflies. Dragonflies, on the other hand, generally hold their wings 'flat', in the same plane as their body. The body of a damselfly is much narrower than that of a dragonfly.

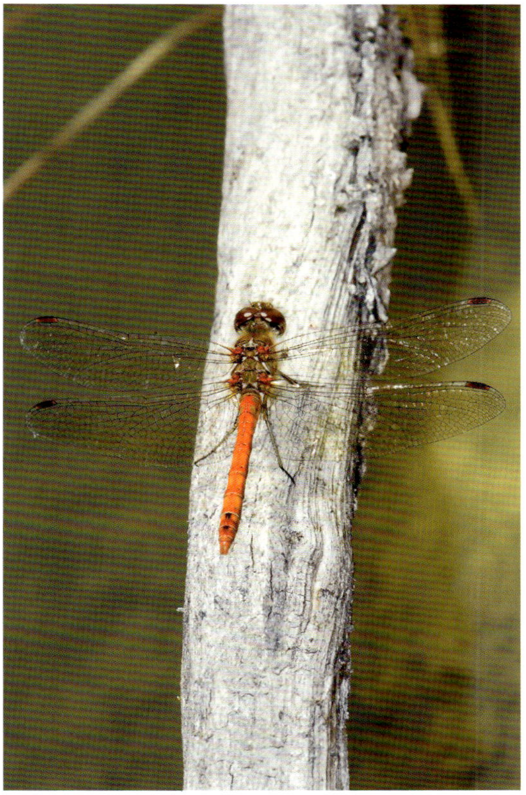

Common Darter

Introduction

There is something compelling about photographing dragonflies. They are dramatic, beautiful, colourful and exciting. And they can move exceedingly fast. Finding them is not too difficult, but photographing them is another matter altogether. You soon discover that they literally have eyes in the back of their head, and these pick up the slightest movement as you approach. Many frustrating hours can be spent getting close, but not quite close enough. These insects always seem suddenly to be on the other side of the pond. However, the challenge can be irresistible, and once bitten (not literally, as dragonflies do not attack humans), you may spend happy hours in the sun stalking these elusive wonders of nature.

Digital photography reveals the complexity of the details of a dragonfly in a way that film never did, and by viewing the images on computer, you can treat yourself to a close-up of the astonishing and intricate detail to be found. Once you have photographed dragonflies, you will wish to spend sunny, summer afternoons happily walking slowly among wildflowers, seeking these royalty of the insect world.

An important factor in dragonfly photography is knowing which species are present at a particular time of year, and how to make use of stalking techniques to photograph them successfully. The structure of this section reflects this.

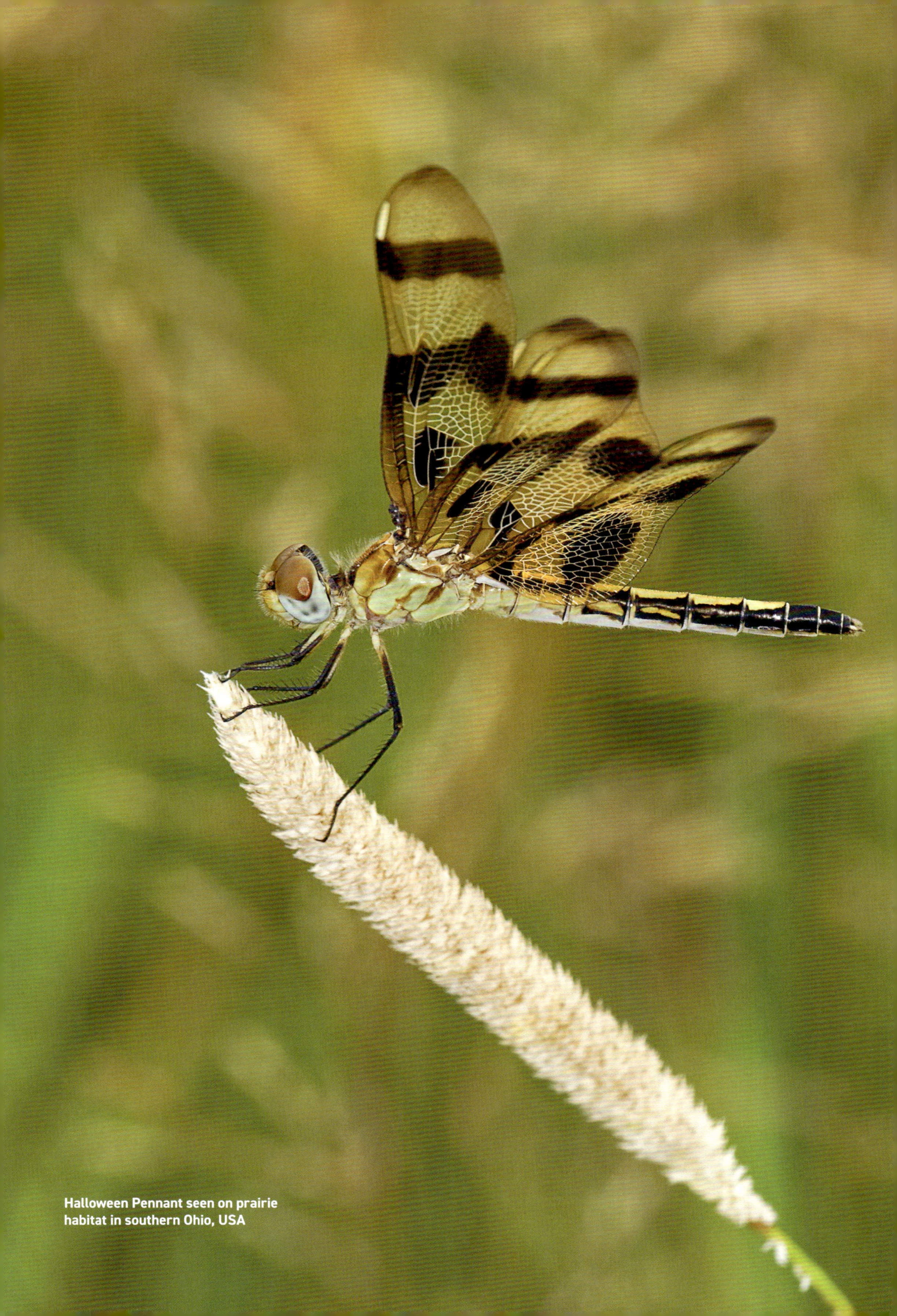

Halloween Pennant seen on prairie habitat in southern Ohio, USA

Habitat

Although most dragonflies are found near water, where they breed, they are also encountered on vegetation where they feed and rest. With the exception of the Golden-ringed Dragonfly and the demoiselles, which prefer running water, most species choose to breed in lakes, ponds, canals, ditches or bogs. Dragonflies prefer a clear path along which to fly, and are less common if there are many trees overhanging the water source.

The greatest number of species is present in the south of England, where the climate is generally warmer, but a number of species are found in Scotland and other areas of the UK as well. A good field guide is essential for determining which dragonflies are likely to be seen in a particular area of the country – a good example is *Britain's Dragonflies* by Dave Smallshire and Andy Swash.

Before you go searching for this one, the Halloween Pennant is a native of America. I have included an image of this species to emphasise that the techniques for photographing dragonflies are much the same the world over.

In the field

Dragonflies spend much of their life as larvae (nymphs) underwater. This period can stretch from several months to as long as five years (as with the Golden-ringed Dragonfly). Their time in the spectacular, colourful adult stage may only be a few weeks, and much of this is spent looking for a mate, mating or egg-laying. Some species, such as the blue damselflies, are gregarious and can be found in large groups, whereas the males of the larger dragonflies are territorial and will lay claim to a specifc area of water, attempting to keep others away.

As a result it will be easy to find, for example, Azure Damselflies to photograph near a stretch of water, but it will be more difficult to locate a male Emperor Dragonfly. Female dragonflies tend to forage in nearby foliage and only venture near water when they are ready to mate or to lay eggs.

Different species behave differently when mating or egg-laying, so knowledge of this can also help the photographer. Many damselflies stay in the mating position for some time, resting on grass, twigs or the ground, which makes them easy to photograph. The male often keeps hold of the female as she lays eggs in plant stems near the water surface, and can often unknowingly strike artistic poses while this process is taking place. The chasers, skimmers and darters mate for a few seconds in mid-air, then the female hovers just above the water, dipping the tip of her abdomen repeatedly as she lays eggs. Males often keep guard during the egg-laying procedure, and sometimes hold onto the female at the same time. As egg-laying may take some time, it can offer good photographic opportunities, albeit with certain technical difficulties as a fast shutter speed (or flash) is required to freeze the rapid motion.

The larger dragonfly females, after their brief mating, employ various egg-laying methods. A female Emperor Dragonfly will spend hours perched on a leaf or branch in water while egg-laying. This

NAME	TIME OF YEAR USUALLY SEEN	COMMENTS
COMMON HAWKER	July–September. Upland areas of the north and west of the UK.	Male is dark with blue and yellow markings. Female is brown with yellow markings. Large. In constant motion, but sometimes hovers at one spot and can then be photographed.
SOUTHERN HAWKER	July–September. Wales and the south of England.	Large hawker. Male is black with blue and green markings. Female is brown with green markings. Rests on foliage at times, but often hovers above the water.
MIGRANT HAWKER	August–October. Southern migrant.	Smaller than other hawkers, but similar in colour to the Common Hawker. Easiest to photograph when mating, as they rest on foliage.

Table 3.1 Common large dragonflies

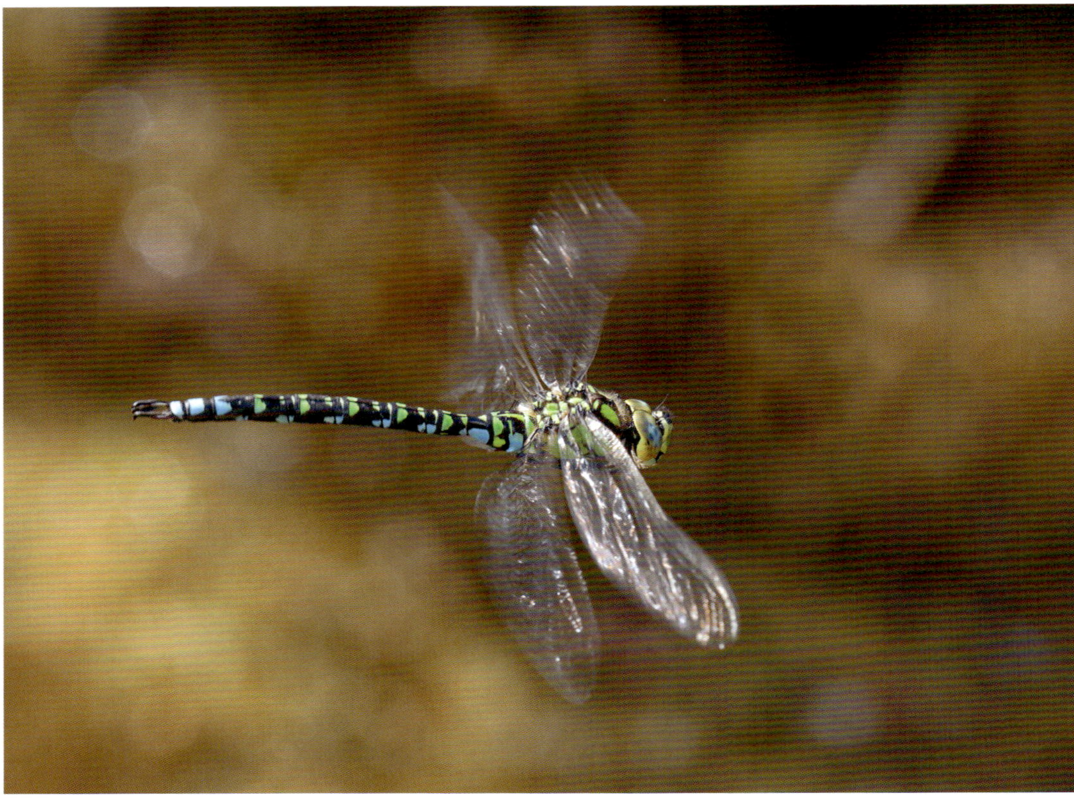

Southern Hawker in flight above a garden pond in Devon

NAME	TIME OF YEAR USUALLY SEEN	COMMENTS
BROAD-BODIED CHASER	May–July. England and Wales.	The male has bright powder blue body and brown head. Very fast moving. The female is yellow and brown and looks like a hornet, but with outstretched wings. Perches often.
FOUR-SPOTTED CHASER	May–August. Most of the UK.	Rather dull brown dragonfly with characteristic dark spots on each wing.
BLACK-TAILED SKIMMER	June–July. England.	The male has a narrow powder blue body with a black tip. The female is yellowish with a dark Adder-like pattern on its body. They perch on bare surfaces, stones or wood.
BLACK DARTER	July–September. Heathland and moorland.	Male is black, female is yellow ochre. Prefers acidic water.
COMMON DARTER	July–October. Found throughout the UK.	The male is bright orange and the female yellower. Easily seen and photographed as it perches often, especially near ponds.

Table 3.2 Common smaller dragonflies

makes an easy photographic target, but for the best pictures you must get down very low to prevent the background from being a distraction, as it is difficult at such close quarters to blur it sufficiently. The female of the Golden-ringed Dragonfly hovers above soft mud, bouncing up and down and laying eggs on each down-strike. This makes it an interesting photographic target.

It is also important to know the time of year at which each species is likely to be seen. Be aware that dragonflies only live a short period in the adult state, and thus the dragonfly you see in May will not be the same one you see in August. Dragonflies can be divided into three groups: large dragonflies, small dragonflies and damselflies. The commoner species are listed below. Other species are rarer or localised.

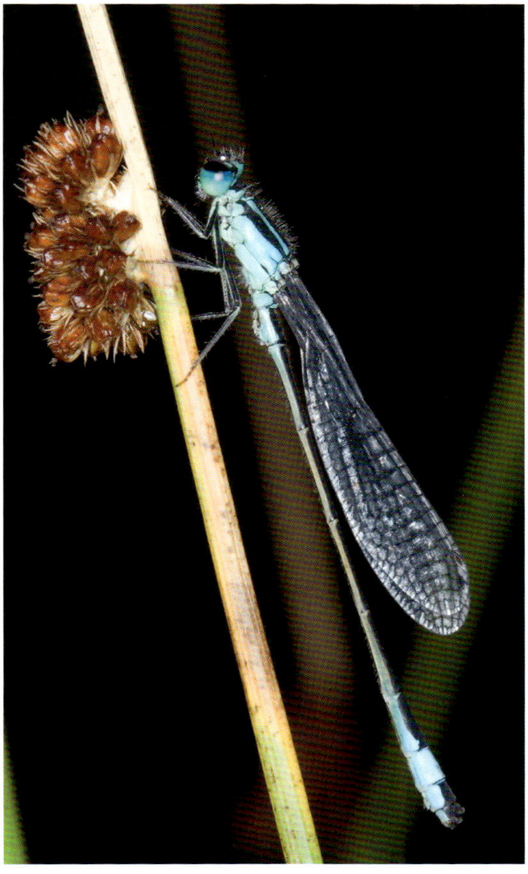

Male Blue-tailed Damselfly

Damselflies

Only the commonest species are described below. Other species are either scarcer or confined to a limited range in particular areas of the country. Damselfly body length is about 25–35 mm.

Time of year seen

Different species emerge and disappear at different times of the year, but most peak in June and July. From my own experience in Devon, there is a succession in terms of the order in which various species peak: damselflies, chasers in spring/early summer; Emperor and Golden-ringed Dragonfly in summer; darters and hawkers in late summer and autumn. The *Field Guide* mentioned above gives details of the peak time for each species.

In the field

Dragonflies offer a great advantage over some other forms of wildlife, in that they are relatively easy to find. Go to almost any area with water on a good day in spring or summer and there will surely be some form of dragonfly present. Building a pond in your garden will attract dragonflies, although the number of species may be restricted compared to larger, more established waterbodies.

Nonetheless, this group of insects does present technical problems in getting a good quality photograph, as they are small and move very quickly. There are two main methods: slow stalking or letting them come to you, although usually a combination of the two is required. Most sources say that they will find a favourite perch and rest on it. This is true to some extent, but it does not guarantee that the background will be attractive or unobtrusive.

When attempting to photograph dragonflies, it is important to wear muted colours and to move very slowly. It is especially important to raise the camera

NAME	TIME OF YEAR USUALLY SEEN	COMMENTS
AZURE DAMSELFLY	May–July. Widespread except in Scotland.	Very common blue damselfly, distinguished from similar species by markings at the top of the tail. Patient stalking is required to get close. Male blue, female green.
BEAUTIFUL DEMOISELLE	May–August. Found in south-west England and in Wales.	Male has an iridescent blue-green body with black wings. The female has a metallic green body and brown wings with a small white spot. Often found on riverbank foliage.
LARGE RED DAMSELFLY	May–August. Widespread in the UK.	A very common damselfly that prefers sheltered ponds and ditches. Relatively easy to photograph provided you can get close enough.
BLUE-TAILED DAMSELFLY	May–August. Common and widespread.	Male black with a blue band at the end of the tail. Female has different colour forms, all distinguished by blue band on a dark tail.
COMMON BLUE DAMSELFLY	May–September. Common and widespread.	This species is similar to other blue damselflies, and a careful study of markings is required to tell them apart.

Table 3.3 Common damselflies

slowly – a reflection from the lens is certain to send your desired subject zooming off. Yet if you move slowly and carefully, it is possible to get very close.

The weather has a major effect on dragonflies. They cannot fly if it is cold or wet, when they rest in grasses and bushes where they are hard to spot. If you can find them, dragonflies can make attractive images when photographed on dewy mornings. Warm sunny summer days, on the other hand, will give a dragonfly bonanza, with the disadvantage that they are much more active and thus difficult to capture.

Photographic techniques for dragonflies and damselflies

Lenses

Use either a 100 mm or 180 mm macro lens, with a ring flash. The 180 mm allows you to stand further back, and thus is less likely to drive off the quarry. For small damselflies, the 100 mm gives a larger image, provided you can get close enough. Other people use a long focal length lens (e.g. 300 mm) and do not use flash, but in this case a tripod is required, which makes stalking much more difficult.

Shutter speed

Set the camera to manual for flash. Choice of shutter speed is a matter of preference. If using flash, you may like to have a fast shutter speed to give a black background and highlight the dragonfly, and this does have the benefit of hiding what might otherwise be an intrusive background. A typical value of shutter speed may be 1/200 s. If the ambient light is very bright, on the other hand, you may wish to adjust shutter speed to give a balanced flash. The value will depend on the light conditions, and the aperture you have chosen, but a typical shutter speed may be around 1/50 s. If uncertain, change the camera to aperture priority and half press the shutter. The shutter speed that appears will be the correct value to use in order to give a bright background with the same exposure as the flash-lit subject. Using balanced flash in dull conditions will mean a longer shutter speed, which may cause blurring, as the subject may move while the shutter is still open after the flash has fired. In other situations, you may wish to select a value between these two extremes of black background and balanced flash.

Aperture

Dragonflies have bits sticking out all over, and even lining the camera up parallel with the insect's body will not remove the requirement for a high depth of field to get it all in focus. Using f/16 usually makes the whole creature sharp, and using flash gives by far the sharpest images. If the background is likely to intrude, because the dragonfly is not as well positioned as you would like, a larger aperture can be employed to reduce the depth of field and thus blur the background.

Flash

Use a ring flash. The best ring flash allows you to adjust the brightness of each half of the ring separately, affording a more natural look. Flash has several advantages. Dragonflies generally fly between 10 am and 3 pm, on sunny days when the light is at its harshest. Using a balanced flash helps to reduce the contrast. A balanced flash means that the background exposure is the same as if no flash were used, so that it is at the same brightness as the subject. See note above for balanced flash in dull conditions.

Tripod/monopod

A tripod greatly restricts flexibility in stalking, and is not recommended. It can, however, be useful if photographing dew-wet and resting dragonflies in the early morning. Monopods can be useful if photographing for long periods, but can still restrict movement.

Butterflies

Butterflies are the living jewels of the garden and countryside. Photographing the commoner species is a pleasant experience, but for the thrill of the chase, try to find and photograph some of the rarer species.

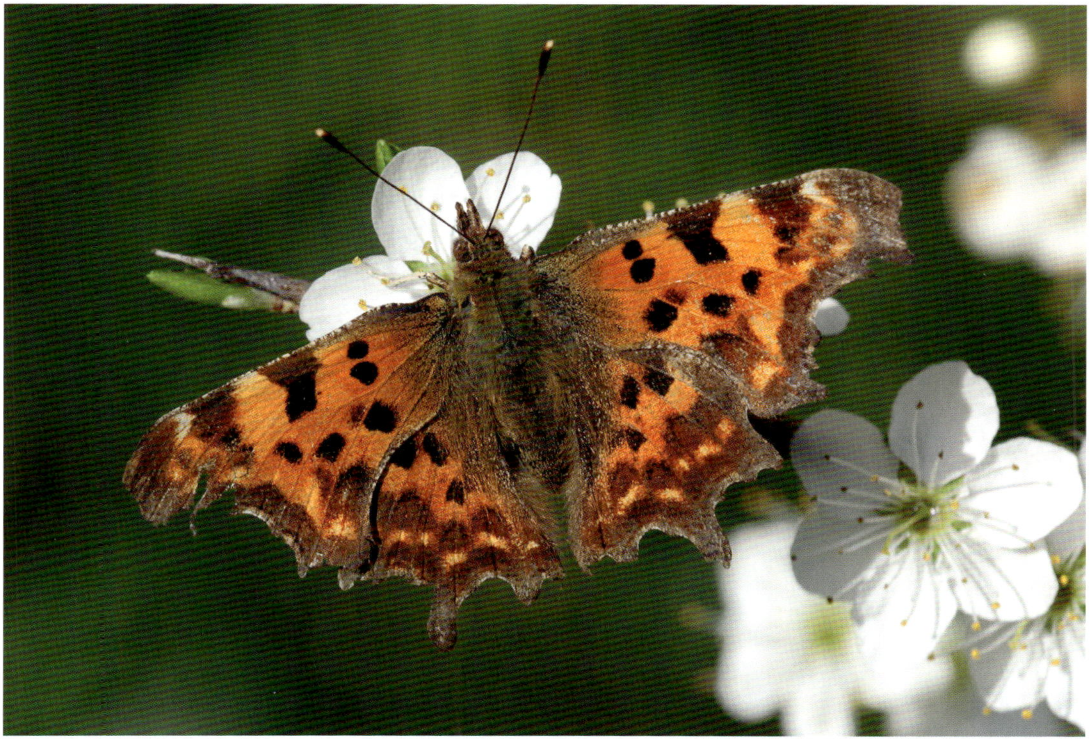

Comma butterfly

Introduction

The techniques and equipment required for the photography of butterflies are almost the same as for dragonflies, although finding them, especially the rarer species, requires research of suitable sites.

In the field

Butterflies move more slowly than dragonflies, but their flight is very erratic which makes it difficult to guess where they will move to next. Watching the butterfly and walking up slowly when it is resting or feeding usually works best. Sometimes standing and waiting next to a flower can work well for skittish butterflies, providing you are not in a field with a large number of similar flowers.

As with dragonflies, a field guide is essential for identification as well as to discover the likely areas where particular butterflies may be found. *Britain's Butterflies* by David Tomlinson is a good guide. Looking for and photographing the rarer species can become something of an obsession, and of course, some high-quality images of rare butterflies always hold a great appeal.

The Butterfly Conservation website lists details of recent sightings. Different species of butterfly are seen at different times of year and in different parts of the country. The rare butterflies are becoming rarer as habitats disappear, so it is worth studying the life histories of the rarer species to find out where and when you might find them. Nature reserves tend to be the best places to encounter the less common, and there is usually information about the butterflies to be found in the reserves signboards or websites. Some nature reserves have conservation programmes for the rarest species, so it is worth finding out what you can about these too.

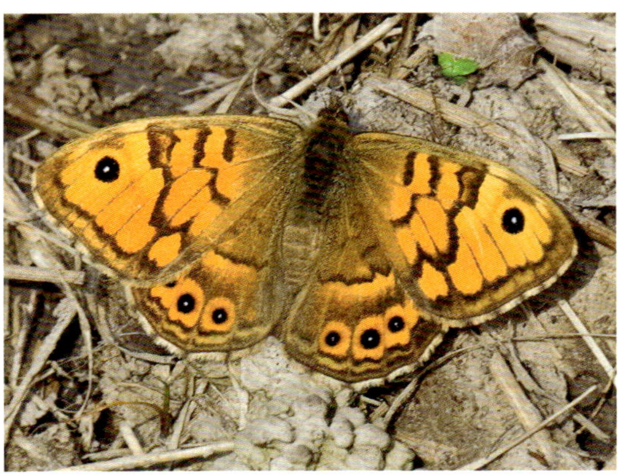

The uncommon Wall butterfly

Photographic techniques for butterflies

Photographic techniques and equipment for butterflies are much the same as for dragonflieas. If you are able to find them on dewy mornings, photography with a tripod and without flash is advised. The light is softer then, and natural light will give a better image. On cool, cloudy days with only occasional sun, butterflies are easier to photograph, as they bask with wings open during the sunny spells and are less likely to move when approached.

Butterflies can be photographed with or without flash, but images are sharper when flash is deployed. If possible, use a ring flash as it gives a softer light than standard flashlights. Aim to get as close as possible for the sharpest images and use a macro lens of between 100 and 180 mm.

Common butterflies

Table 3.4 shows the more colourful of the common butterflies. In many cases the female is larger than the male.

Rare butterflies

Even if you find a site with these butterflies, you may need to undertake several visits before you see them. Consult the Butterfly Conservation website for sightings.

Declining butterflies

Butterflies are declining in number across the British Isles, and the Wall is an example of a once-common species that has fallen sharply in numbers. It prefers bare ground or stone when resting, hence its name.

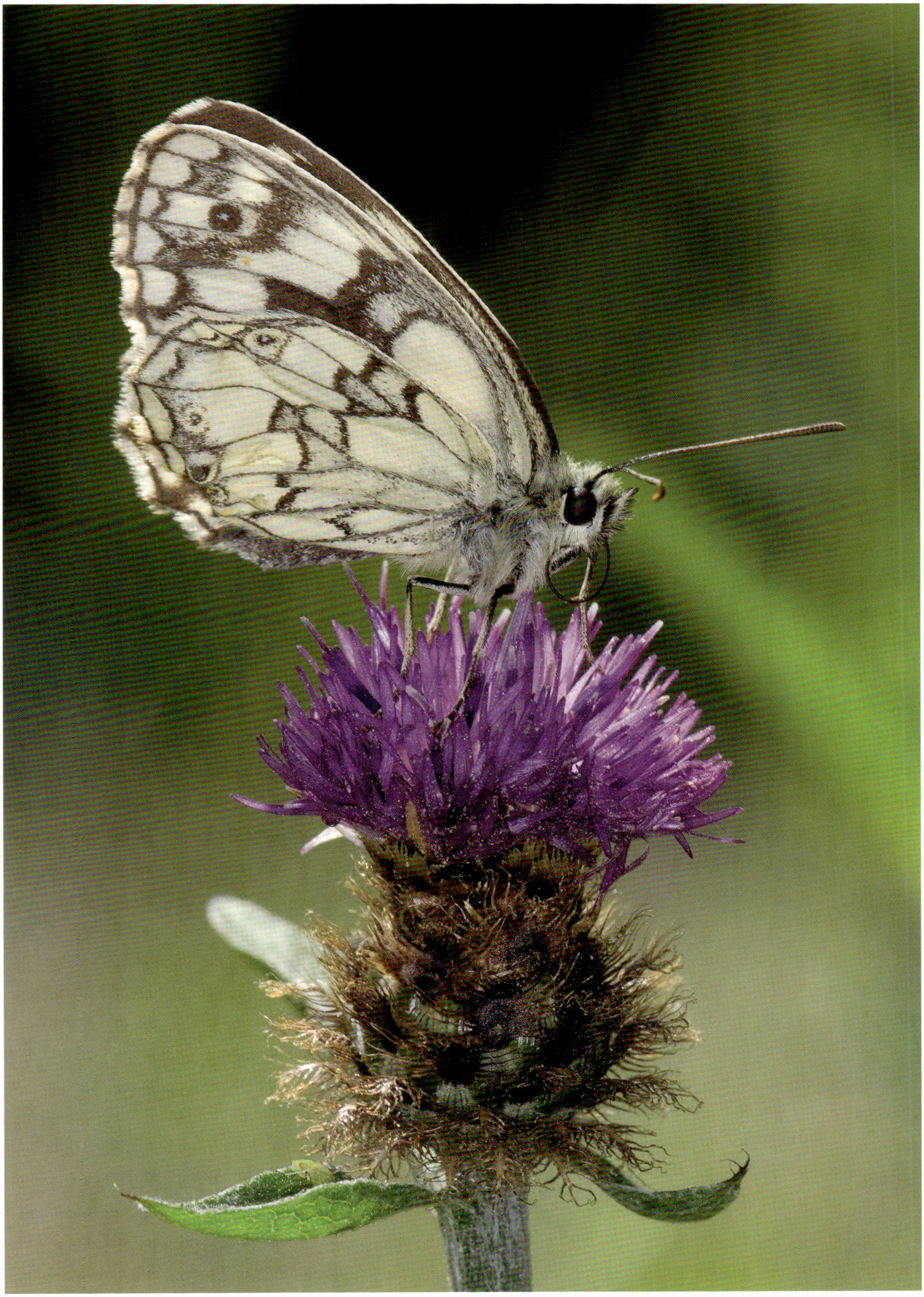

Marbled White on Knapweed in a Devon wildflower garden

NAME	TIME OF YEAR USUALLY SEEN	COMMENTS	WINGSPAN
BRIMSTONE	Spring to autumn in England.	Favours scrubby woodland and hedges.	60–75 mm
COMMA	Spring to autumn in England and Wales.	Found in gardens and woodland edges.	50–65 mm
RED ADMIRAL	Spring to autumn in most of the UK.	Migrates from the continent each year. Likes flower- rich gardens.	65–80 mm
PEACOCK	Spring to autumn in England and Wales.	Found in many habitats. Lays eggs on nettles.	65–75 mm
SMALL TORTOISESHELL	Spring to autumn in much of the UK.	Found in a wide variety of habitats.	45–60 mm
COMMON BLUE	May–September in most of the UK.	Likes sheltered areas. Has beautifully marked under wings.	30–35 mm
LARGE SKIPPER	June–July in England and Wales	Found on rough grassland but only active in hot weather.	30–35 mm

Table 3.4 Common butterflies in order of appearance

NAME	TIME OF YEAR USUALLY SEEN	COMMENTS/EXAMPLE LOCATIONS	WINGSPAN
DINGY SKIPPER	May/June	Likes bare earth for basking. Magdalen Hill Down, Hampshire.	25–35 mm
PEARL-BORDERED FRITILLARY	May/June	Recently coppiced or cleared woodland in the south of England and west Scotland.	35–45 mm
ADONIS BLUE	May to September, but August best.	Fontmell Down and Purbeck Hills, Dorset on chalk or limestone.	30–40 mm
BLACK HAIRSTREAK	June/July	Very rare, but seen in Monks Wood National Nature Reserve, Cambridgeshire.	35–40 mm
LARGE BLUE	July when sunny	Collard Hill, Somerset is managed for this butterfly.	35–50 mm
WHITE ADMIRAL	July	Deciduous woodland in Southern England.	55–65 mm

Table 3.5 Rare butterflies in order of appearance

CASE STUDY: Pearl-bordered Fritillary

The commoner butterfly species can be found in many gardens, so the challenge for the wildlife photographer rests in finding and photographing the scarcer species. The principles described here can be applied to any of the rarer butterflies and dragonflies.

I had to find this butterfly to photograph for a book, and was given information by a local ecologist on likely locations. The main place specified was a private site in south Devon, several acres of which had been managed for the Pearl-bordered Fritillary. Scrub had been cleared, leaving an open area surrounded by trees. Permission was easy to obtain in this case as the land was owned by the company that had commissioned the photographs.

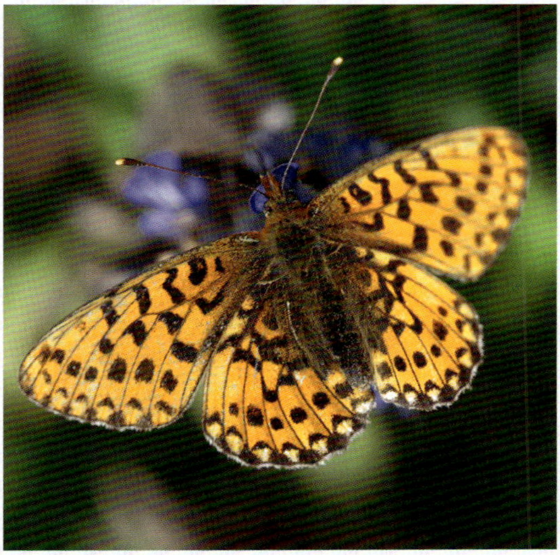

Pearl-bordered Fritillary

Initial research

Location

The Pearl-bordered Fritillary is only found in open habitats, and it favours recently coppiced or cleared woodland where violets grow in good numbers. Many sites manage the habitat specifically for this butterfly, others, such as in Scotland, are grazed by sheep and deer. Examples are the RSPB site at Leighton Moss in Lancashire and parts of Dartmoor, with recent sightings across the country being published on the Butterfly Conservation website. *I was fortunate in that I was armed with information of a likely site.*

Basic facts

Description: Many fritillaries are similar in appearance, being orange-brown with dark patterning on the wings – it is the underside of the wing that is key to identification. The Pearl-bordered Fritillary has seven white spots (pearls) on the outer edge on the wing's underside, together with two other white marks, plus several red patches. The wingspan is 45 mm on average. *Description alone would not make identification clear, so the other facts had to be taken into account.*

Feeding: This species is attracted to purple or yellow flowers for nectar, such as bugle, bird's-foot-trefoil and bluebell. The caterpillar feeds mainly on violets. *This information would help with identification.*

Breeding: Eggs are laid on the foodplant (violets) and hatch after 10–15 days. The caterpillars grow until the first frosts, at which point they hibernate among the leaf litter until March of the next year. They then enter the pupa stage then emerge as butterflies in May. *Early May would be the best time to start looking.*

Habitat: The preferred habitat is open areas within deciduous woodland, where the caterpillar's foodplant and adult's nectar plants are available. There is often bracken growth present, with the adult being camouflaged by dead bracken stems. It is essential that habitat areas remain open, either by rotational coppicing or grazing. *The site I was directed to had been cleared in the previous year.*

Distribution: This butterfly is found in isolated pockets within areas of suitable habitat. Lack of woodland management, and lack of woods themselves, are regarded as the main reasons for its decline. It is found in the south and west of England and the west of Scotland, with small groups in other parts of western England and Wales. *Devon is a suitable place to look,*

Population: Butterfly populations are often described in terms of range rather than numbers. The fact that this species is no longer seen in sites that once held large numbers has led to the conclusion that it is in steep decline. *Small numbers would likely mean more than one visit to increase the chances of seeing the butterfly.*

Equipment

Opinions are divided between those who use long lenses (300 mm) and those who use macro lenses and flash to capture images of butterflies. I prefer the latter, as the resulting photographs are much sharper. Wearing clothing in shades of green and brown are best for butterfly photography. A monopod can be used if you are photographing for long periods, although it can be restrictive: *as the Pearl-bordered Fritillary can be skittish, a monopod would make it difficult to react quickly, so I opted for flash.*

Habits

The Pearl-bordered Fritillary has a rapid fluttering flight, making it a difficult subject. It often flies low down, just above the growth, or else glides towards a plant. This can make it difficult to see. *Careful observation on the ground was required.*

In the field

Looking for a particular species of butterfly is a more intense experience than looking for butterflies in general. In this case, it was important to be familiar with the caterpillar's foodplant, as that was where the adult female would lay her eggs. Finding the butterfly depended on several factors:

- whether the adults had emerged from their pupae;
- whether the caterpillar's foodplants and adult's nectar plants were present;
- the weather had to be sunny and reasonably warm with little wind.

Butterflies can appear in less favourable conditions, but the chance of seeing them will be greatly increased if all of the conditions are met. When I first arrived at the site in question, in April, bracken growth was starting to unfurl and common dog-violets beginning to flower. There was a variety of wildflowers around including bird's-foot

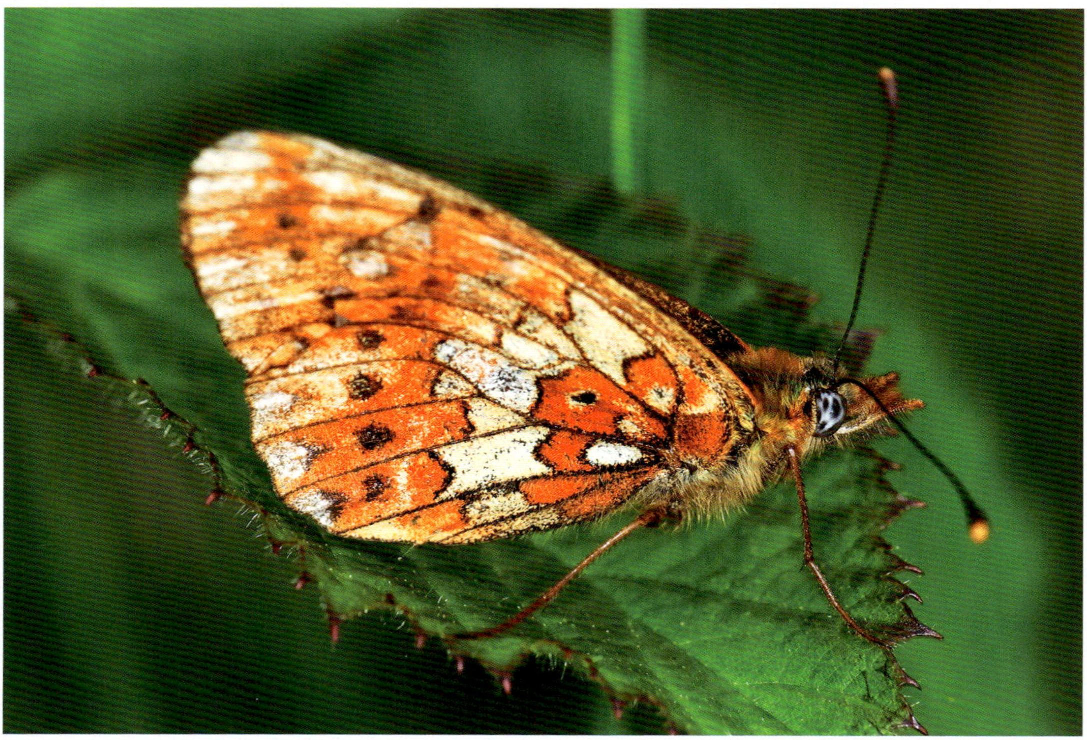

Pearl-bordered Fritillary underside

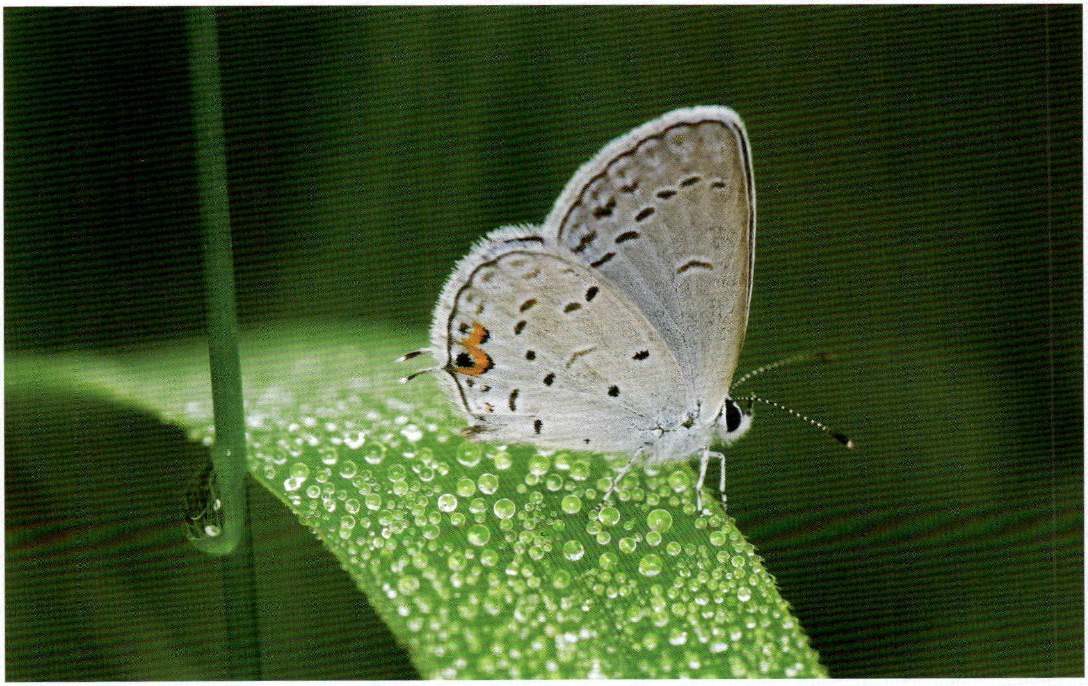

Blue butterfly and dew, Ohio

trefoil, bugle and bluebells. The weather was reasonably warm, although patchy cloud meant that the sun only appeared now and then. That was not a problem, as the butterflies would be less active in cloudy conditions, and would spend more time with wings outstretched, warming up during the sunny intervals. It was windy, but the cleared areas were on a slope on the leeward side, and so were sheltered.

I walked slowly back and forth across the site, so that I covered the whole area. After each few steps I peered around to see if the butterflies were flying, and then looked down to see if there were any on the ground. There were several large patches of bugle and I concentrated my efforts in that area. I did not see any Pearl-bordered Fritillaries, although I did find several other species of butterfly.

I repeated the visit once a week over a period of six weeks, and on the fourth visit I finally saw the butterflies! It was another cloudy day with sunny spells, and each time the sun came out, the butterflies rose from the ground and could be seen feeding on the bugle. Several times I approached and they flew off, so eventually I stayed next to the bugle patch and waited. After ten minutes or so, the butterflies returned, and I was able to photograph them for several minutes. I also found one on dead bracken stems, with wings outstretched, warming up in the sun, where it stayed for some time.

It would have been very easy to have missed the target species, as they were only present on one of my six visits, despite information that they were likely to be there. This shows that even with the best information and research, patience is required, but if you have to obtain an image as I had, the motivation to persevere is strong.

Be aware that at times and especially towards the end of their season, butterfly wing markings can became faint and washed out, making identification more difficult, which is the case with the photograph of the underside of the fritillary shown here.

The butterfly shown above is a North American species, the Eastern Tailed Blue, although it looks very similar to some blue butterflies found in the UK. The technique for photographing butterflies is the same wherever you go.

Chapter 4

OTHER ANIMAL GROUPS

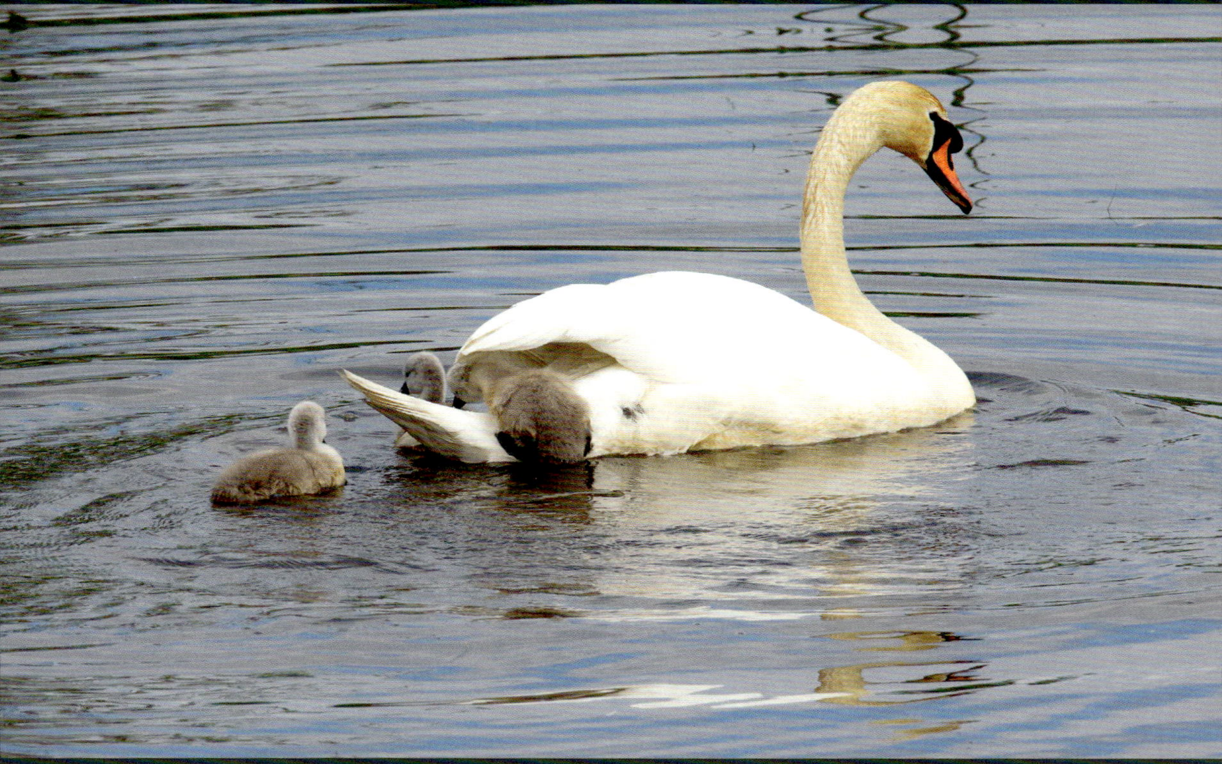

Mute Swan and cygnets

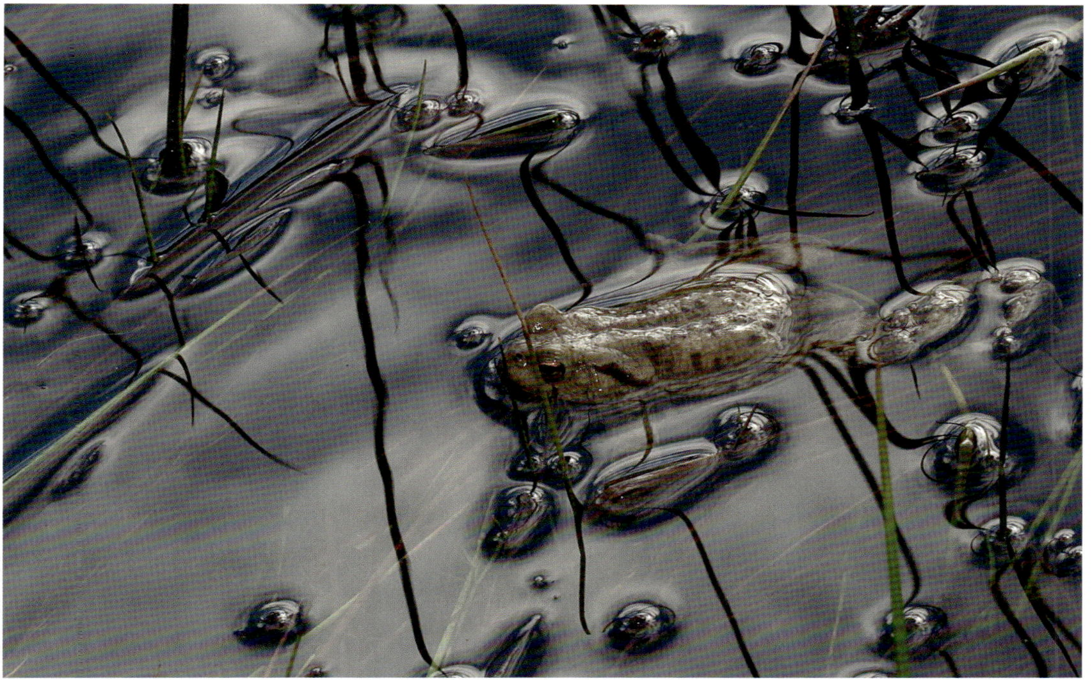

Toad in a rushy pool

This chapter covers reptiles, dormice and bats, which are protected, and thus their photography is not generally legal, as well as rare species of mammals that are hard to locate. I give a little information about each of these species.

The easy ones

I have not included Grey Squirrels or Rabbits in the main mammal section as they are so easy to find that there is little need for fieldcraft knowledge. Grey Squirrels will come into any garden if food is supplied (often that meant for birds), and Rabbits can be seen in many green spaces. The challenge for the photographer is to aim for something different, and if you wish to enter wildlife photography competitions, an unusual image of a common animal can do well. After a while you may find the fact they are so easy to find makes them less of a challenge, but for the new photographer they make an excellent first subject.

As I have not included water-based wildlife in this book, this has excluded frogs and toads. However, these amphibians do spend some time on land and on the water surface, and are well worth considering as photographic subjects too.

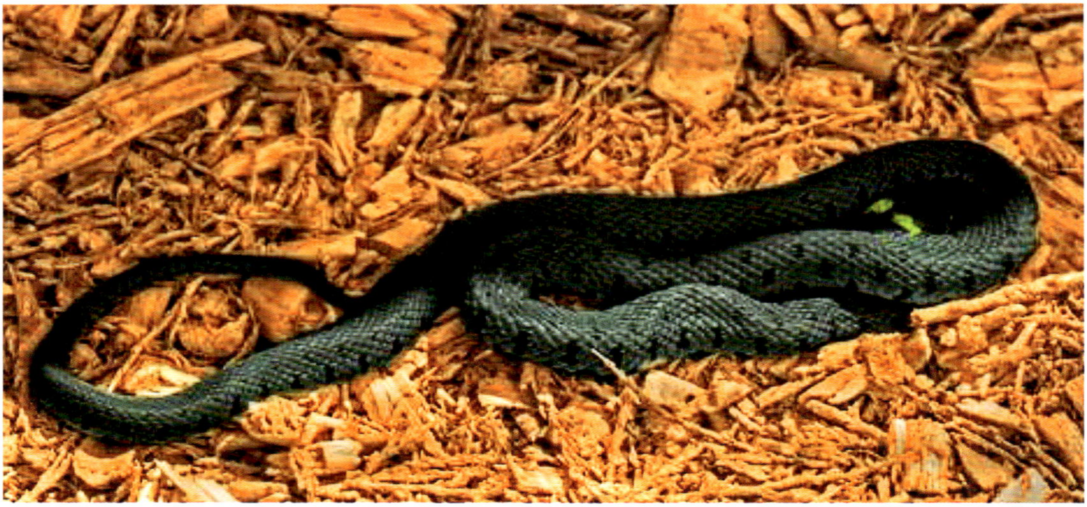

Grass Snake

Reptiles

Britain is home to relatively few reptile species, and the ones most likely to be seen are the Grass Snake and the Slow Worm, which are described below. Our only venomous snake is the Adder which is found on heathland, and is uncommon in many areas. Other species include Smooth Snake and Sand Lizard, which are very rare, and the Common Lizard which is less so but which is nonetheless often elusive.

Reptiles are cold-blooded and must gain heat from their surroundings. As a result they hibernate in winter, often underground. Once the weather gets warmer, they become more active and will bask on sunny embankments to warm up, especially in March and April. All British reptiles are protected species and it is an offence to kill or injure them.

Grass snake

Our commonest snake in England and Wales, but still elusive.

Basic facts

Description: The adult snake is up to a metre long when fully grown. Colour varies from green to brown, with black marks mainly on the side. The Grass Snake is distinguished by a yellow 'collar' on the neck. Young snakes are miniatures of the adult.

Breeding: Mating takes place soon after emergence in spring, with up to 40 eggs being laid in warm places. Eggs hatch from August to September.

Feeding: Fish, frogs, newts.

Habitat: Wetlands, meadows, open woodland, where there is water nearby.

Distribution: England and Wales.

Population: Around 350,000.

Habits

The Grass Snake survives British winters by hibernating underground or in log piles, emerging in early spring. The rotting vegetation in compost heaps produces heat, and because eggs must be laid in warm places in order for them to hatch, compost heaps are a favoured place for egg-laying. The snakes can swim well, and can often be seen in water. They are sensitive to disturbance, and will quickly move into the undergrowth on sighting a human. The snakes bask in warm places to raise their body temperature, especially in the morning, and this is the best time to observe them.

It is difficult to photograph these sensitive and fast-moving subjects, and even more difficult to produce quality images. The Grass Snake photographed here was under a piece of corrogated sheet which cast a shadow when lifted. I did not have flash with me, and although the image looks fine on a computer screen, and is good for identification as the yellow collar is easy to see, it is not of a high enough quality for reproduction in photographic books.

Ideally, I should have focused the camera on the ground next to the sheet to estimate the exposure, aperture and shutter speed and prepared the flash before I approached the corrogated sheet. I should have asked someone else to lift the sheet so I was immediately ready to take the shot. Preparing beforehand means that only the matter of focusing needs attention before pressing the shutter.

Adder

This is our only venomous snake. Although found throughout the UK, it is generally confined to heathland areas, and so is uncommon in most regions.

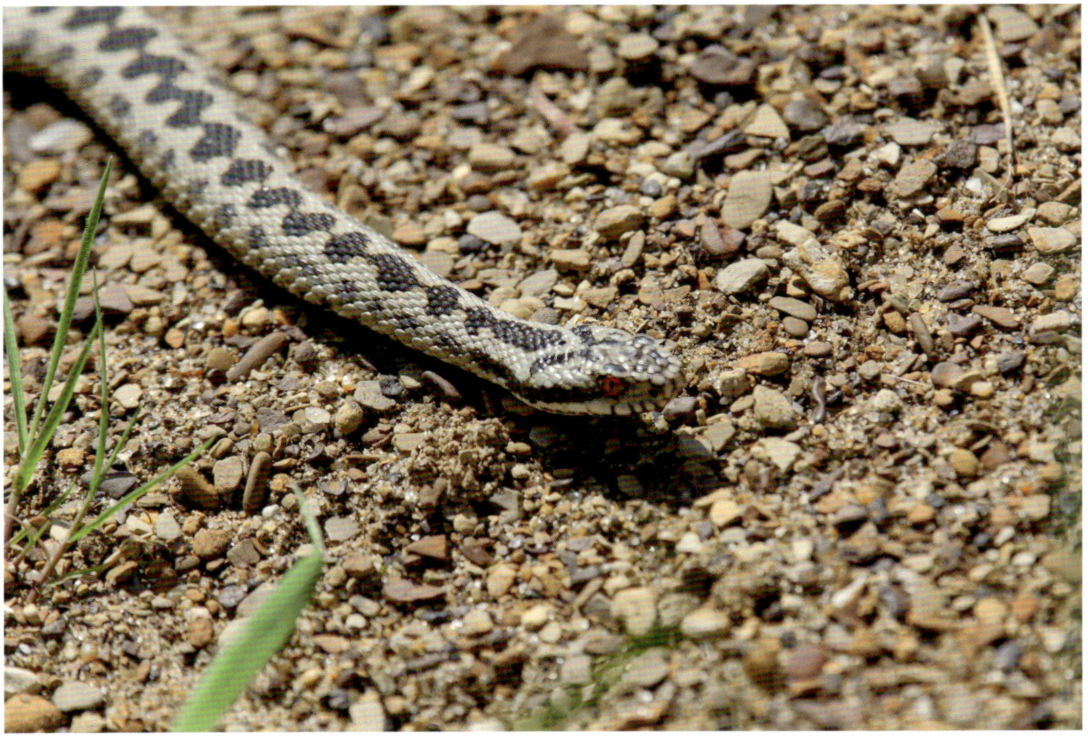

Male Adder

Basic facts

Description: The Adder is smaller than the Grass Snake, being less than 80 cm when fully grown. The female is brown with a distinctive dark zigzag pattern along its back. The male is smaller and much paler in colour, but also has the dark zigzag stripe.

Breeding: Mating takes place during warm spells in early spring. Sometimes males will wrestle each other for supremacy. The Adder does not lay eggs like the Grass Snake: the young are born at the end of August, as miniatures of the adult.

Feeding: Voles, frogs, lizards.

Habitat: Heathland, woodland edges, rough grassland, sea cliffs.

Distribution: Throughout the UK except for Ireland.

Population: Actual numbers are not known, but they are found in fewer sites than in the past, and thus are regarded as in decline, probably due to loss of habitat.

Habits

The Adder hibernates in winter and emerges in early spring. Like other reptiles, the Adder basks in sunny, sheltered positions, especially on early spring mornings when it has to raise its body temperature. Also like other reptiles, the Adder cannot regulate its body temperature internally, relying on external heat sources. In very hot weather it may become almost dormant in order to keep cool. The Adder kills its prey with its venomous bite, then slowly swallows and digests it.

Photographing Adders is even more difficult than Grass Snakes, as the venemous nature of this species has to be taken into account. It would be unwise to approach close enough to use a ring flash, so a conventional flashgun may be more suitable.

The Adder in the photograph featured on the previous page seems OK until you look closer and see that the head is out of focus. Once the Adder starts moving, not only is focusing a problem but there is also a powerful instinct to get out of the way fast!

When I took this picture I had actually set out with a plan to photograph mammals and had a 400 mm telephoto lens with me, and no flash. The extra weight also made it more difficult to react quickly.

Slow Worm

The Slow Worm is a legless lizard, not a snake, and is by far our commonest reptile, found throughout mainland Britain. It does not always move off when disturbed. Its colour varies from silver to gold. It is fond of sunny embankments, but is decreasing in numbers, probably due to habitat loss.

Basic facts

Description: The Slow Worm is narrow and less than 50 cm in length. It can take several different colour forms, with the females being silver to gold in colour and with a black stripe along the back. Males are often paler, without the dark stripe. Sometimes, if they have been feeding in ants' nests, the males can even have bluish spots.

Breeding: Mating takes place in May once the adults have emerged from hibernation and warmed up. Live young are born in late summer, often only every second year. The young are born in an egg membrane, but this breaks soon after birth, releasing miniatures of the adult.

Feeding: Slugs, snails and other invertebrates.

Habitat: Rough grassland and sunny banks.

Distribution: Throughout the UK, but commoner in England and Wales.

Population: Common but declining, probably as a result of habitat loss.

Habits

Like other reptiles in the UK, the Slow Worm hibernates from October to March. On emerging in spring it has to gain heat from its surroundings, and will bask on sunny banks. It will move into the undergrowth when disturbed, but is not as sensitive to human presence as snakes, which makes this species much easier subject to photograph. They can often be found in gardens with rough grassy areas, although many people are unaware of their presence.

In the field: general points for common reptiles

The easiest way to find reptiles is to offer them suitable shelter. A sheet of corrugated iron, or other corrugated roofing material, placed in an open position where there is vegetation such as long grass, heather or gorse, will eventually attract any reptiles present in your area, as it will be warmer under the sheet. They may move away in very hot weather, but will return when it is cooler. Slow Worms are the commonest inhabitants, but Grass Snakes will also appear, especially if there is water nearby. I have found that Grass Snakes are more often present around the time that they shed their skin (which they may do more than once a year, especially when still growing). Be careful to lay the corrugated sheets so that they will not slip and trap the reptile underneath.

Adders will only be present if you place the sheets in heathland, or similar habitats. Some nature reserves have sheets placed around for reptile shelter already, but they are usually off the beaten track. Ask the rangers if there are any such sheets around and seek their permission to carefully lift them; on private land, ask the landowner if you want to place sheets on land that is not your own. Felt roofing tiles are commonly used for reptile surveys, although it can take several months or even a year before they are used. Be aware that Field Voles and Wood Mice often nest under the sheets, so you may have photographic opportunities for more than one group!

If you do not use sheets/tiles, but want to find reptiles in the wild, first research your location to find the most likely areas. Most nature reserves

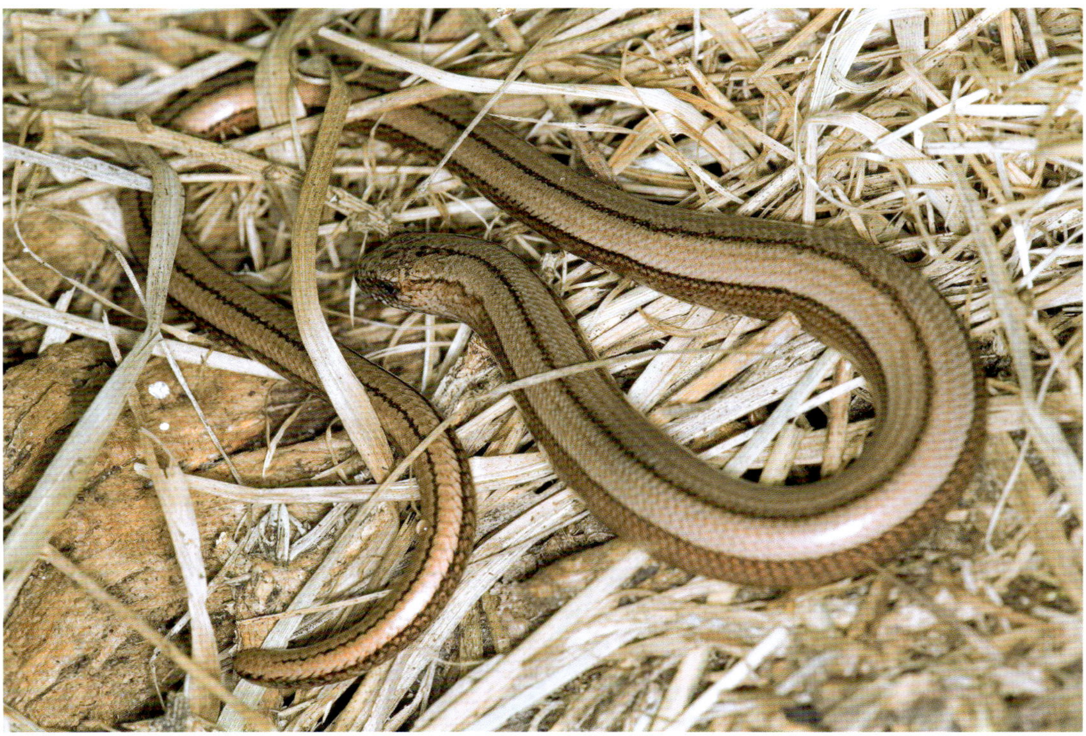

Slow Worm

will have information as to which reptiles are present. The best time to see them is early in the morning in March or April, when they are likely recently to have emerged from hibernation. They will be found basking on dry sunny banks in order to warm up. You will have to walk very slowly and place your feet carefully as they can feel vibrations before they see you. The Grass Snake is often close to water which has vegetation nearby so that they can swiftly move into cover. Be aware that snakes are often curled up, so are not immediately obvious as snakes, and can appear more like something left by a rather unhealthy dog!

Photography

Reptiles are very fast moving unless the conditions are cool, so flash may be your best option to avoid a blurred image. If you are looking under sheets, it is much easier if there is someone with you to lift up the sheet (safer with gloves if Adders are likely to be present). Pre-focus first as there may not be much time to take the shot. In this case a 100 mm macro lens, or similar, is suitable, together with flash. I tend to use a ring flash in this situation, as the subject is close.

If you are looking for reptiles in the countryside, you may not be able to get very close, so a longer lens will probably be more suitable. Choose a lens that you can hold easily as there is unlikely to be time to set up a tripod.

Rare reptiles

Table 4.1 gives some details of less common reptiles.

NAME	TIME OF YEAR SEEN	LOCATION	COMMENTS
COMMON LIZARD	Warm, sunny days in summer. Hibernates in winter.	Lowland heath is the most popular habitat.	Fast moving and difficult to find and photograph. Look for them in sunny sheltered spots on rocks or tree stumps.
SAND LIZARD	Warm, sunny days in summer. Hibernates in winter.	Sandy heaths in Dorset, Hampshire and Surrey.	Extremely rare and difficult to find. A guide is advised. A protected species.
SMOOTH SNAKE	Warm, sunny days in summer. Hibernates in winter.	Dry Lowland heath and sand dunes in Dorset, Surrey and Hampshire.	Very rare and difficult to find and photograph. A guide is advised. A protected species.

Table 4.1 Rare reptiles of Britain

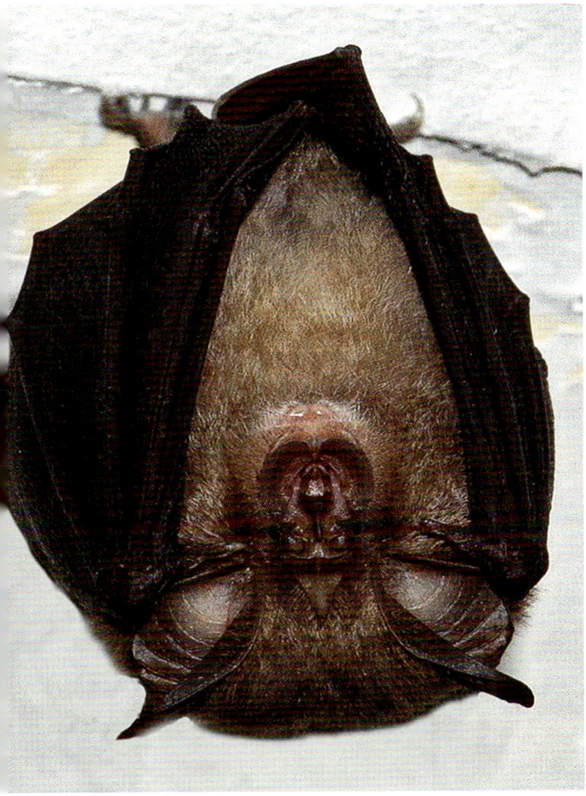

Lesser Horseshoe Bat

Other rare and protected species

This section describes species that you would be very lucky to find in the wild. For this reason I only put dowr the basic facts; my aim is to be realistic and not raise false hopes, but that does not mean you should not try to find these special animals.

The challenges

Wildlife in general is becoming rarer in the UK, but fortunately there are still some hotspots, mainly in Wales and Scotland. In these countries it is possible to see Polecats and Water Voles (Wales) or Pine Martens and Wildcats (Scotland). Some areas have also seen the introduction of Beavers and Wild Boar. Wild Boar and Water Voles can be found using research and local knowledge, but it is very unlikely you will see Wildcats in the wild.

It is not all bad news though, as the population of some rarities is increasing, due either to natural processes or by introductions.

The very photogenic Polecat has recolonised large parts of southern England, and the equally attractive Pine Marten can be found in Wales and has also been reported in some parts of England.

By harnessing local knowledge it is not impossible to find rare species, although the vast majority of images of rarities that you see are of captive animals. If you are prepared to devote a large part of your time to researching these rare species, any resulting photographs are likely to be rather special.

Bats

All British bat species are very heavily protected, and it is an offence to disturb them at their roosts. They can be photographed away from the roost, though, and if you are lucky enough to have them drink from your pond, it is possible to set up automatic triggered flash to photograph them. Otherwise, it is a matter of taking many photographs if you see them in flight, and hoping for the best as these animals move very quickly and are difficult to see in the dark. Another way to photograph bats is to join a bat group. Many groups look after injured bats and it is not an offence to photograph them, although care should be taken not to stress such individuals.

The image of the Lesser Horseshoe Bat was photographed in an old building. I was with a

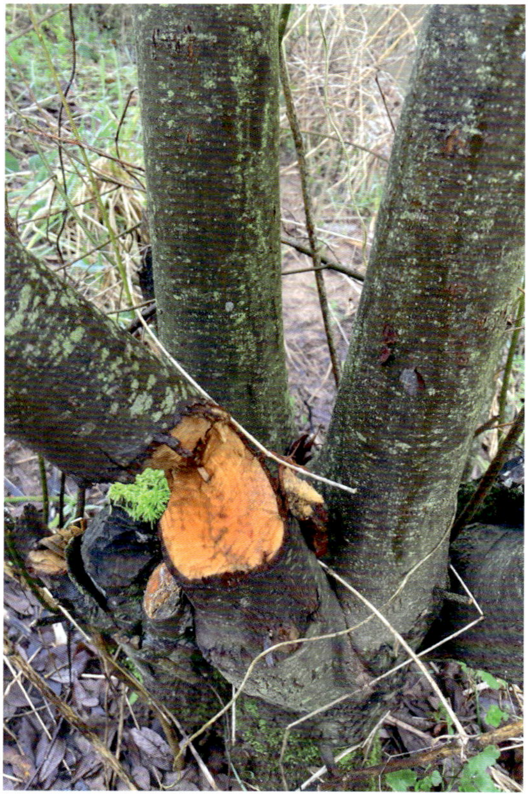
Tree branch chewed by Beaver by the River Otter, Devon

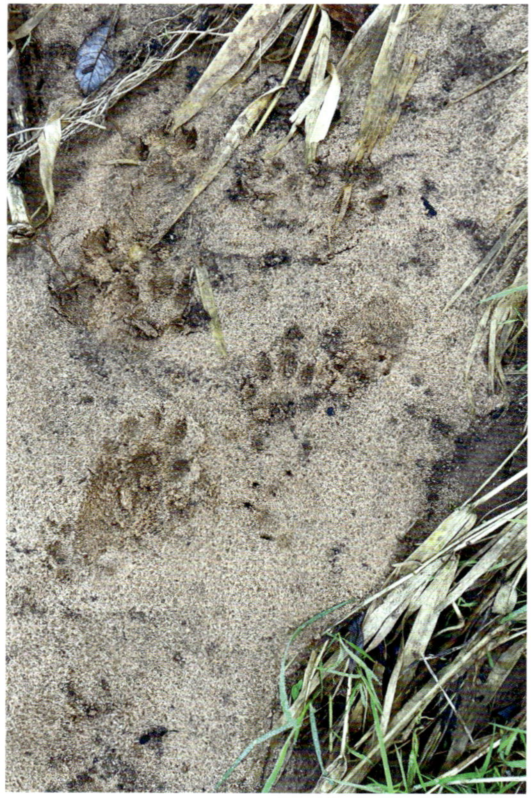
Beaver front tracks

licensed bat worker who ensured that the bat was not disturbed, so it was a fleeting visit. In such situations make sure you know exactly what camera settings to use as you may have to work quickly.

Beaver

The Beaver became extinct in the UK in the sixteenth century, but through escapes and reintroductions it is now increasing in some parts. The largest concentrations are in Scotland, especially along the River Tay.

Basic facts

Description: The Eurasian Beaver found in the UK is around 120 cm in length including the flattened tail. Its hindfeet are webbed, whereas the front feet have long fingers used to hold food. It is a large rodent with orange incisors and brown fur.

Weight: Variable, up to 35 kg.

Feeding: Beavers are vegetarian and do not eat fish. Their diet consists of waterplants, ferns, leaves and, in winter, bark, especially of willow.

Habitat: In the UK they are found along wide rivers, such as the River Tay in Scotland and the River Otter in Devon.

Distribution: At present in Scotland and Devon, but likely to be introduced in (or spread to) other parts of the UK.

Population: Possibly around 400 in the UK.

They were recently found in East Devon, and Devon Wildlife Trust successfully monitored them over a period of time. This study led to the conclusion that Beavers increase biodiversity and help reduce flood risks in the surrounding landscape. The Trust also invested time to ensure that farmers were kept informed and were compensated for any damage to their land, and methods to avoid damage were developed.

The Devon Beavers have expanded their range rapidly to at least 18 family groups, and are a great local attraction. The success of this trial has now led to other Wildlife Trusts wishing to reintroduce Beavers.

These are large mammals, and although mainly nocturnal, they can be seen during the day, and are now a relatively common sight in some parts of Scotland. This is an exciting success story, and photographers can also reap the benefits. Soon, it seems, Beavers may leave the rare species list.

Tracks and signs

Although early morning in spring or summer is the best time for photographers to see Beavers in the wild, a walk at other times along a river in a Beaver area to spot signs can be successful.

Looking along a watercourse in Beaver territory should reveal signs of Beaver-chewed trees, footprints in sand or soft mud bordering the river, and drag marks from the the animal's tail. Beaver front tracks measure about 6 cm long and show five toes, although sometimes only four are clear. The hind feet are webbed and are about twice as long and wide as the front tracks. Trees chewed by Beavers have a chacteristic triangular shape and the grooves left by the large front teeth can be seen.

In order to watch for Beavers, the best viewpoints are elevated areas with foliage to give some camouflage to the photographer. It would be necessary to arrive around 5 or 6 am in spring/summer and to sit quietly for some time. Early

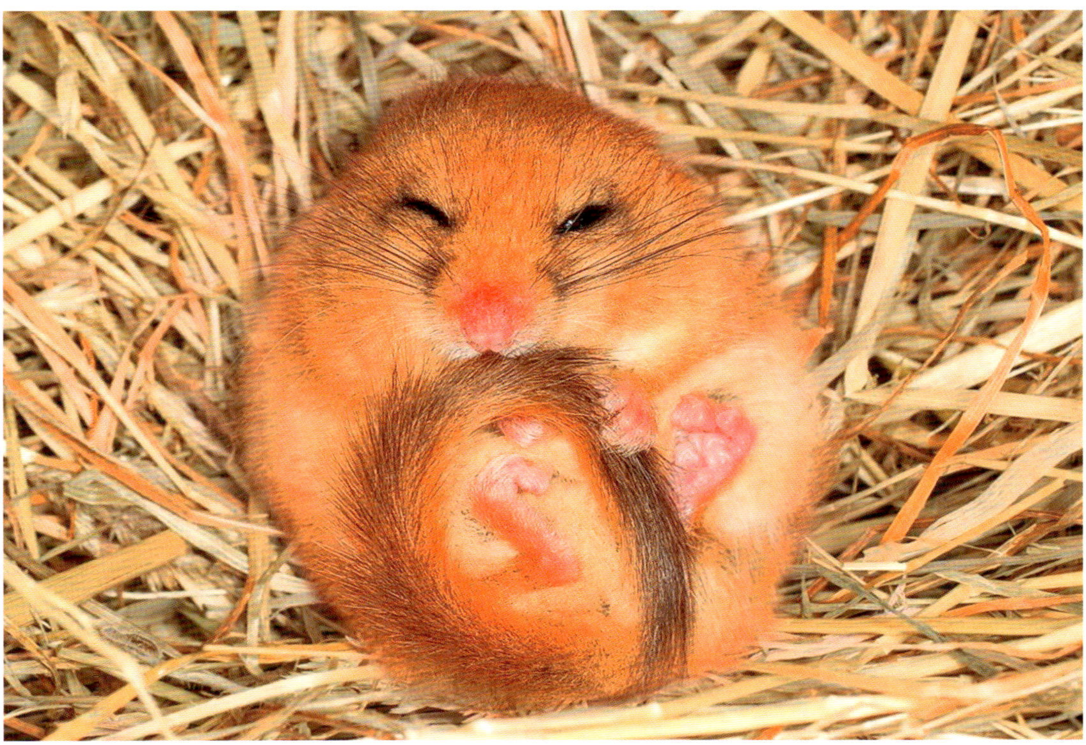

Dormouse

evenings are also possible in summer, but may mean leaving in the dark, which can be hazardous. Repeating this several times over a few days is likely to increase the chance of success, but as always, perseverance is required.

The main Beaver areas do have conducted tours, but as they could well cause disturbance, it is advisable to avoid the times of such events.

Dormouse

Basic facts

Description: A small mammal with golden-orange fur and a long furry tail. They have large dark eyes and their small feet have fleshy pads. Around 8 cm long, with another 8 cm of tail.

Weight: About 20g, but can be more than 50% more in autumn.

Feeding: Hazel Dormice eat a variety of food depending on what is available. The diet includes fruit, flowers, pollen, small insects and nuts, especially hazelnuts.

Habitat: Deciduous woodland is preferred, but bushy hedges and conifer plantations can contain Dormice.

Distribution: Predominantly found in the south of England, with smaller populations in other parts of the UK except for Scotland.

Population: The actual population is not known, but surveys have shown this species to be decreasing.

The Dormouse is a heavily protected species, and the only sure way to find Dormice in the wild is to carry out surveys with a licensed surveyor. If you help with or observe Dormouse box checks, you are likely to have the opportunity to photograph box inhabitants. As in this case you would see them at close quarters, a short-focus lens would be suitable. They do sometimes appear in gardens near suitable wild habitat and a hanging table feeder in a tree, with hazelnuts or seed, may attract them.

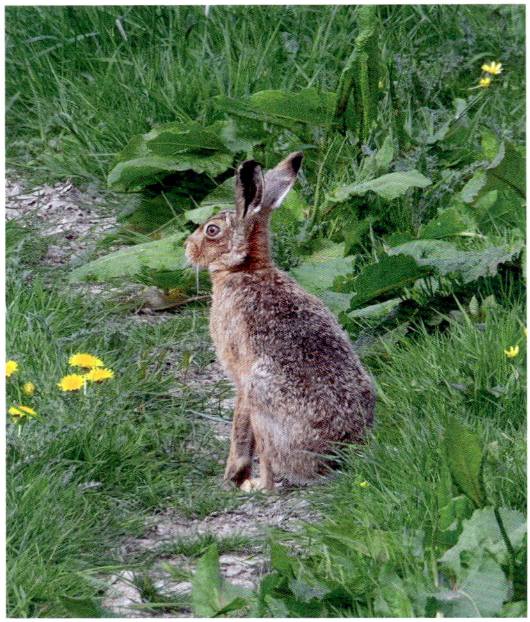

Brown Hare seen on a wildlife reserve in Wales

Hare

Basic facts

Description: The Brown Hare is distinguished from rabbits by its long ears and long back legs, which give it a somewhat ungainly appearance – until it starts running that is! It is also larger than a Rabbit, being around 55 cm long.

Weight: Around 3–5 kg

Feeding: Young shoots of grass and cereal crops.

Habitat: Grassland and farmland, especially with cereal crops.

Distribution: Low-lying areas of the UK.

Population: Around 575,000.

The Brown Hare is best observed on early mornings from March to April in its stronghold of Norfolk and Suffolk, although it can be seen in other parts of the UK where cereals are cultivated or where there are large uncultivated fields. The photograph here was taken from a hide in a nature reserve in west Wales where there were extensive rough grassy areas.

The Mountain Hare is a different species and is much rarer; it is only found in numbers in the Scottish Highlands such as the Cairngorms. In such areas a guide is the best and safest way to find these shy but enchanting animals. They are at their most photogenic in their white winter coat, when, unfortunately, the Scottish mountains are at their most inhospitable.

Mink

Basic facts

Description: Similar in appearance to a small otter, with dark fur that looks black when wet. They are around 36 cm in length, with a tail adding half that length.

Weight: Males are 0.8 to 1.5 kg, with females about half that.

Feeding: A wide range of prey including mammals, birds and fish.

Habitat: Close to wet areas – river, marshland, coasts.

Distribution: Throughout much of the UK.

Population: Around 100,000.

The American Mink was introduced in the wild as a result of escapes or illegal releases from Mink farms, which no longer exist in the UK. These are voracious predators and are known to exact a heavy toll on Water Vole populations. Mink are generally regarded as a serious pest and are trapped in sensitive areas.

It is not uncommon for Mink to be seen when one is looking for Otters, as they are found in similar habitats and require similar photographic techniques. Although mainly nocturnal, they are sometimes seen during the day. The photograph here was taken in Wales whilst I was watching for waterbirds. In this case, the Mink had a den with young near to the river, and had been observed there on several occasions. This photograph also shows how Mink are at home in water.

Pine Marten

Basic facts

Description: Dark reddish-brown fur, with a yellow-orange patch under the chin. A triangular-shaped face and relatively large ears. They are around 50 cm in length, with a bushy tail about 25 cm long.

Weight: At 1.5 kg to over 2 kg, males are roughly twice the weight of females.

Feeding: A wide range of foods, including mammals, birds, eggs and berries.

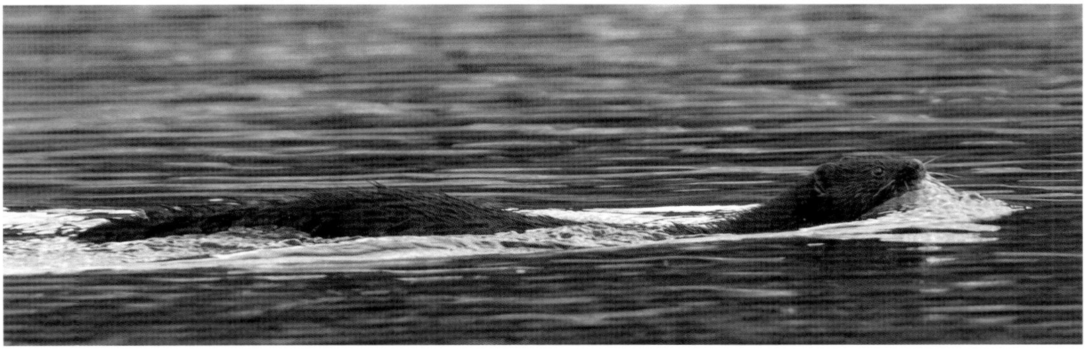

Mink swimming with prey

Habitat: Predominantly woodland, including conifer plantations.

Distribution: Until recently, Scotland was the main stronghold, but they are now found in parts of England and have been reintroduced into Wales.

Population: Around 4,000, but increasing.

Pine Martens are still rare and only found in quantity in northern Scotland. An Internet search on Pine Marten watching will bring up a list of venues, including guesthouses, that leave food out for Pine Martens, especially to help wildlife watchers and photographers see these elusive mammals.

A few years ago I stayed in a cottage in Kylerhea on the Isle of Skye. Each evening I left out peanut butter, a few slices of banana and/or an egg, as suggested by the cottage owner. The first night, a Pine Marten came visiting, followed by a Hedgehog. On its initial visit, the Pine Marten left very little for the Hedgehog, so the next evening the Hedgehog came earlier. Each evening the Hedgehog came that little bit earlier, until it managed to eat much of the food before the Pine Marten arrived. However, the Pine Marten always had the egg as it was too difficult for the Hedgehog to break the shell. It was a thrill to watch – although, as it was wet most evenings, photographs in the dark were not feasible.

Pine Martens are mainly nocturnal, and are still relatively uncommon. They are spreading into northern England and have been reintroduced into Wales. Pine Martens in Wales have been reported as reducing Grey Squirrel numbers but not affecting Red Squirrels adversely. This has increased interest in reintroductions. Reports from conservationists suggest that Grey Squirrels are a good meal for Pine Martens, whereas Red Squirrels are much less so – plus they are harder to catch. It has been suggested that the lesser weight of Red Squirrels means they can escape to branches that would not support the weight of a Pine Marten.

If you do not live near a hotspot, a visit to a wildlife centre may be the best way forward. It is also possible to book a place in a hide in Rothiemurchus in the Cairngorms where Pine Marten are regular evening visitors.

Polecat

Basic facts

Description: The brown-and-white marked face of the Polecat distinguishes it from other similar mustelids, such as Stoats and Pine Martens. Polecats have dark brown fur and are around 40 cm in length, with another 15 cm for the bushy tail.

Weight: At 1 to 2 kg, males are roughly twice the weight of females.

Feeding: Mainly rabbits and rats.

Habitat: Woodland, grassland, farmland. They can also be found in urban areas.

Distribution: Throughout Wales and in many parts of England, especially in the West.

Population: Around 45,000.

Polecats were once abundant, but persecution by humans greatly reduced their numbers, almost to extinction. They are making a comeback and are now spreading to many parts of England from their stronghold in Wales. Polecats can be confused with Ferrets, and due to interbreeding between these species, hybrid forms also occur. Finding them is difficult, especially as they are mainly nocturnal, and local knowledge is required. Reserve rangers are probably the best source of information. In areas where they are known to be present, a trail camera is a good method for finding their location, and where to set up a night vigil in the hope of capturing them on camera. If the landowners or local rangers allow it, setting out bait may attract Polecats.

Water Vole

Basic facts

Description: Dark reddish-brown fur, rounded ears and blunt nose. Length around 20 cm with a tail roughly half that length. The tail is covered with hair but is not bushy.

Weight: 200–300 g.

Feeding: A wide range of vegetation and grasses, mostly found near water.

Habitat: Slow-moving watercourses or lakes.

Distribution: Much of England and large areas of Scotland and Wales. Recently reintroduced to Devon.

Population: 875,000.

The Water Vole is described as an endangered species, with Mink being blamed for its severe decline. Water Vole nests are protected by law and it is an offence to disturb them in any way. Their stronghold is in the south-east of England, while some reserves, such as the London Wetland Centre, have successfully introduced the species. Such locations are the best places for successful photography 'in the wild'.

Walking slowly along watercourses known to harbour Water Voles may bring photographic luck. Sitting quietly across a slow-moving section of a suitable river may also be successful, using similar techniques to those described for the Dipper.

Populations appear to be stabilised in some areas, partly due to the reduction in Mink numbers and with reintroductions, but they are vulnerable to pollution and habitat loss.

Wildcat

Basic facts

Description: Similar to a large tabby cat, but distinguished by a thickly furred tail with dark concentric rings. Approximately 55 cm in length, with the tail adding another 30 cm.

Weight: Males weigh around 5 kg with females being about 4 kg.

Feeding: Mammals, especially rabbits, roadkill and birds.

Habitat: Moorland and woodland.

Distribution: Northern Scotland.

Population: 300–400.

The Scottish Wildcat is exceedingly rare and has been declining rapidly, its genetic purity also being damaged by interbreeding with feral cats. It can only be found in Scotland, where the most recent counts put its numbers at a few hundred and still decreasing. There is a faint chance you might see one if you find a source of local knowledge. However, for a photograph of a Wildcat, a visit to a wildlife centre is the best option.

Chapter 5

EQUIPMENT

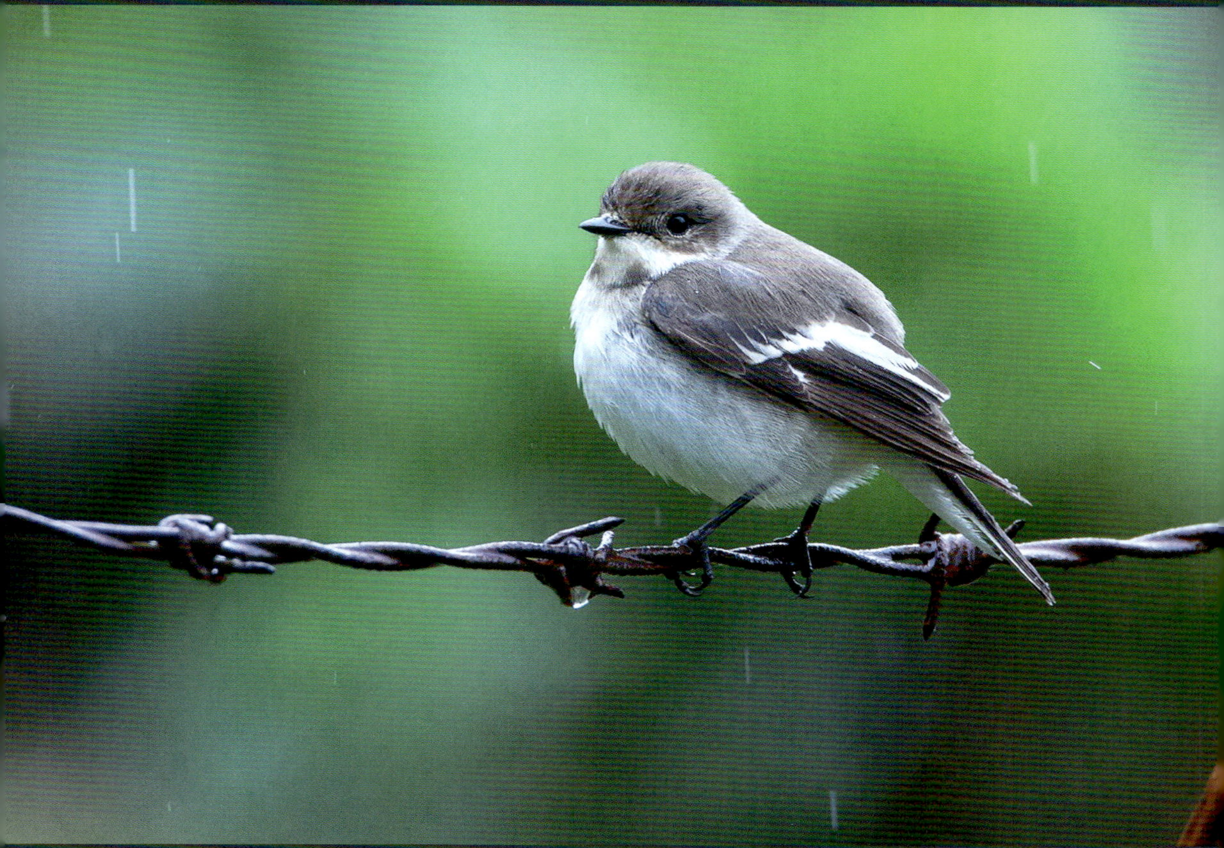

Female Pied Flycatcher

It is possible to spend more on photographic equipment than a quality car, but the most important piece of equipment is... the photographer themselves.

Camera equipment

Expensive equipment is not essential in wildlife photography. It will not help you find wildlife, and it will not guarantee good pictures, but there is no doubt that good equipment can make things easier and more comfortable. The equipment described below is what I have found to be the best, and something to aspire to – not something you must get. I name various manufacturers that I have used. Please note that I have no affiliation with any company mentioned.

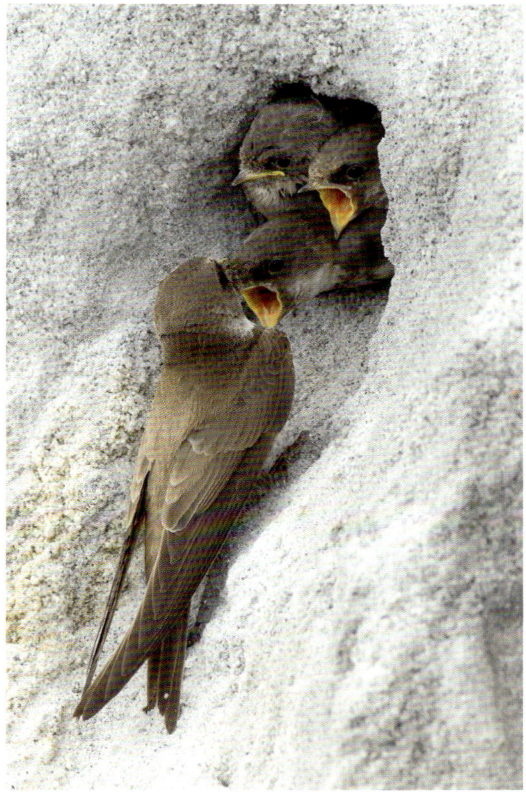

Sand Martin feeding chicks in a clay quarry, Devon

Tripods

Always employ a tripod if you can. However good you are at handholding, an image taken using a tripod will always be sharper, provided you hold the camera firmly, both to stop movement by the wind, and also to prevent vibrations from the mirror movement when the camera opens the shutter (unless you have a mirrorless camera). This is especially important when using a long lens. If you magnify a live image on the camera LCD screen, you will be horrified by how much the lens vibrates, even in a slight breeze. Put your hand over the body of the lens (avoiding the focusing ring) and press down firmly, bracing your arm over the tripod. Try taking the same shot with and without holding down the camera/lens combination to see the effect of vibrations. Avoid burst photography whenever possible, as this is another source of vibration, not to mention noise. A high shutter speed will help counteract the effects of camera/lens movement, but such speeds are not always practicable.

Although this may all seem obvious, from what I have seen many photographers often fail to realise the importance of these simple steps.

There are many sizes and types of tripod, but I would recommend carbon fibre as it is lighter. There are two main methods for adjusting the tripod leg, either lifting a catch or twisting a barrel on the legs. I prefer the twist action to release the tripod legs as it is much easier to adjust and can be done with one hand. Make sure the tripod is strong enough to support your camera and biggest lens, allowing some extra for those lenses you plan to buy in the future. Of course there are situations where you may not wish to use a tripod, such as when climbing mountains or when stalking dragonflies, but a good tripod is well worth the expense. The main brands are Manfrotto or Gitzo (now owned by the same company). There are cheaper makes, but a good quality tripod should last a lifetime, and spares will also be available.

Tripod heads

Ball head: There are many types of ball head, so it is important to choose one that fits your tripod and that you find easy to adjust. The advantage of a ball head is that it is much easier and quicker to rotate the camera to a suitable position. Ball heads are only suitable with shorter/medium focal length lenses, as the weight of longer lenses tends to cause them to overbalance the tripod, in my experience.

Gimbal head: These are more expensive than ball heads, but are necessary to carry the weight of long telephoto lenses. If used with quick-release plates, they are easy to handle. The big advantage of the gimbal head is the ease with which a heavy lens/camera combination can be moved in any plane. Gimbal heads can be bought from a variety of websites in the UK. I use the Wimberley. It is very expensive, but in my experience, worth the cost.

Cameras and lenses

There is a vast range of cameras to choose from, and they are continually being updated and improved. Select the best DSLR camera that you can afford and that has a good range of compatible high-quality lenses. You will probably keep good lenses for many years, whereas you may change or upgrade your camera several times. However, remember that once you have invested in lenses, you will find it very expensive to change to another brand of camera as you may have to change your lenses to be compatible as well.

I hope the section below on sensor size will dispel the myths surrounding the difference between full-frame cameras and those with smaller sensors. It is important to try to understand this, although it is a confusing subject, because it will affect your choice of camera. The choice of camera manufacturer should be driven by the quality of lenses they produce, as most of the top brands of camera are good. The leading manufacturers are Canon and Nikon, who also make high-quality lenses. These are expensive, although the greatest costs are attached to a telephoto lenses. The best site I have found for reviews of the cameras of these and other manufacturers is dpreview.com.

Mirrorless cameras are a relatively recent entry to the camera market. At the time of writing, there is not yet a great range of telephoto lenses, especially second hand, but this is an area you may wish to explore.

It is usually cheaper to buy cameras over the Internet, but for the more expensive cameras, it is advisable to see the camera first to be sure it is what you want. Most manufacturers have official stockists, which is a safer way to buy, especially as they are helpful and knowledgeable, but there are also some good camera shops around. If in doubt ask around or contact your local camera club for advice. Be wary of buying from ‘cheap’ sites as you may be buying an import that is not covered by warranty in the UK.

Flash

Flash may be required for the photography of nocturnal animals, but in that case should be used sparingly to avoid distress. However, flash is very useful when it comes to the photography of dragonflies and butterflies, as it gives much sharper images, and also reduces the unsatisfactory effect of high contrast in bright sun.

If you are some distance from the subject, a flash gun, either mounted on the camera, or off-camera and radio controlled, is more suitable. If you are closer to the subject, a ring flash will give better results, especially if the ring is in two sections which can be illuminated in different ratios.

Monopods

A monopod can be a good compromise between using a tripod and handholding the camera (but is not suitable for telephoto lenses as they will unbalance the monopod). They are useful, for instance, if you are photographing dragonflies or insects for long periods, as the support is welcome relief from handholding camera, lens and flash all day.

Beanbags

Beanbags are very useful for supporting a camera and lens, especially in situations where a tripod is not practical, such as when stalking or when using a car as a hide. They also offer an advantage in some public hides, especially those that do not have space for tripods or which have very narrow window slots. It is not necessary to buy anything expensive, as a small rectangular cushion cover filled with rice or beans will do the trick, although double beanbags shaped like saddlebags are better for use on car window frames.

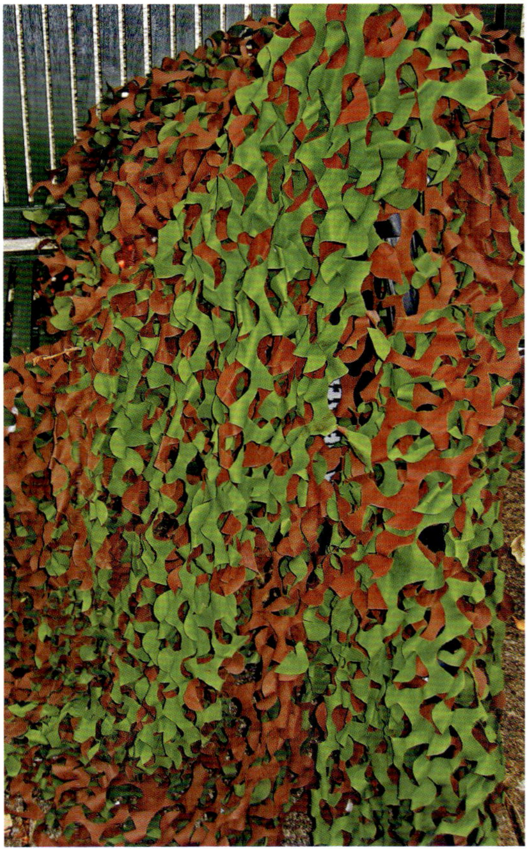

Seat and pigeon net camouflage

In other situations, a camera bag can be useful, especially if you want to minimise weight. I used my camera bag to the support camera and the telephoto lens when photographing Ptarmigan in the Cairngorms. I wanted to minimise weight as the trip entailed climbing several thousand feet up some steep slopes. Much of the time taking photographs was spent kneeling in the snow behind rocks, and a camera bag was as good as a beanbag would have been, but without the extra weight.

Fieldcraft equipment

Seat and pigeon net

Making yourself invisible to wildlife is an important part of wildlife photography. There are many cases where a low seat and camouflage cloth are sufficient, and this is the best method for short visits, especially if you want to move position at some point. It is also a very lightweight option.

I have used a small, three-legged stool and pigeon net with great success when photographing birds and even deer. The net is light, easily squashed into a camera bag and is very resilient. Provided you are very still, your quarry will not see you, and provided the wind is blowing towards you, they will not scent you either. Larger nets can be used to cover both you and your tripod if you want to stand, but in this case it is best to position yourself under a tree so that you appear to be part of the tree. I use Jack Pyke pigeon net (readily available from many places on the Internet). The net breaks up the outline of whatever is underneath, so if an animal looks at you, it will not recognise a human. In the image shown, the pigeon net hides the fact that it is covering a tripod and three large cushions on a garden bench. The best net is a different colour on each side, giving a more natural appearance.

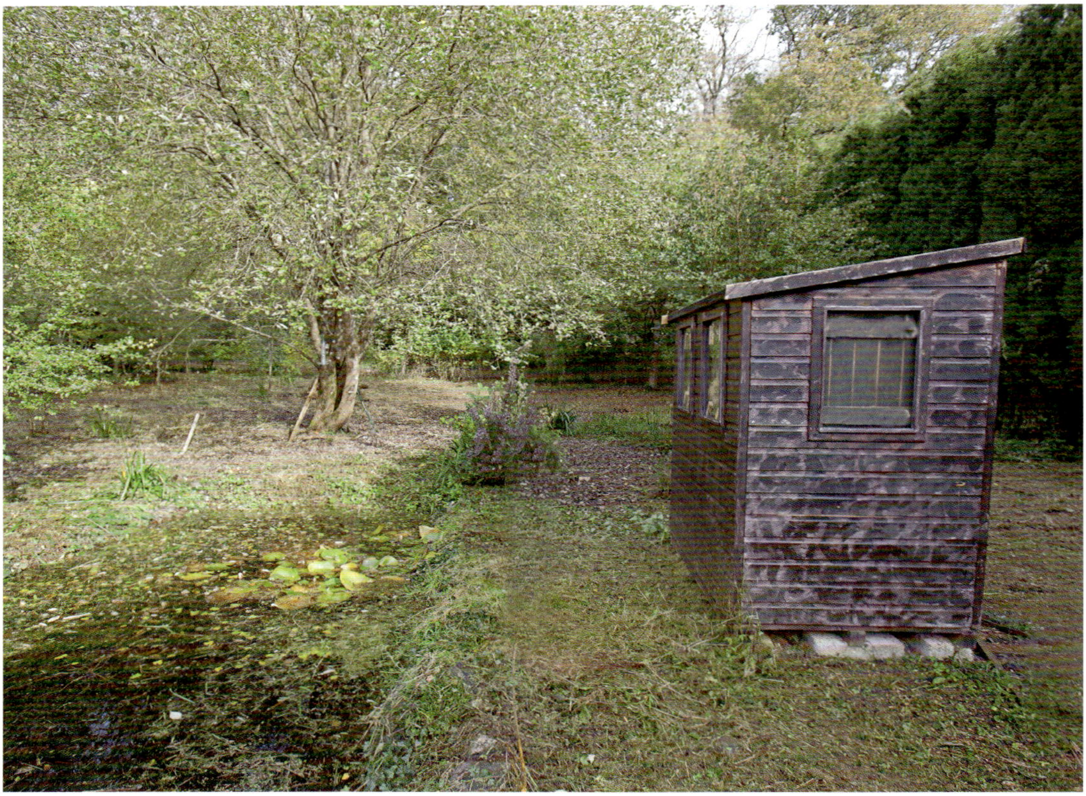

Basic shed hide

Hides

In most other situations, hides (or blinds, to use the American term) are by far the best option. You will be more comfortable, protected from the weather and able to move without being seen, provided your quarry is not too close. There are many types of hides, and the choice depends on the situation. At one time, public hides tended to be created for birders with binoculars and the dimensions were inconvenient for cameras, with the window slots being at the wrong height and/or too narrow. However, perhaps due to the increasing popularity of wildlife photography, hide design is often now more suitable for photography.

Wooden hides – for permanent positions

The photograph shows a wooden shed with the windows removed, leaving a wide gap ideal for tripods and giving long lenses plenty of room for movement.

A collection of feeders and perches is situated about 5 m from the hide, with a pond in between. This allows photography of birds on the perches, as well as when they are in or around the pond. It can also be used for mammals, but the large windows make it more difficult to conceal movement and to prevent the scent of humans from escaping.

I use wooden flaps to close the 'windows' when the hide is not in use, to stop rain entering. As an added precaution against rain I have also added perspex insets, held in place tightly by the flap. This design is suited for tripod use, and I use it for bird photography.

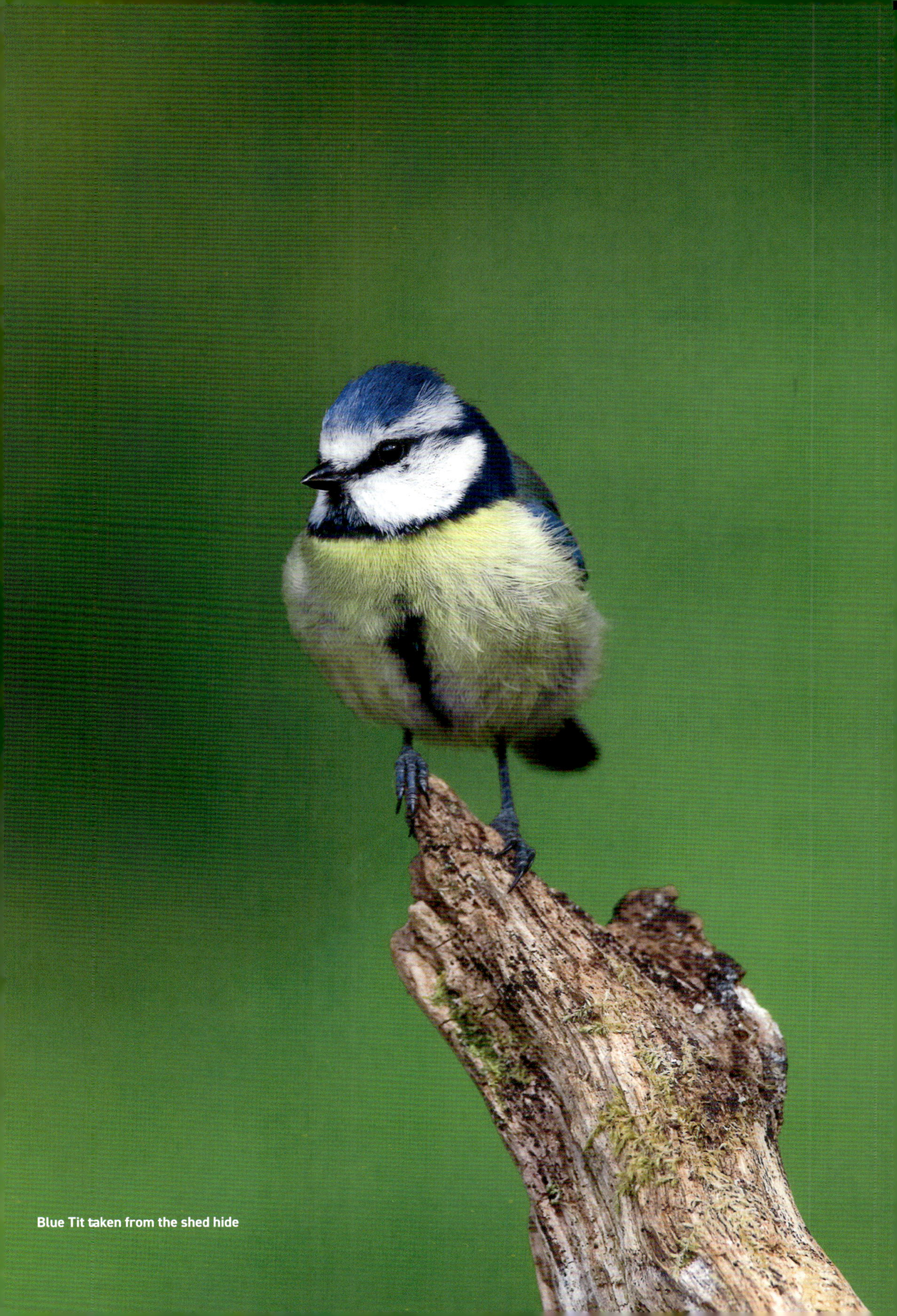

Blue Tit taken from the shed hide

The hides found in nature reserves tend to be high quality as they have to last for years. The roof usually slopes back so that water does not drip in front of the windows, and it also overhangs the viewing slots so that a camera lens stays dry in rain and is also less visible to birds from above. The hides usually have hinged opening windows held in place when open by a simple bolt or twist hinge method. The flaps fit tightly when closed and keep out rain, at least in the better built hides. These hides are more suitable for use with beanbags, and a shelf just below the slot opening is usually at the right height to be comfortable for leaning on when seated. Not all hides have the correct shelf or window height for a camera, so check first. The ideal measurement will vary depending on your height and the height of your seat. It is important that the distance below the opening will allow camera and lens on a beanbag to clear the slot, and still afford room for height adjustment. Public hides can often accommodate tripods, but they tend to be unpopular with other hide users as they take up a lot of space.

There is no reason why you should not commission such a hide from a reputable shed builder. You have to make sure that shelf height, window height and window opening height are correct. These measurements are critical, but will be different for different people, so if you go down this road, make sure the dimensions suit you. Visit a public hide and estimate what your ideal measurements should be.

Cup hooks above the slots can be used to hook on a pigeon net, which will conceal you and most of your camera but still allow you to see out of the slot. Make sure that the hide is made from treated wood so that it is protected from wet.

I had such a hide constructed and used it mainly for photographing mammals, as the narrower slots and use of beanbag minimise camera movement.

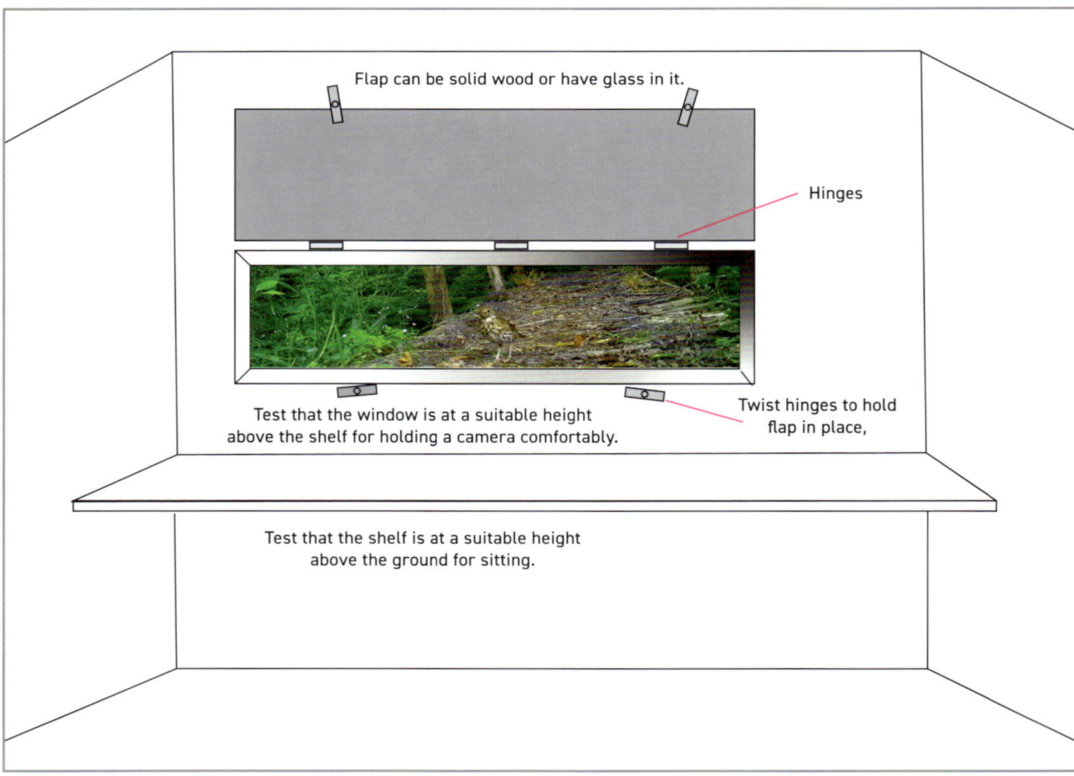

Inside a typical hide

I used this hide with shorter focal lengths, as the Badgers and Foxes came quite close. It is possible to have slots in the side walls or in the door to allow viewing in more directions or when using a tripod.

By chance I situated the hide near some horizontal branches on the edge of woodland, so as a bonus was able to use it for photographing Tawny Owls.

Cloth hides – for portability

These are suited to situations where the hide will be in position for some hours, days or weeks, as they need to be fixed to the ground with tent pegs to prevent them blowing away. There are many types: pop-up hides which are easy to erect but which can be very difficult to fold away again, despite the marketing claims; and hides that are more like small tents. The good quality ones are quite expensive and even the best can be rather cramped, as generally you cannot stand up in them; however, they will give many years of good reliable service, and it is possible to use a low seat for comfort. Cheaper hides will not last as long and may be so thin as to allow your shadow to be seen, which rather defeats the purpose of having a hide.

Car hides – for simplicity

A car makes an excellent hide in areas where there are handily placed car parks, and makes use of the fact that birds generally ignore cars. The simplest method is to lower the car door window, rest a beanbag on the car door and place the camera on top with the lens pointing out. The only precaution necessary in most cases is to avoid sudden lens movements, although hanging some pigeon net across the gap may be helpful for sensitive wildlife. If you have an old car, you might even consider removing the passenger seat, so that you can sit in the well and be even less visible, but that would only be necessary for very sensitive wildlife. A simple beanbag can be used, but for long lenses, the greater security of a saddle-shaped beanbag may be preferred. It is also possible to buy more expensive window mounts, but the cost is only justified if you intend to use this kit a great deal.

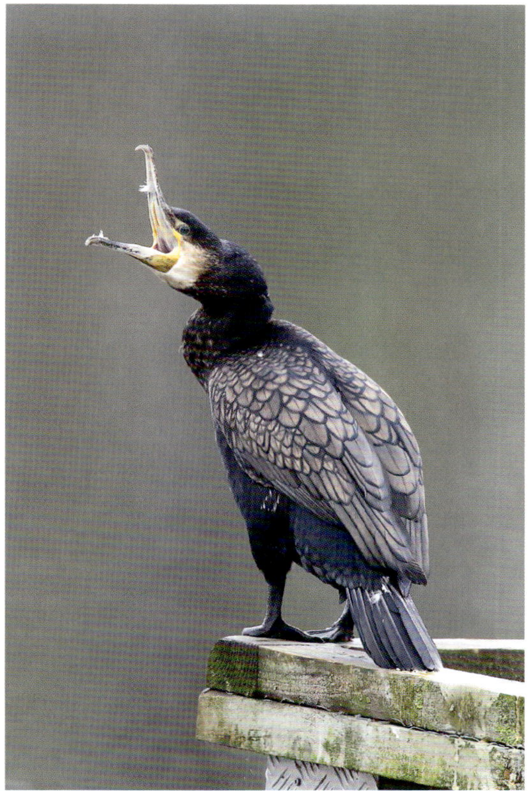

Cormorant – hides allow closer access to wildlife

Portable pipe hides – for flexibility

These hides are made by building a framework of thick-walled PVC pipes and covering it either with pigeon net or with a camouflage cover, which you sew yourself. I discovered these after a trip to America and had to carry out extensive Internet research to find a UK supplier at the time. There are several advantages to this type of hide: they can be made to a variety of sizes; they are more flexible than a fixed wooden hide; they are easy to put up and take down again. These 'furniture-grade' pipes and fittings are not made in the UK and are imported from the USA, but they can be obtained from several UK online suppliers, and are still cheaper than the other options, as well as being very flexible in design. The pipes, which are easy to cut, are joined by PVC connectors and can either be glued together for a permanent but easily portable structure, or left unglued and taken apart when required. I know someone who uses the pipes for a fruit cage when not in use as a hide.

Making a portable hide

There are many methods for making hides, but thick-walled PVC tubing gives a lightweight yet strong structure. There are various diameters from 0.5 inch upwards, but 0.75 inch is a good compromise between strength and weight. (As the pipe is imported from the USA, diameters are in inches not cm.)

Diameter dimensions are in inches, but the pipe is sold in 1.25 m and 2.5 m lengths. This hide is lightweight, but still too heavy to carry long distances. It is very quick to assemble. The pipe is designed for use in structures and so is thick-walled and rigid. Connectors can be obtained with the pipe. The size of the hide is a matter of preference, but assume width and depth are X m, and height Y m.

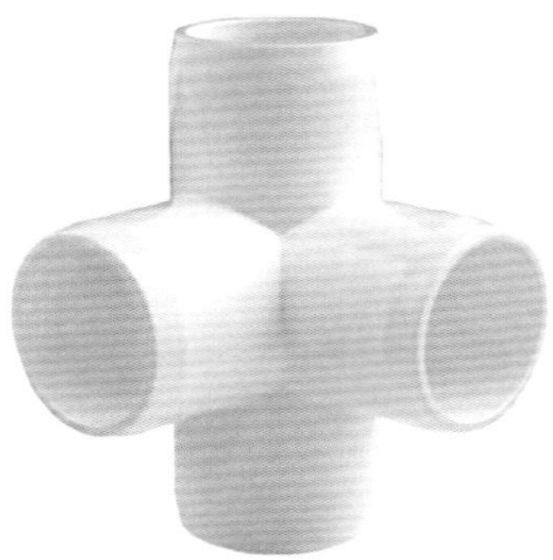

Four-way elbow connector

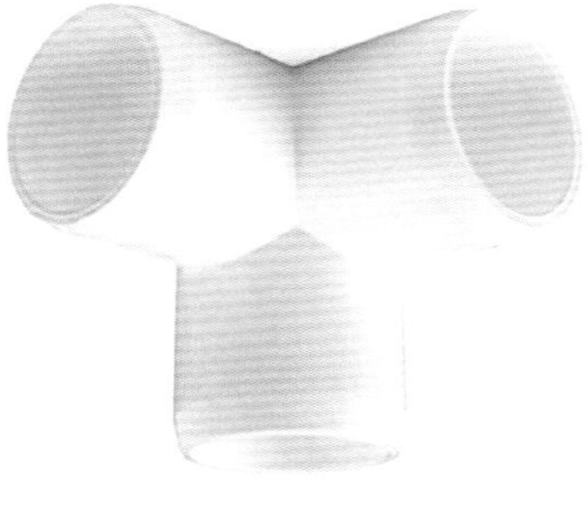

Three-way elbow connector

Instructions

- Cut eight pipes of length X m, diameter 0.75 inches.
- Cut four pipes of length Y m, diameter 0.75 inches.
- Connect up the four base pipes, length X, using four-way elbow connectors, diameter 0.75 inches. The structure will rest on these and not on the pipe, which makes it easier to sit it in a level position on rough ground.
- Connect up the four top pipes, length X, using three-way elbow connectors, diameter 0.75 inches.
- Connect the height bars, length Y, to the base then add the top.
- The frame can be secured using tent pegs if required.

Example

If you want to build a 0.75 inch pipe hide of 1 m square base and 1.25 m in height, you will need:

- Eight 1 m lengths of 0.75 inch pipe for top and bottom
- Four 1.25 m lengths of 0.75 inch pipe for the sides
- Four three-way elbow connectors, diameter 0.75 inches for the top
- Four four-way elbow connectors, diameter 0.75 inches for the base.

For a semi-permanent position, the base bars can be filled with sand for stability. For a permanent structure, PVC glue may be used. The structure will still be moveable if glued together.

Add the cover.

The cover consists of a rectangle 4X + 8 cm long (includes seams), and Y + 8 cm wide, for the sides of the cover. For the roof, cut a square X + 8 cm wide and X + 8 cm long.

Portable pipe hide

The hide is made from 4 vertical and 8 horizontal pipes, 4 three-way connectors and 4 four-way connectors.

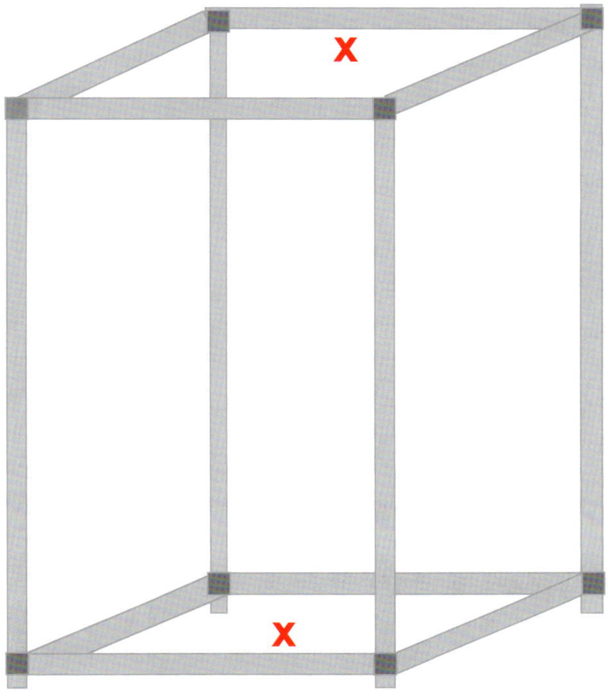

In the example above, 4X + 8 = 408 cm (4.08 m), X + 8 =108 cm (1.08 m) and Y + 8 = 133 cm (1.33 m).

Any camouflage material will do, with lightweight showerproof material being easier to work and more suitable than heavy camouflage twill, as well as being much cheaper. The best source for such camouflage material is eBay.

- Fold under and stitch 4 cm at each end of the rectangle (i.e. on the Y + 8 cm sides).
- Fold under and stitch 4 cm along the bottom edge of the rectangle.
- Pin the top length of the rectangle round the edges of the roof, starting in the middle of one side of the roof, and put over the hide frame.
- Mark the ideal position for the window opening.
- Remove the cover and cut out the window.

Cover for pipe hide

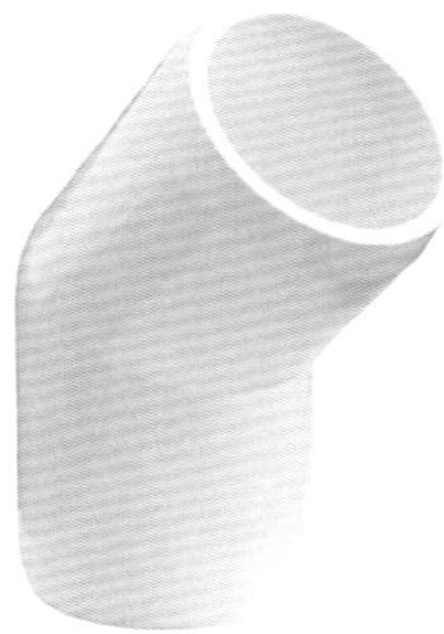

45° angled connector

- Turn under and sew the window edges to prevent fraying.
- Sew the long rectangle to the edges of the roof square.
- The entrance should be in the middle of one of the sides, with the window on the opposite side
- If needed, use velcro to attach net across the top of the window opening.
- For stability, attach loops to the cover at the top edges, and attach cord for guy ropes.
- Add loops to the bottom of the cover. The loops can be hooked over tent pegs.

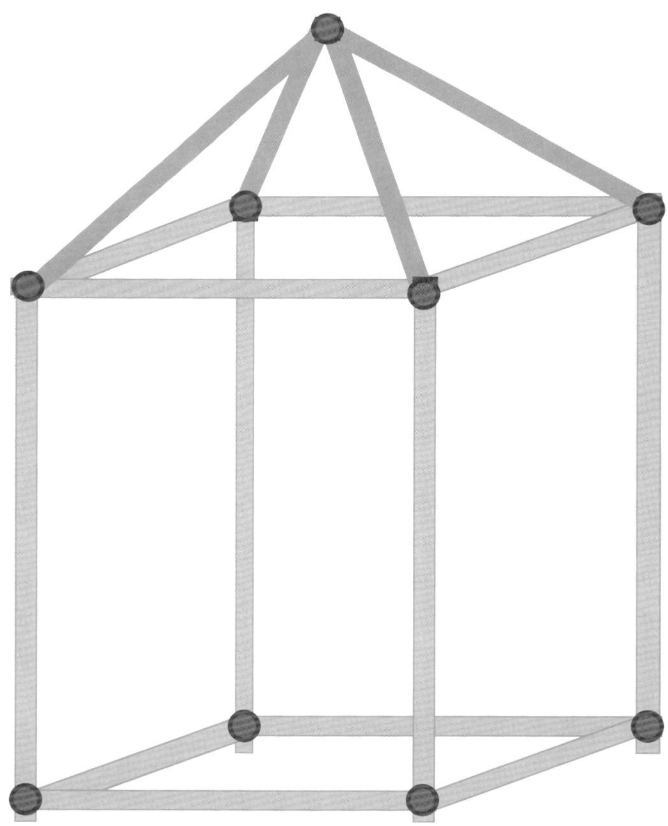

Pipe hide with pitched roof

A pitched roof can be added using 4 additional tubes, 4 angled connectors fitted to 4 four-way connectors (to replace the top connectors) and glueing the 4 pipes at the top.

Using a net cover

Instead of a cover, camouflage net, such as Jack Pyke pigeon net, can be used. The net can be held in place with snap clamp fixings available from the pipe manufacturer, though they are best cut in half for easy use. This is a quick and easy option, but the net will not hide movement or keep in human scent as well as a solid cover.

If you intend leaving the hide outside, it is a good idea to remove the cover and only fit it when you use the hide. This will prevent water from collecting on the fabric roof. Alternatively, you could fashion a sloping roof from pipe, attach a cover to it, then fit it on top of the hide. The range of connectors may make that tricky, but one suggestion is:

- change the top three-way elbow connectors for four-way elbow connectors;
- connect 45° angled connectors to the top of each of the four-way connectors and turn them to point to the centre;
- connect the premade roof to the angled connectors.

Trail cameras

One of the most useful pieces of equipment for fieldwork is the trail camera. There are several different types, with Bushnell being the best known, but all photograph animals (and indeed humans!) automatically when triggered. The trigger is usually a heat sensor in the camera which detects changes in the heat pattern when animals move, starts up the camera and records a video or takes a photograph.

Trail cameras usually work using visible light during the day, and infrared light at night, the latter giving a black and white image. Initially, trail cameras were deployed in hunting, especially of deer, and originated in the USA. Nowadays, they are utiltised by ecologists to detect and monitor the presence of wildlife.

For the wildlife photographer, they are useful at showing the time of day that wildlife is present, and especially whether it is present at all. This can greatly reduce the time spent looking for wildlife. Care should be taken with the camera location as they can be a target for thieves, although it is possible to use brackets or padlock cables to fix the camera to a tree or similar to reduce the risk of theft.

Image quality is very variable as you do not have much control over exposure or composition, and the internal camera is relatively simple, so this technology is best used to signify the presence of wildlife rather than as a method of obtaining high-quality wildlife images.

High-speed photography

If high-quality automatic images are what you want, it is possible to buy triggering devices that attach to your camera and which automatically take a picture when a beam (such as a pen laser or infrared beam) is broken by wildlife passing through. It is possible to obtain high-quality images this way, and it is especially useful for birds in flight. The devices can be left unattended for short periods as long as the camera and equipment are protected from the weather and safe from thieves.

Automatic triggering with a separate camera is a big subject with specialised techniques, so any further detail is beyond the scope of this book. Devices available at present are Stopshot or MIOPS.

CCTV

If you wish to move into taking videos of wildlife, CCTV has many advantages. It is a much cheaper medium than the DSLR camera, and takes high-quality videos at night as well as during the day, unlike trail cameras. There is a huge range of equipment due to the size of the CCTV security market, although this can make choice difficult. Possibly the greatest advantage is that the cameras are weatherproof and can be left outside for long periods. The greatest disadvantage is that for subjects in the wild, battery power is required.

I have been using CCTV for some years, mainly for conservation monitoring, and now take far fewer still photographs.

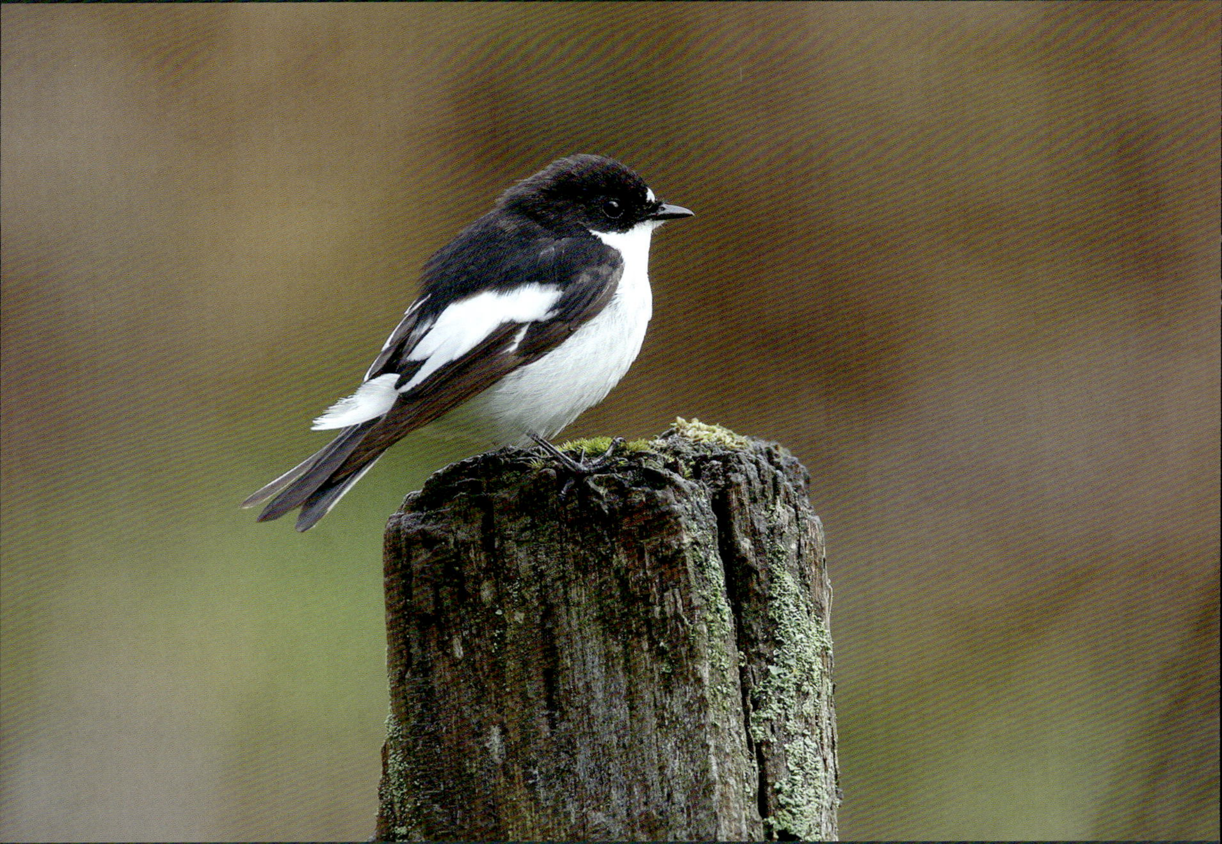

Male Pied Flycatcher

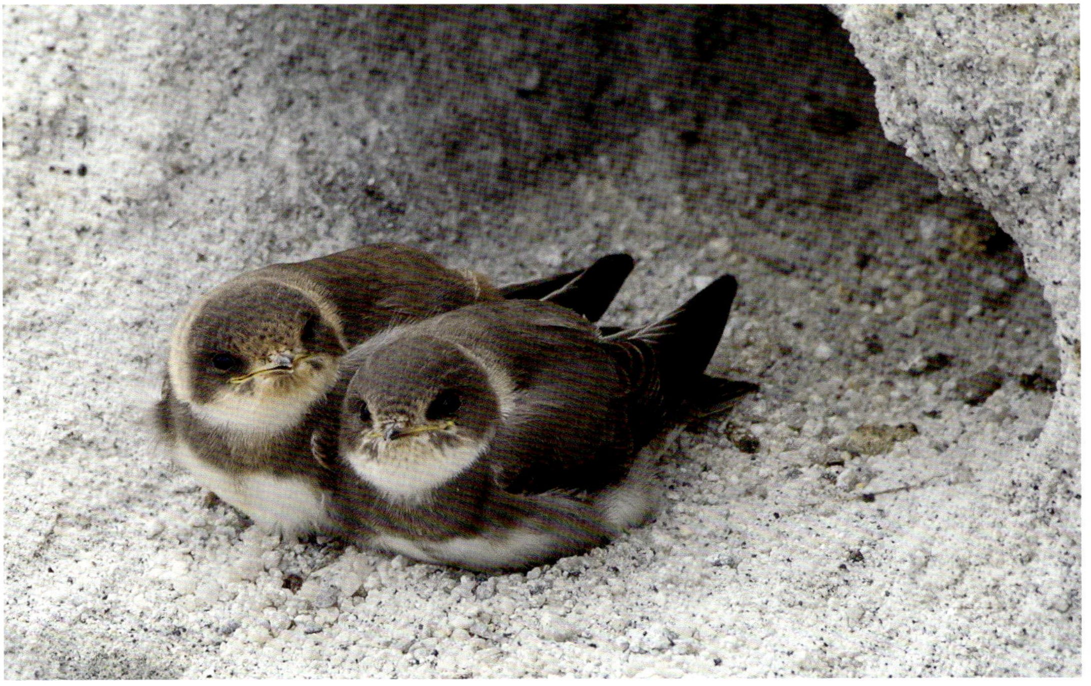

Sand Martin chicks

Most books on wildlife photography emphasise equipment and post-processing in Photoshop or equivalent software. I believe, however, that the cameras of today are capable of producing very good images, and very little work should be required after taking the shot if it is done well.

For the new photographer

Wildlife photography is particularly problematic for the new photographer, as not only have field techniques to be learned, but the basic requirement for a telephoto lens is costly. It is unlikely you would want to spend £8,000 or more on a prime 500 mm lens until you were sure that wildlife photography was for you. Zoom lenses which extend to 300 or 400 mm are cheaper, especially if you can get them second hand, but it will limit you with the photography of small birds. Using a portable hide can help to get closer to the birds, and can be helpful, but for serious bird photography, quality lenses are a must.

In the beginning...

There is a tremendous learning curve with digital photography, but it is not as complex as the camera manuals can make it appear, since many of the features of digital cameras are not absolutely necessary. Below are the main points only, as there are many tutorials on the Internet that will explain the basic terms. The important things to know as far as wildlife photography goes are:

- Make sure you understand what exposure is and how it depends on aperture and shutter speed.
- Aperture priority is the most useful mode, so make sure you know how to select that on your camera.
- Make sure you know how to change the aperture and that you understand depth of field.
- ISO in a digital camera is an electronic function to amplify the reading created by light hitting the sensor (similar to turning up the volume). When the aperture is fixed (say at f/5.6), increasing ISO is the best way to increase shutter speed, so make sure you know how to increase ISO. Experiencing noisy images will show you if you have overdone it.
- Use a tripod and avoid handholding the camera. Make sure the camera is firmly fixed to the tripod (seems obvious but it is easy to make mistakes).
- Make sure to hold the camera and lens combination very firmly.
- In the beginning it is easier to copy other photographers' aperture and ISO values for similar situations. The end of this section lists the main photographs in this book and gives the camera values used.
- Start off with easier subjects, such as garden birds, or animals in wildlife centres.
- Don't be intimidated by photographers with a great deal of expensive gear. It does not guarantee they will be better than you.
- Remember that the keen amateur photographer with lots of time can often achieve more with rare animals than a time-strapped professional photographer.

For the more experienced

This book does not intend to provide a detailed manual on digital photography, but I include the fundamentals below, based on using Photoshop. The tendency today seems to be to take a shot then process it heavily in Photoshop. This is not to be recommended, as not all errors can be corrected and it is bad practice. Try to get as much right as possible before pressing the shutter: this includes holding the tripod firmly; testing exposure and focusing; carefully choosing equipment; and selecting the correct camera settings.

Before taking the shot

If you are careful before you take the photograph, minimal processing will be required. If you have to spend a great deal of time improving an image in Photoshop, then perhaps the image is not worth saving.

RAW files

Most cameras have the facility to photograph in RAW, and this is to be recommended unless you only wish to produce snapshot-size photographs. Detail is lost if the file is in JPEG format, making it more difficult to produce images of the size and quality requested by magazines and image libraries. Even if you do not have such ambitions now, it is, I believe, important to aim for the highest quality possible each time. A super high-quality image will also help to futureproof your work, ensuring that the photographs will still look good for many years to come.

Aperture

Aperture size is of great importance in wildlife photography, and aperture priority is frequently the most suitable mode. Large apertures are often required, partly to give a suitably low depth of

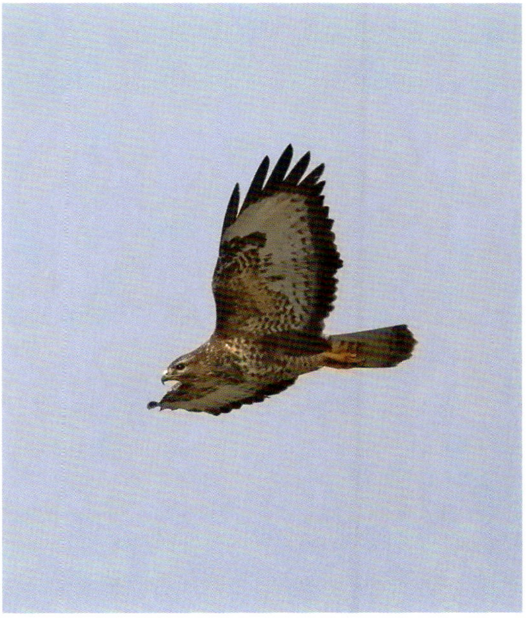

Spot metering (bird of prey on the Isle of Mull)

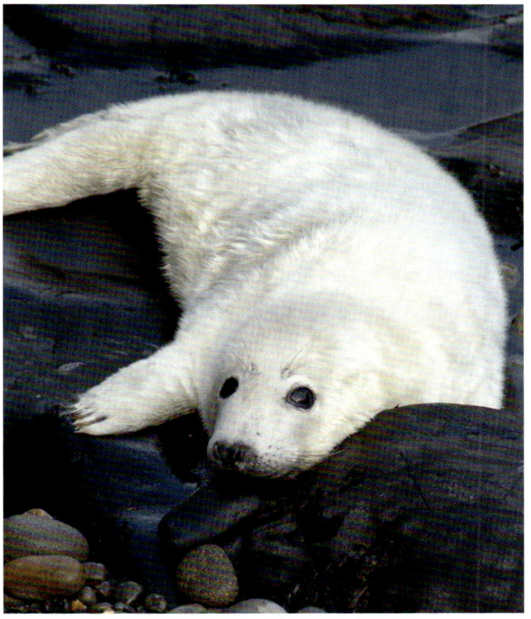

Partial metering (Grey Seal pup)

field – important for making the subject stand out clearly from the background – and partly to ensure a high shutter speed. This is highly necessary, as most wildlife tends to move! A typical aperture for a 500 mm lens is f/5.6.

Shutter Speed

Shutter speeds of greater than 1/250 s are required to freeze motion, although much higher speeds are recommended for fast-moving subjects.

ISO

ISO increases the sensitivity of the sensor by amplifying the signal, but it also amplifies noise. A typical low noise value of ISO is 200 to 400. The newer cameras have excellent noise-reduction electronics, allowing much higher ISOs, but it is still better to use as low an ISO as the light conditions allow.

Exposure metering mode

You can usually adjust your camera so that it meters the correct exposure from part or all of the view. Different cameras have different terms and symbols, but do much the same job. Take care to read your camera manual for information on how your camera deals with metering and focusing. With some, half-pressing the shutter will fix exposure and focusing, with others it will not.

Spot metering is best when the subject is a small part of the view. Check your camera manual to see if half pressing the shutter fixes the exposure when using this setting, as it may only fix the focus.

Partial Metering is best when the subject is larger. This weights exposure calculations to the central 10–20% of the view. Use if there is a large difference in brightness between the subject and the background.

Evaluative metering is best when the subject takes up a large part of the frame. Use if the brightness of the scene is reasonably uniform, as in this shot of a Chiffchaff. Exposure is metered and averaged over the whole scene.

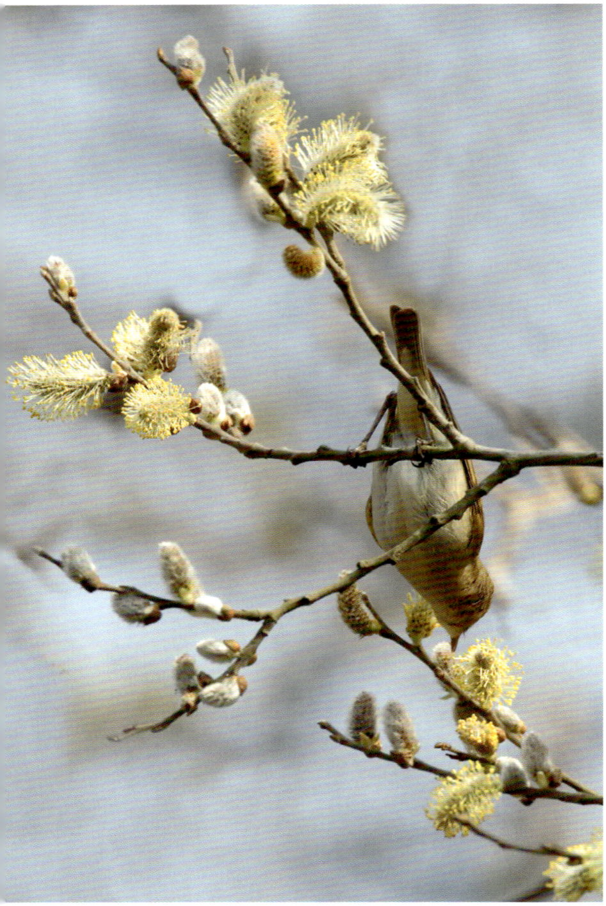

Evaluative metering (Chiffchaff on willow)

Using the Histogram

Most DSLR cameras show a histogram on the LCD screen once an image has been taken.

If, for example, the image has been overexposed, the histogram will be pushed to the right and you should try reducing exposure compensation, by about −1EV.

Different cameras will achieve exposure compensation in slightly different ways, so once again, study your camera manual.

Focus mode

Even more important than exposure metering is focusing. Most DSLRs allow you to select focus points, that is the point or area of the subject that the camera actually focuses on. Read your manual carefully to find out how to do this, as it is different for different makes of camera. In very difficult situations, such as when the subject and background are close to each other, manual focusing may be the easiest. This is achieved on DSLRs by making the adjustment from AF to MF on the lens. Compact, mirror or bridge cameras will have a different method, if they allow it at all.

Moving objects

The normal mode for DSLR cameras is Single Shot; in other words, one image is taken when the shutter is pressed.

You may also have a mode for moving objects. This may be called AI servo or similar and is only available with automatic focusing. With AI servo, focusing and exposure will constantly change when the shutter is half pressed, and are only finally fixed when the shutter is fully pressed. However, if the moving object is small, it can be easier to switch to manual focus, otherwise the image may go out of focus just when you are about to press the shutter, especially if the object is moving quickly.

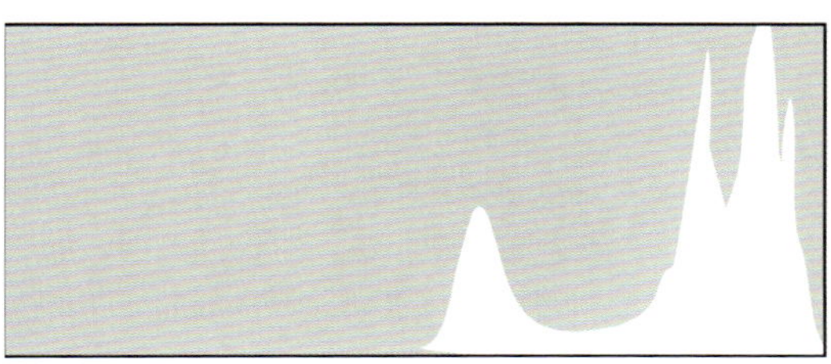

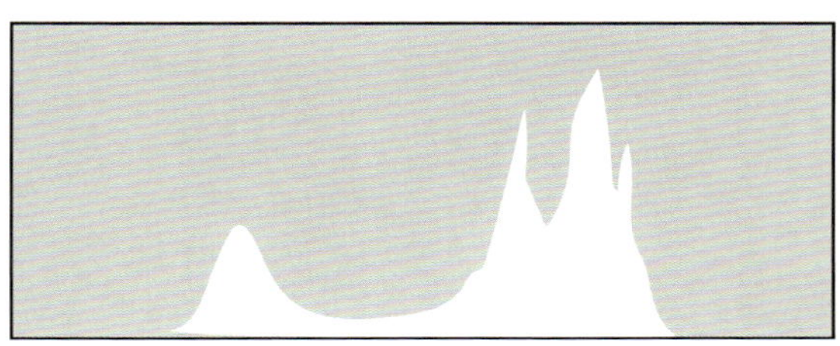

Exposure histograms, the one on the left is overexposed

Burst mode

This mode seems very popular with wildlife photographers, and entails taking several shots with one press of the shutter. However, it shakes the camera and makes accurate focusing between shots more difficult, with the result that the images are not always as sharp as they should be – but most of all it makes a dreadful noise: not loud by human standards, but deafening and very disturbing to wildlife. There are very few occasions when burst mode is essential, and those are mostly concerned with the photography of a sequence of images of fast-moving subjects.

Lens use

Choosing the correct lens to take with you when going into the field can be a nightmare. Just about every photographer will say at some time 'I had the wrong lens, so couldn't get the picture'. When I first started photography, I found this aspect very difficult. Nowadays, I find it easier to target a particular species and take the most suitable lens for that. For example:

- A 500 mm lens plus extender is essential for much bird photography, especially if the birds are small.
- A 100–400 mm lens is good for just about every other situation, especially if a lot of walking is required. I usually take a 1.4× extender as well.
- A 100 mm or 180 mm macro lens I find best for dragonflies and butterflies or insects.

Some photographers take everything with them wherever they go. That may work for you, but to me it signifies lack of intent when going into the field. Even if something different goes by, you are unlikely to have time to change lenses anyway, as wildlife is usually quick to disappear!

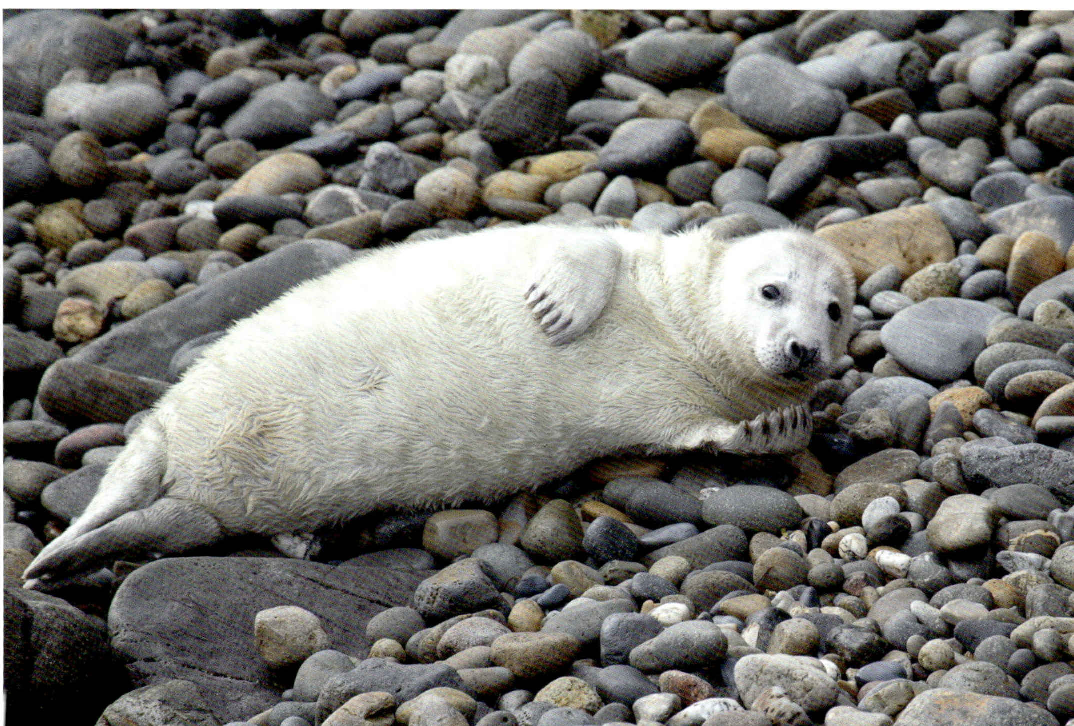

Two-week-old Grey Seal pup, Ramsey Island, Wales

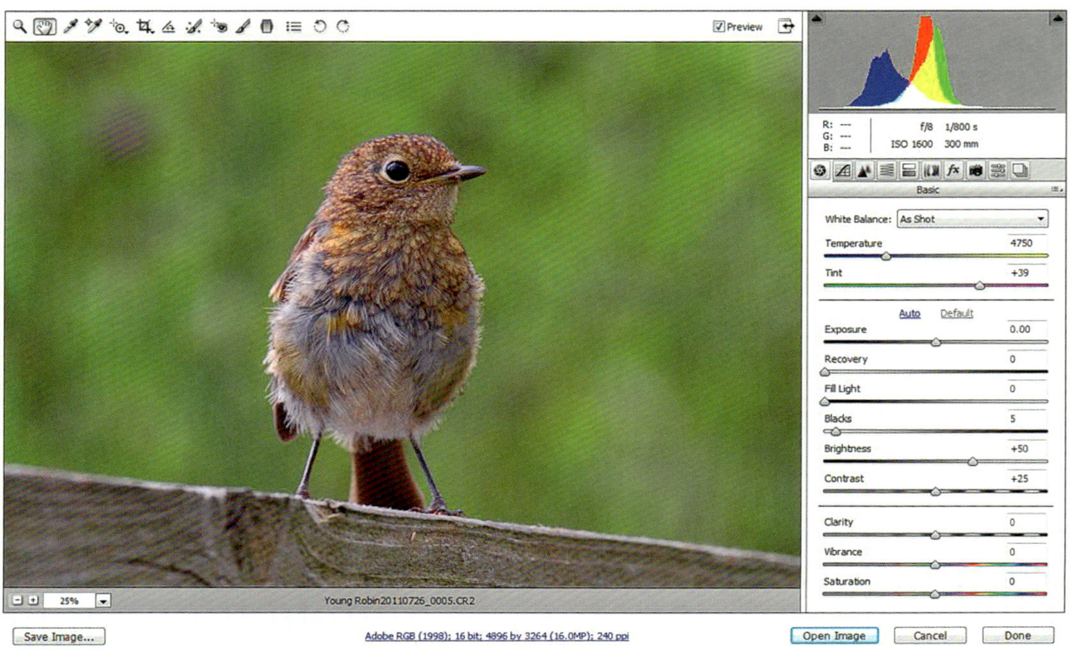

An example of RAW image processing

Basic processing in Photoshop

JPEG files are fine for snaps, but if you want to produce images of high quality, you should take images in RAW and process them in the software that came with your camera.

If images are in RAW, then Adobe Bridge, Photoshop or the equivalent post-processing software will automatically open them in the correct mode for processing. Each software program will have different screens and use different terms, but the processes will be similar. The main steps to carry out are:

- Adjust the Exposure slider so that the image is bright without the histogram edge being too close to the right.
- Adjust Blacks if shadow areas are too dark or not dark enough. Ensure the histogram edge is not too far to the left.
- Adjust Fill light to lighten areas that are too dark
- Adjust Recovery if highlights are too bright
- Make small changes in Contrast and Brightness if required, then Open the image and Crop if required.

You can do much more in Photoshop using adjustment layers for levels, curves, brightness, contrast, saturation etc., but if the image was correctly exposed, all you should need to do is a little sharpening.

Images can be saved in various formats. I usually save in TIF format (which is not compressed), although this makes for very large files.

Before you upgrade your camera....

Sensor size and magnification

There is a great deal of confusion over the effects of sensor size on image size. I have often heard people talk about the 'magnifying effect' of smaller sensors and the fact that one can obtain the same image size as a full-frame sensor but using a lens of shorter focal length. The truth is much more complicated, depending as it does on pixel density as well as sensor size and quality.

If a bird, say, is photographed with a full-frame camera (blue line) and a smaller sensor camera (red line), from the same distance, with the same lens, the subject in the smaller sensor (APS-C) camera will appear larger in the viewfinder.

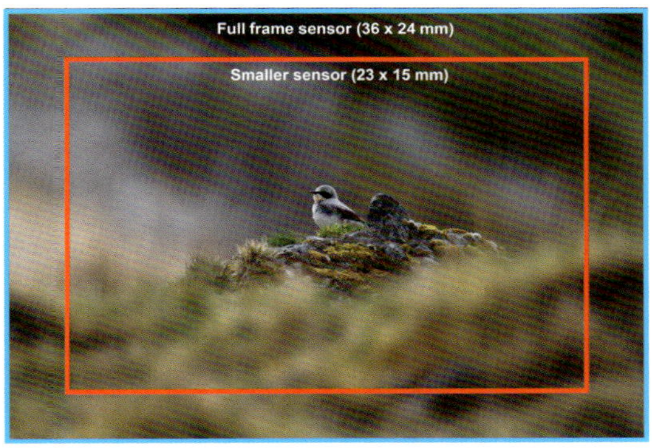

Comparison of image size for a full-frame sensor and a smaller sensor

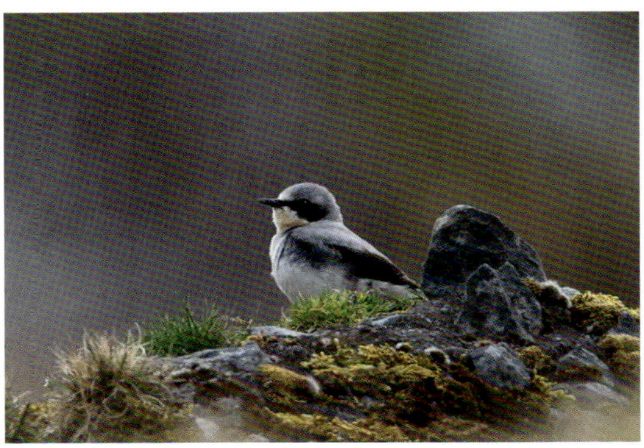

Cropped image

If I cropped the image with the full-frame sensor to show the same view as that of the smaller sensor camera (i.e. cropped to the red line), the image from each camera would be identical in size when printed (assuming each has the same pixel density). The only apparent advantage of the smaller sensor camera would be that the image of the bird would appear larger in the viewfinder and possibly easier to focus on. In the photograph here, the bird is a small part of the frame and this might be an advantage.

This particular image, however, is not a good composition as there is too much uninteresting background which detracts from the main subject. Further cropping is required but this gives a small image.

In reality, things are complicated by the fact that APS-C cameras tend to have smaller sensors which receive less light and there is a higher propotion of 'noise' (spurious signals). In general, larger sensors have a much better signal-to-noise ratio and thus better quality images. Different cameras have different pixel densities, so the difference in quality would vary from camera to camera.

If the aim is to print the above image, it would need to be enlarged by resampling. If the size of the final images in Photoshop were resampled or 'rezzed up', the final image from the full-frame camera would show much less noise than the final image from the smaller sensor camera.

But be aware: because smaller pixels have a lower signal-to-noise ratio, the image from the smaller sensor camera will have more noise and the detail would be degraded, which would be apparent when enlarging the final composition by resampling, and the image from the smaller sensor may have to be printed smaller to hide this degradation.

In other cases, I might not want a large image of a bird, and might want more background, and a full-frame camera gives me the facility to crop in different ways.

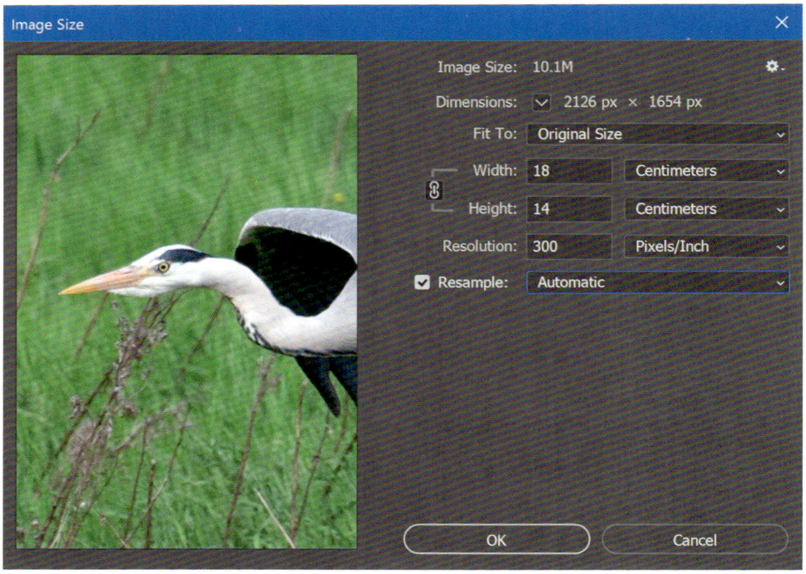

Initial image size

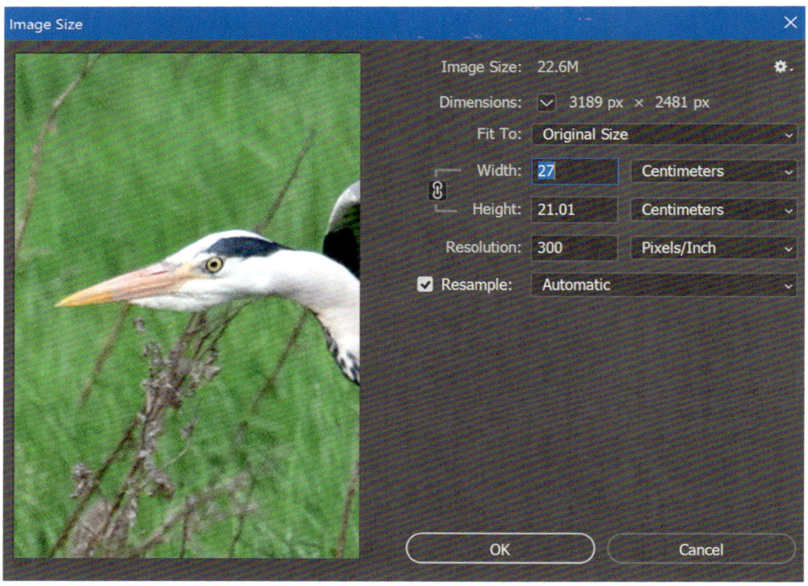

The previous image 'rezzed up'

It is impossible to generalise, as sensors vary from one camera to another, but the major manufacturers are moving towards full-frame sensors with their high-end cameras.

Another, similar, confusion arises from the megapixel count of a camera. 'Surely more pixels means more detail?' I have been asked. The answer is: perhaps, but it depends on the quality of the sensor. However, the major camera manufacturers have realised that pixel quality matters a great deal, and some have even slightly reduced the pixel count of their full-frame cameras, putting quality of detail first.

Rezzing up an image

The heron image was cropped and so was rather small. If printed at 300 ppi the print would be 18 cm wide. The measurement pixels per inch is abbreviated to ppi and relates to how the printer presents the image. When printing images, 300 ppi is generally taken to be the highest resolution that the eye can resolve, i.e. at which it can determine individual pixels. Thus, a typical photographic print – if reproduced at or smaller than the size of the original file – at 300 ppi will appear to be detailed. Lower ppi measurements will show less detail and be perceived as of lower quality. In this case, the image was high resolution to start with, and the 'rezzed up' image would be larger but could still be printed at high quality even though the pixel count has been enlarged digitally and does not represent more actual detail.

To do this, I check the 'Resample' box to change the size to suit. It is best if Width and Height are linked (as shown), so that the image is scaled up properly without size distortion.

If I 'rez up' the images in Photoshop, the printed image could, for instance, be 27 cm wide. The number of pixels appear to have been increased from 2,126 × 1,654 to 3,189 × 2,481. This is only as far as the printer is required, as of course you cannot increase the actual number of pixels in the sensor.

Note: The 'rez up' boxes above select a section of the image for adjusment and do not show the whole of the image.

Images and their camera values

This section lists the main images in the book together with their camera data, shown in the order they appear. This is of most use to the less experienced photographer. Photographs were taken in Devon, except where specified. All images are copyright of the author, and were taken with either a Canon 1D MKIV or a Canon 1Ds MKIII.

Table 6.1 Camera values

Cover and prelims

IMAGE	LENS FOCAL LENGTH (mm)	APERTURE	SHUTTER SPEED (s)	ISO	COMMENTS
Front cover. Red Squirrel	500	f/4.5	1/80	640	Cairngorms
Frontispiece: Young Roebuck	500+1.4×	f/5.6	1/160	1,250	
Preface: Tiger Swallowtail	180	f/16	1/250	200	flash used
0.1 Blue Tits	500+1.4×	f/5.7	1/500	200	
0.2 Coot chick in reeds	500+1.4×	f/5.7	1/125	400	

Chapter 1

IMAGE	LENS FOCAL LENGTH (mm)	APERTURE	SHUTTER SPEED (s)	ISO	COMMENTS
1.1 Heron takes off	500+1.4×	f/11	1/1,600	2,000	Wales
1.2 Chiffchaff	500	f/5.6	1/250	400	
1.3 Chaffinch in rain	500	f/5.6	1/320	400	Cairngorms
1.4 Curious Robin	500+1.4×	f/5.6	1/640	400	
1.5 Great Crested Grebe dance	500+1.4×	f/6.3	1/640	200	

IMAGE	LENS FOCAL LENGTH (mm)	APERTURE	SHUTTER SPEED (s)	ISO	COMMENTS
1.6 Great Crested Grebe pair	500+1.4×	f/6.3	1/2,000	400	
1.7 Grebe carrying nest material	500+1.4×	f/5.6	1/640	400	
1.8 Grebe pair at nest	500+1.4×	f/5.6	1/320	640	
1.9 Grebe feeding young	500+1.4×	f/6.3	1/1,000	400	
1.10 Coots and chicks	500+1.4×	1/5.7	1/160	640	
1.11 Coot with young on nest	500+1.4×	f/8.0	1/100	640	
1.12 Dipper with food	500+1.4×	f/5.6	1/250	2,500	
1.13 Young Grey Wagtail	500+1.4×	f/6.3	1/250	3,200	
1.14 Redstart	500+1.4×	f/5.6	1/2,000	800	Wales
1.15 Great Spotted Woodpecker on log feeder	500+1.4×	f/5.6	1/320	400	
1.16 Great Spotted Woodpecker on power pole	500+1.4×	f/8	1/2,000	400	
1.17 Capercaillie	190	f/5.6	1/160	640	Cairngorms
1.18 Linnet	500+1.4×	f/5.6	1/2,000	400	
1.19 Long-tailed Tit	500	f/5.6	1/1,600	800	
1.20 Yellowhammer	500+1.4×	f/5.6	1/3,200	400	
1.21 Male Wheatear	500+1.4×	f/5.6	1/2,000	400	
1.22 Wheatear at nest hole	500+1.4×	f/8	1/400	400	Wales
1.23 Puffin	560	f/9	1/2,000	640	Shetland
1.24 Curlew	500+2×	f/8	1/400	400	Dawlish Warren, Devon
1.25 Choughs on a cliff	400	f/5.6	1/400	400	Wales
1.26 Heron with outstretched wings	500+1.4×	f/5.6	1/2,500	400	
1.27 Little Egret preening	500+2×	f/8	1/1,000	400	
1.28 Great Egret	500+2×	f/13	1/250	400	

IMAGE	LENS FOCAL LENGTH (mm)	APERTURE	SHUTTER SPEED (s)	ISO	COMMENTS
1.29 Sanderlings	500+2×	f/5.6	1/2,500	640	
1.30 Barn Owl	100	f/16	1/40	250	Barn Owl Trust
1.34 Osprey with fish	400+1.4×	f/11	1/8,000	3,200	Cairngorms
1.39 Buzzard on alert	500+1.4×	f/5.6	1/1,000	400	
1.40 Unsteady Buzzard fledgling	500+1.4×	f/5.6	1/160	1,000	
1.41 Buzzard in flight	500+1.4×	f/5.6	1/400	640	
1.43 Kestrel with prey	500	f/4	1/400	400	
1.44 Kestrel	500+1.4×	f/8	1/4,000	1,000	Cairngorms (captive bird)
1.45 Peregrine	500	f/4.5	1/320	800	Cairngorms (captive bird)
1.46 Osprey at nest	400+1.4×	f/11	1/2,000	1,600	Cairngorms
1.47 Osprey with fish at nest	400+1.4×	f/8	1/1,600	800	Cairngorms
1.48 Ptarmigan and blue sky	400+1.4×	f/8	1/800	200	Cairngorms, high up
1.50 Golden Eagle in rain	500	f/4	1/500	200	Cairngorms (captive bird)
1.51 Red Kite	400+1.4×	f/8	1/6,400	2,500	Gigrin farm, Wales
1.53 Redshank	500+1.4×	f/8	1/1,000	200	Dawlish Warren, Devon
1.54 Ptarmigan in winter	400+1.4×	f/8	1/800	200	Cairngorms, high up

Chapter 2

IMAGE	LENS FOCAL LENGTH (mm)	APERTURE	SHUTTER SPEED (s)	ISO	COMMENTS
2.1 Brown Hare	500+1.4×	f/11	1/2,500	2,000	Wales
2.2 Young Roe deer	500+1.4×	f/5.6	1/320	400	
2.8 Young Roe jumping	500+1.4×	f.5.6	1/500	400	
2.9 Fallow doe	23	f/4.9	1/60	72	

IMAGE	LENS FOCAL LENGTH (mm)	APERTURE	SHUTTER SPEED (s)	ISO	COMMENTS
2.12 Red Deer on Mull	400+1.4×	f/8	1/320	250	
2.14 Roebuck and Roe doe	500+1.4×	f/5.6	1/640	400	
2.15 Fox with Rabbit	500+1.4×	f/5.6	1/200	400	
2.18 Baby fox	100	f/5.6	1/40 (flash)	250	Wildlife Hospital
2.19 Sibling Fox cubs at play	500+1.4×	f/5.6	1/500	640	
2.20 Badger and nuts	50	f/5.6	1/100	400	
2.24 Badger	50	f/5.6	1/100	400	
2.25 Hedgehog	50	f/11	1/250	200	Flash used
2.27 Baby Hedgehog	100	f/16	1/50	400	Wildlife Hospital. Flash
2.28 Wood Mouse	50	f/16	1/200	200	Flash used
2.30 Weasel	100	f/13	1/200	400	
2.31 Stoat	100	f/13	1/200	400	
2.36 Young weasel	100	f/11	1/250	400	
2.37 Curious Red Squirrel	500	f/4	1/50	400	Cairngorms
2.39 Red Squirrel on branch	500	f/4	1/50	400	Cairngorms
2.40 Otter on Mull	500+1.4×	f/5.6	1/1,250	1,250	Isle of Mull
2.42 Otter chews and cub watches	400+1.4×	f/5.6	1/2,500	400	Shetland
2.23 Otter and cub, Shetland	500+1.4×	f/5.6	1/1,000	400	Shetland
2.44 Two otter cubs	500+1.4×	f/5.6	1/2,500	400	Shetland
2.45 Otter sniffs out its path	560	f/8	1/2,500	2,000	Shetland. ISO too high
2.46 One-week-old Grey Seal pup	400	f/5.6	1/1,000	400	Ramsey Island, Wales
2.47 Sleeping female Grey Seal	400	f/5.6	1/1,000	400	Ramsey Island, Wales
2.48 Badger cub yawning	50	f/16	1/60	400	Wildlife Hospital. Flash used

Chapter 3

IMAGE	LENS FOCAL LENGTH (mm)	APERTURE	SHUTTER SPEED (s)	ISO	COMMENTS
3.1 Beautiful Demoiselle	180	f/16	1/250	200	Ring flash
3.2 Common Darter	180	f/16	1/250	200	Ring flash
3.3 Halloween Pennant	180	f/16	1/60	200	Ring flash
3.4 Southern Hawker	180	f/8	1/200	400	Ring flash
3.5 Male Blue-tailed Damselfly	100	f/16	1/250	200	Ring flash
3.6 Comma Butterfly	180	f/11	1/400	400	
3.7 Marbled White butterfly	180	f/16	1/60	200	Sunny morning, balanced flash
3.8 Wall butterfly	180	f/11	1/100	200	Ring flash
3.9 Pearl-bordered Fritillary	180	f/6.3	1/125	200	Ring flash
3.10 Pearl-bordered Fritillary underside	180	f/6.3	1/125	200	Ring flash
3.11 Butterfly and dew	180	f/7.1	1/250	400	

Chapter 4

IMAGE	LENS FOCAL LENGTH (mm)	APERTURE	SHUTTER SPEED (s)	ISO	COMMENTS
4.1 Mute Swan and cygnets	500+1.4×	f/11	1/2,500	2,000	
4.2 Toad in a rushy pool	100	f/16	1/40	200	Flash
4.4 Male Adder	400+1.4×	f/9	1/640	200	
4.5 Slow Worm	180	f/16	1/250	200	Flash
4.6 Lesser Horseshoe Bat	300	f/16	1/250	1,640	Flash
4.9 Dormouse	50	f/11	1/50	200	Wildlife Hospital. Flash
4.10 Brown Hare	500+1.4×	f/11	1/1,600	2,000	Wales
4.11 Mink swimming	500+1.4×	f/5.6	1/1,000	800	Wales

Chapter 5

IMAGE	LENS FOCAL LENGTH (mm)	APERTURE	SHUTTER SPEED (s)	ISO	COMMENTS
5.1 Female Pied Flycatcher	500	f/5.6	1/400	1,600	
5.2 Sand Martin and chicks	500	f/8	1/800	1,000	
5.5 Blue Tit taken from the shed hide	500	f/5.6	1/1,600	400	
5.7 Cormorant	500+1.4×	f/5.6	1/400	640	

Chapter 6

IMAGE	LENS FOCAL LENGTH (mm)	APERTURE	SHUTTER SPEED (s)	ISO	COMMENTS
6.1 Male Pied Flycatcher	500+1.4×	f/5.6	1/1,000	800	Wales
6.2 Sand Martin chicks	500	f/8	1/800	1,000	
6.3 Spot metering	500+1.4×	f/8	1/8,000	1,600	Mull
6.4 Partial metering	400	f/5.6	1/640	400	Ramsey Island
6.5 Evaluative metering	500+1.4×	f/6.3	1/1,250	400	
6.7 Two-week-old Grey Seal pup	400	f/5.6	1/320	400	Ramsey Island

Appendix

IMAGE	LENS FOCAL LENGTH (mm)	APERTURE	SHUTTER SPEED (s)	ISO	COMMENTS
A1 Golden Eagle portrait	500	f/5.6	1/200	400	
A2 Canada Geese and goslings	180	f/6.3	1/5,000	1,640	
A3 Golden Eagle with prey	500	f/5.6	1/100	400	Cairngorms (Captive bird)

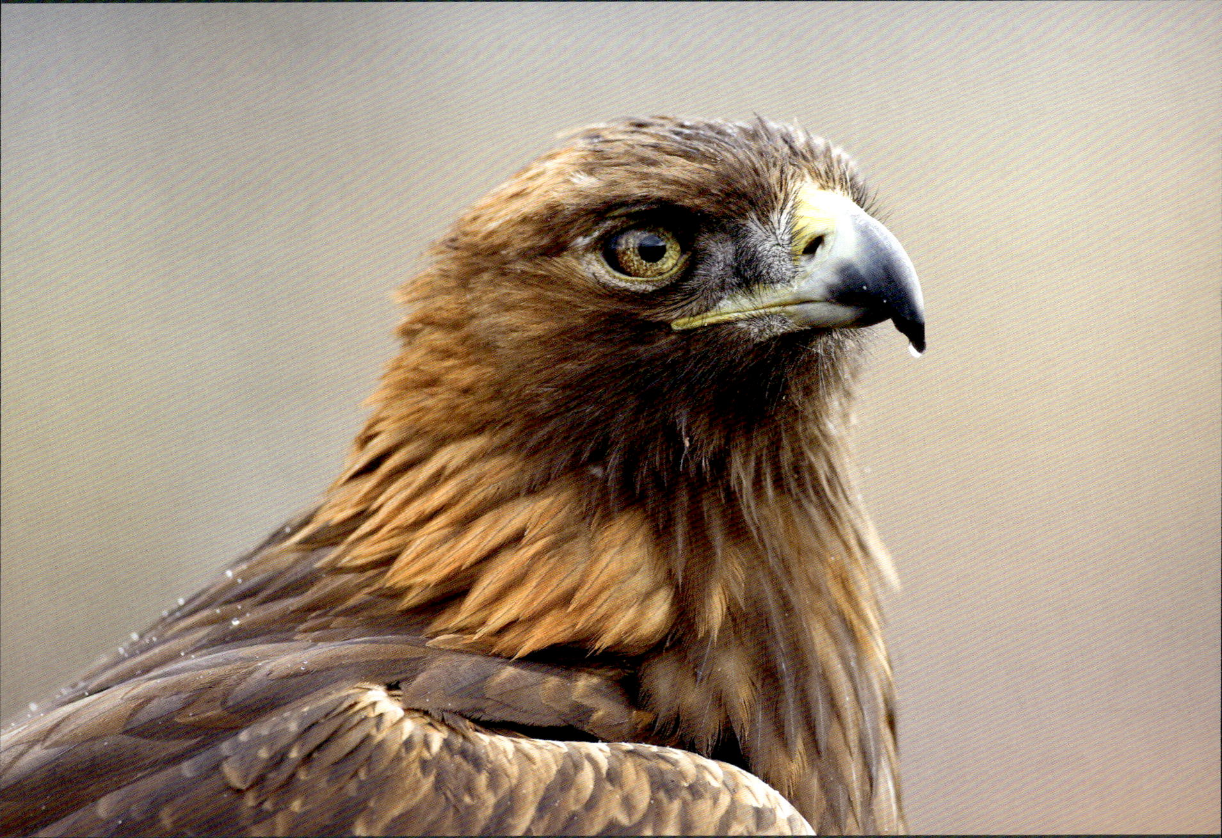

Golden Eagle portrait

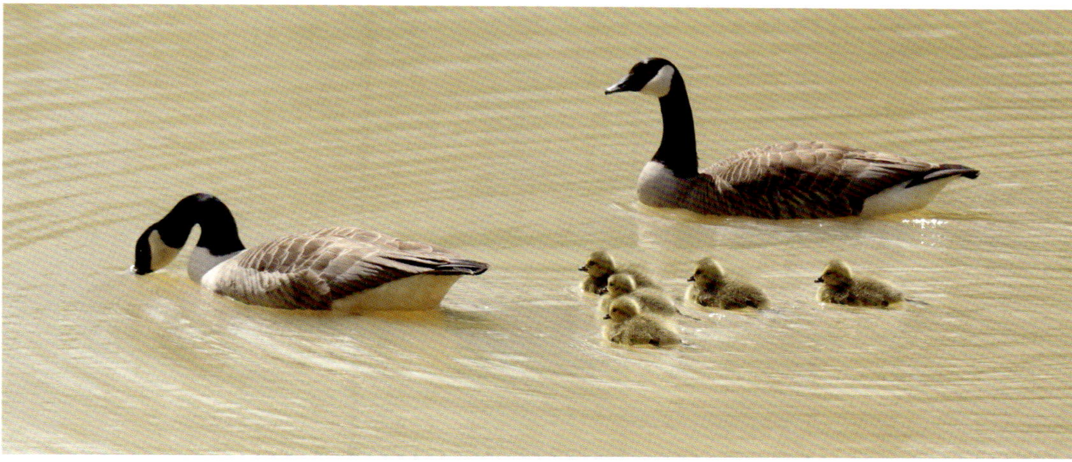

Canada Geese and goslings

Ethical issues

The most important aspect of wildlife photography is to ensure that your presence does not harm or disturb your subject in any way. Below I have detailed some ethically questionable methods that some photographers use and which, in my opinion, should be avoided.

Getting close to the animals

Many photographers have different interpretations of this, and for some, getting the photograph matters more than the wellbeing of the animal. A recent example of this occurred at a favoured spot for photographing seals and their young when hauled out on the beach. There are often viewing areas set up for the public by Wildlife Trusts, but some professional photographers in the past have taken groups across to other areas favoured by seals with pups. The reserves have tried to ban this, as they feel that the seals are being disturbed. Several professional photographers objected strongly as they seemed to feel that they had a special right, having visited the site for many years and being well known. Personally, I think well-known photographers should set a good example and show how it is possible to get good photographs without causing disturbance.

Other animals are very sensitive to the presence of humans, and even though you may not think you are disturbing the animal, it may leave a favoured feeding area because of your presence. Otters are an example, and Otters in coastal districts in particular have a tough battle to survive. This battle can be made even harder if they are disturbed. Make sure you are familiar with the natural history of such animals to ensure that you take the correct steps to avoid disturbance.

Baiting

I regard this as different from feeding birds on a regular basis, as that is for the benefit of the birds with a potential added advantage to photographers. To me, the term baiting implies short-term supplying of animal flesh to attract birds of prey or mammals for photographic purposes. Whether you wish to do this or not is up to you, but use only dead animals (for example road-kill rabbit). Some photographic workshops supply dead lambs for larger captive birds of prey in order to allow 'authentic photography'. Look at the photographs of the Golden Eagle opposite and on pages 182–3 and decide if you think they were created in an ethical fashion.

Others have used live fish in a tank to attract Kingfishers. Under the Animal Welfare Act of 2006 it is an offence to cause unnecessary suffering to wildlife, and supplying of live bait would be covered by this. Some photographic organisations will not accept photographs where live bait has been used.

Playing birdsong

There was an incident reported recently in which some wildlife photographers used bird calls to lure a rare bird from its nest so that they could photograph it. The bird in question was a protected species, but the photographers were let off with a caution – the reason given being that they 'did not realise they were doing wrong'. I find that hard to believe and think a mere caution gives out the wrong message. Ethical wildlife photographers should put the bird first and their needs second. If a bird is lured from its nest, the eggs it was sitting on may not hatch, or the bird may become exhausted from continual disturbance. Despite all this, there are some well-known photographers who use birdsong to attract birds for photography.

Rushing to see rarities

A few years ago an extremely rare bird arrived at Dawlish Warren. Over 3,000 photographers descended on the scene to see the bird. Fortunately, as a waterbird it was a little safer than if it had been a landbird. There have been stories of such birds being hounded almost to death. If you find a rare bird, take a photograph safely, then keep the knowledge to yourself until it has flown off!

Legal issues

All wildlife in the UK has protection under the Wildlife and Countryside Act 1981 and some have additional protection under the Conservation of Habitats and Species Regulations, together with other Acts.

The Natural England website has details of the law relating to wildlife, and in particular details of protected species and when a licence is required. In general, the emphasis is on disturbance and how to avoid it.

Animals with additional protection include: reptiles, bats, Dormouse, Red Squirrel, Pine Marten, Otter, Mountain Hare, Wildcat, Polecat, Badger and Water Vole.

There are several codes of practice for the wildlife photographer, with the most comprehensive possibly being that from the Royal Photographic Society Nature Group, which can be found on their website.

Schedule 1 birds have special protection at all times. A licence is required from Natural England to photograph these birds at or near the nest unless it can be guaranteed that there will be no disturbance.

A list of Schedule 1 bird species is given in Table A.1.

Table A.1 Schedule 1 bird species

Avocet	Grebe, Slavonian	Sandpiper, Wood
Bee-eater	Greenshank	Scaup
Bittern	Gull, Little	Scoter, Common
Bittern, Little	Gull, Mediterranean	Scoter, Velvet
Bluethroat	Harriers, all species	Serin
Brambling	Heron, Purple	Shorelark
Bunting, Cirl	Hobby	Shrike, Red-backed
Bunting, Lapland	Hoopoe	Spoonbill
Bunting, Snow	Kingfisher	Stilt, Black-winged
Buzzard, Honey	Kite, Red	Stint, Temminck's
Capercaillie	Merlin	Stone-curlew
Chough	Oriole, Golden	Swan, Bewick's
Corncrake	Osprey	Swan, Whooper
Crake, Spotted	Owl, Barn	Tern, Black
Crossbills	Owl, Snowy	Tern, Little
Divers, all species	Peregrine	Tern, Roseate
Dotterel	Petrel, Leach's	Tit, Bearded
Duck, Long-tailed	Phalarope, Red-necked	Tit, Crested
Eagle, Golden	Plover, Kentish	Treecreeper, Short-toed
Eagle, White-tailed	Plover, Little Ringed	Warbler, Cetti's
Falcon, Gyr	Quail, Common	Warbler, Dartford
Fieldfare	Redstart, Black	Warbler, Marsh
Firecrest	Redwing	Warbler, Savi's
Garganey	Rosefinch, Scarlet	Whimbrel
Goshawk	Ruff	Woodlark
Godwit, Black-tailed	Sandpiper, Green	Wryneck
Grebe, Black-necked	Sandpiper, Purple	

Golden Eagle with prey (captive bird supplied with dead lamb)

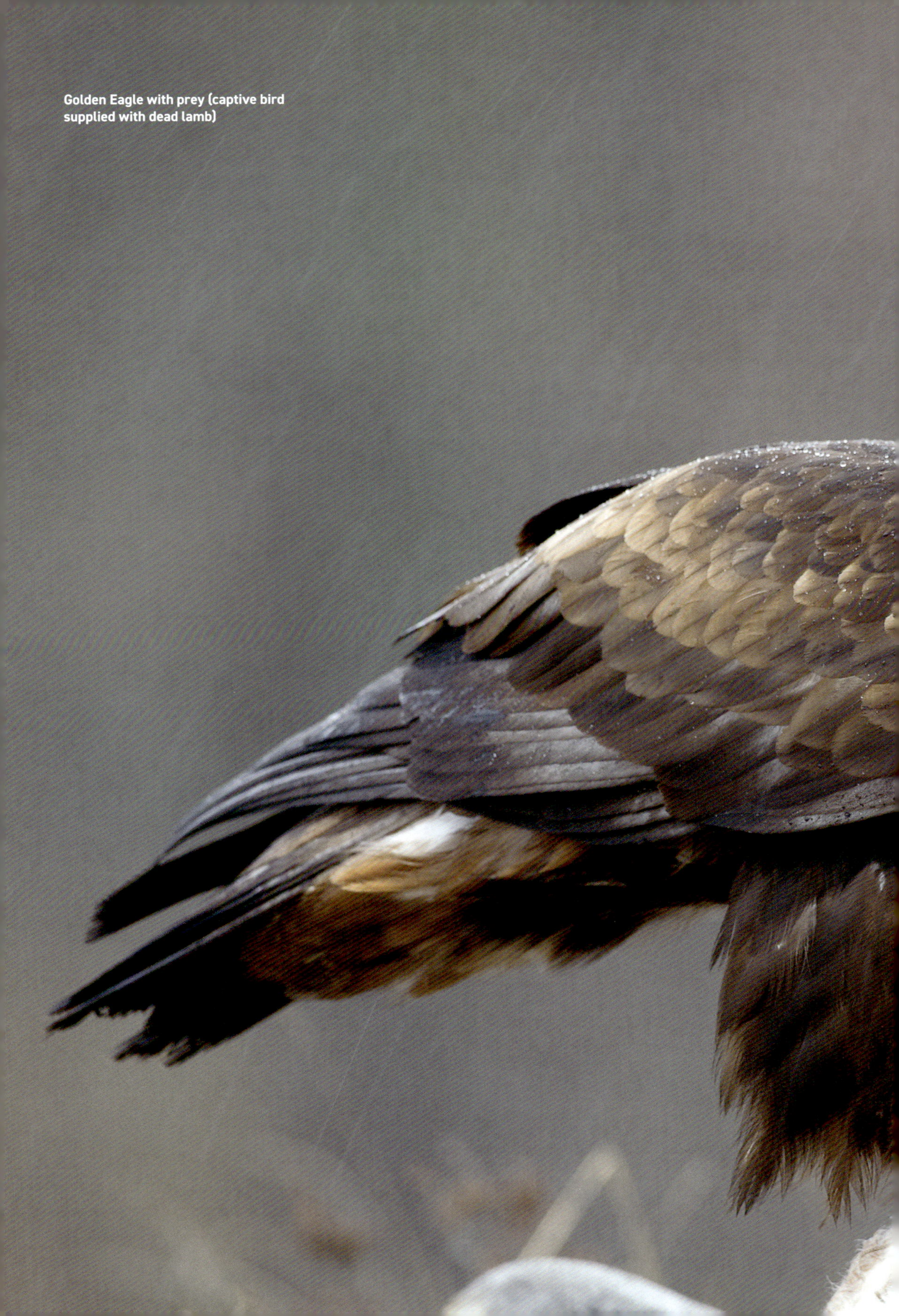

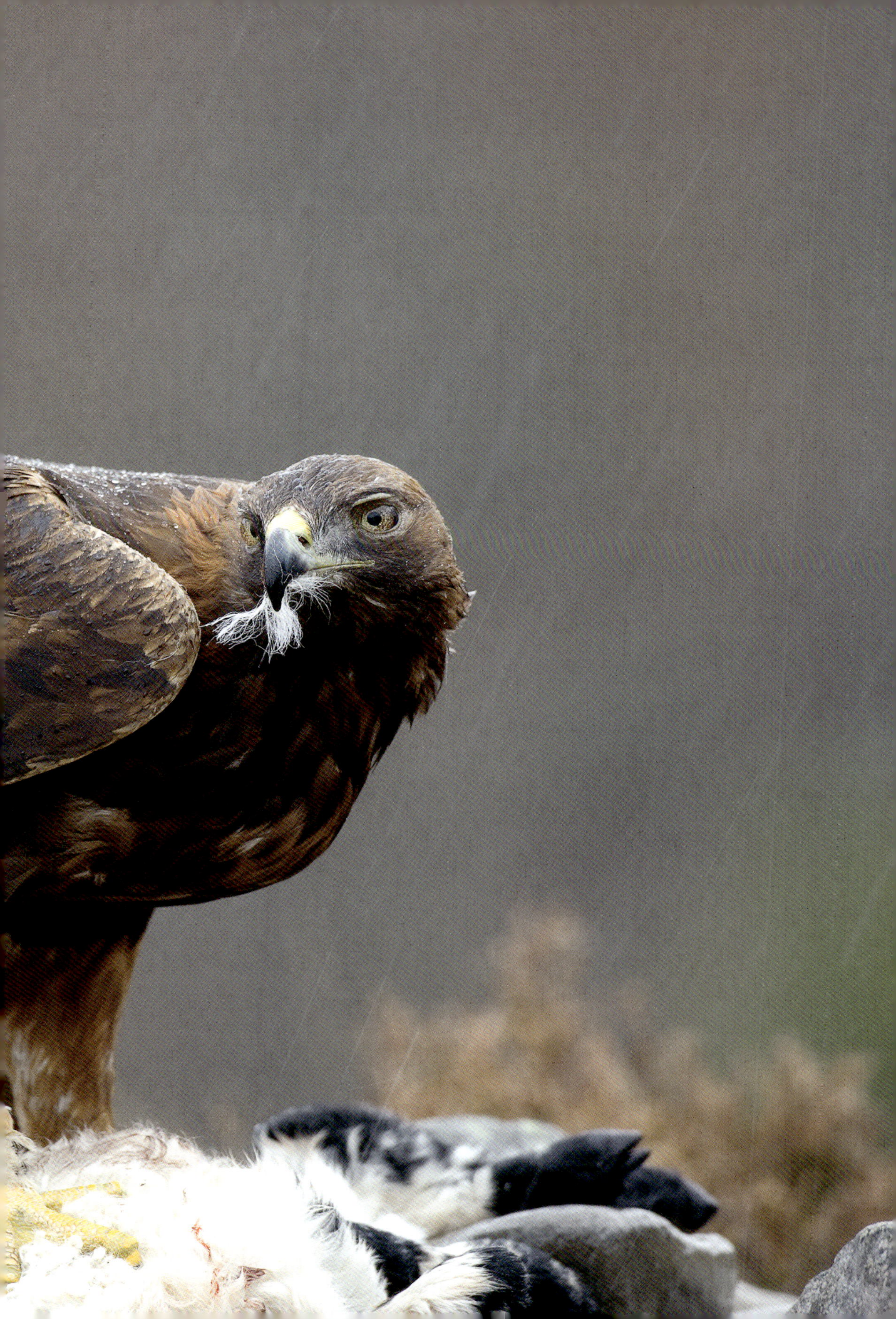

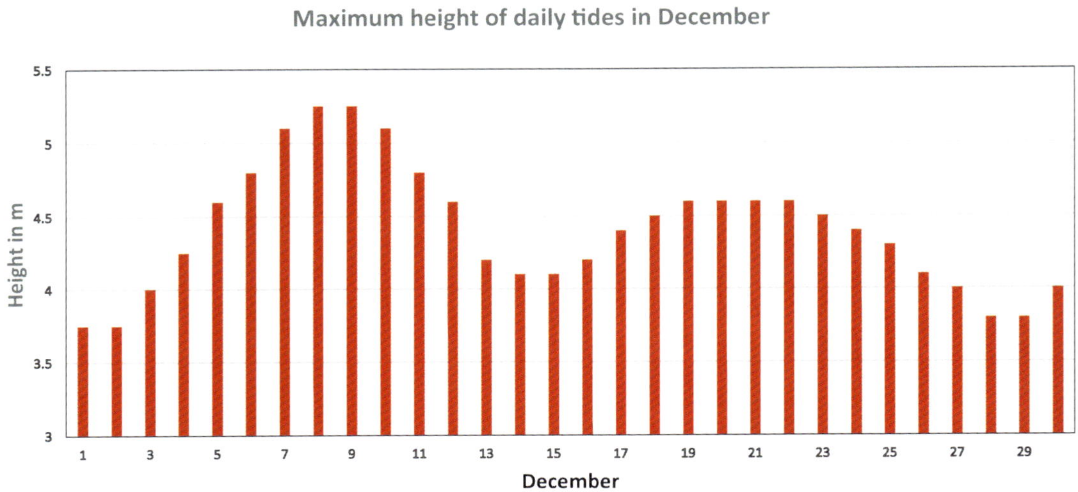

Typical high tide variation in December for the River Teign

Tides

It is important to remember that not only do the times of the two daily high tides vary from day to day, being approximately an hour later each day, but the exact height of the high tide shifts too. The maximum height of the high tides varies from day to day and from month to month. Tides are also affected by wind and barometric pressure. If you travel to an unfamiliar coastal district, especially if visiting a river estuary, consult tide tables to find out the position of the highest tide, so that you can gauge when it would be safe to walk along the estuary. This chart gives an example, but actual numbers will depend on your location. Tide timetables can be obtained from newsagents in coastal areas, or from online bookshops.

Recommended books

Balmer, D., Gillings, S., Caffrey, B., Swann, B., Downie, I., and Fuller, R. (2013) *Bird Atlas 2007–11: The Breeding and Wintering Birds of Britain and Ireland*. Norfolk: BTO Books.

Bang, P. and Dahlstrom, P. (2001) *Animal Tracks and Signs*. Oxford: Oxford University Press.

Brown, R., Ferguson, J., Lawrence, M. and Lees, D. (2009) *Tracks and Signs of the Birds of Britain & Europe*. London: Bloomsbury Press.

Moores, R. (2007) *Where to Watch Mammals in Britain and Ireland*. London: A&C Black.

Mullarney, K. et al. (2010) *Collins Bird Guide*. London: Collins Publishers.

Smallshire, D. and Swash, A. (2010) *Britain's Dragonflies*. Princeton: Princeton University Press – WILDGuides.

Tomlinson, D. (2020) *Britain's Butterflies*. Princeton: Princeton University Press – WILDGuides.

Young, S. (2016) *CCTV for Wildlife Monitoring*. Exeter: Pelagic Publishing.

Some useful websites

Wildlife Trust sites

There are 46 trusts in England and Wales, administering 2,300 reserves in 100,000 hectares, and there are also 18 in Northern Island. Details are on the Wildlife Trusts' website where you can search for the Trusts nearest to you.

Scotland is covered by the Scottish Wildlife Trusts organisation, which administers 120 of the reserves amounting to 20,000 hectares. Details of the Trusts can be found on the Scottish Wildlife Trust's website.

Urban reserves

Those who live in cities may think there is no wildlife around, but a quick Internet search for wildlife in each of the major cities will reap rewards, for example:

- The London Wetland Centre, owned by the Wildfowl and Wetlands Trust, is near Richmond upon Thames. It has several large hides.
- Birmingham has 35 hectares of nature reserves, as described on the Birmingham local government website.
- Glasgow has many large parks and there is a great deal of wildlife on or near the River Clyde.
- It is useful to remember that almost all major cities are built close to rivers, and rivers attract wildlife more than almost anything else.

National Parks

- Details of the 15 National Parks in the UK can be found on the National Parks websites.
- The National Parks include Dartmoor, Lake District, New Forest, Cairngorms, Peak District and the Brecon Beacons.

Bird and wildlife charities

- The British Trust for Ornithology (BTO) is a science-based charity and gives impartial advice on birds. There is information on its website about bird identification videos and training courses.
- The Royal Society for the Protection of Birds has a large number of reserves and gives out popular advice. Some believe it to be more political and less scientific than the BTO.
- The Mammal Society has a strong science base and publishes excellent booklets and fact sheets on mammals, which can be found on its website.
- The Dragonfly Society has a great deal of information about dragonflies and has a membership base. There will be a local group near you.
- Butterfly sightings and other information can be found at the Butterfly Conservation site, including details of local groups.
- The Field Studies Council has centres throughout the UK and gives excellent courses, some at professional level. Their laminated foldout identification charts are the best around.

Websites for birdwatchers

There are many birdwatching clubs in the UK, plus several birding magazines. These sites can be very useful for up-to-date information about where birds can be found. Bird Guides also publishes a list of bird groups county by county.

Wildlife holidays and guides

If you wish to have experienced guiding rather than a mainly social holiday, look for trips that aim to show you wildlife rather than teach you how to use your camera. One to one is the better option, and can work out cheaper in the long run, as you will need fewer days. Read the descriptions carefully to gauge how successful the guide claims to be. It is impossible to guarantee the presence of wildlife, so there is always a risk of disappointment. For this reason, mammal guides are few and far between, and are mainly found in Scotland. Otter guides in Shetland, for example, prefer to have at least two or three days as it is so difficult to find these animals.

Some examples of guides and/or hides:

- The Aigas Field Centre near Inverness has hides for Pine Marten, Badger, Otter, Beaver, deer and birds. Guides are also available.
- Shetland Nature conducts photographic holidays in Shetland with the UK's best Otter guides. It has hides available.
- Guided Bird Watching has details of companies and individuals providing guides for birdwatching.
- Red Kites can be seen in large numbers at Gigrin Farm and Llanddeusant in Wales.

An Internet search will bring up lists of guides and wildlife holidays, but careful reading is required to gauge the likelihood of seeing what you want. Nature reserves often have set days in the year for wildlife walks for deer, Red Squirrels and other animals, so study their websites carefully. Although photography on such events is not always successful, you will gain a better idea of what can be seen where. As I have emphasised many times, the best method for finding wildlife is to get to know a particular nature reserve well and develop good relationships with the local rangers.

INDEX

References to figures and photographs appear in *italic* type; those in **bold** refer to tables.

N

O

P

R

S

T

Also available from Pelagic

Wild Mull: A Natural History of the Island and its People
by Stephen Littlewood and Martin Jones

The Hen Harrier's Year
by Ian Carter and Dan Powell

A Field Guide to Harlequins and Other Common Ladybirds of Britain and Ireland
by Helen Boyce

A Natural History of Insects in 100 Limericks
by Richard A. Jones and Calvin Ure-Jones

Essex Rock: Geology Beneath the Landscape
by Ian Mercer and Ros Mercer

Bat Calls of Britain and Europe
edited by Jon Russ

Pollinators and Pollination
by Jeff Ollerton

A Hair Scale Identification Guide to Terrestrial Mammalian Carnivores of Canada
by Justin Kestler

Rhythms of Nature: Wildlife and Wild Places Between the Moors
by Ian Carter

The Wryneck
by Gerard Gorman

Low-Carbon Birding
edited by Javier Caletrío

A Miscellany of Bats
by M. Brock Fenton and Jens Rydell

Ancient Woods, Trees and Forests
edited by Alper H. Colak, Simay Kırca and Ian D. Rotherham

101 Curious Tales of East African Birds
by Colin Beale